FAMILY INVOLVEMENT IN LITERACY

Also available from Cassell:

E. Bearne, M. Styles and V. Watson: *The Prose and the Passion: Children and Their Reading*
E. Bearne (ed.): *Greater Expectations: Children Reading Writing*
R. Andrews: *Teaching and Learning Argument*
J.I. Schwartz: *Encouraging Early Literacy*
A. Stables: *An Approach to English*
K. Topping: *Paired Reading, Spelling and Writing*
C. Weaver: *Understanding Whole Language*

Family Involvement in Literacy

Effective Partnerships in Education

Edited by
Sheila Wolfendale and
Keith Topping

CASSELL

Cassell
Wellington House   215 Park Avenue South
125 Strand   New York
London WC2R 0BB   NY 10003

First published 1996

British Library Cataloguing-in-Publication Data
A catalogue record for this book is available from the British Library.

ISBN 0–304–33422–7 (hardback)
      0–304–33423–5 (paperback)

Typeset by Mayhew Typesetting, Rhayader, Powys
Printed and bound in Great Britain by Redwood Books, Trowbridge, Wiltshire

Contents

Foreword

Unless nostalgia is truly 'not what it used to be!' the widespread tapping of parental interest and involvement in their children's reading during the late 1970s/early 1980s seems to have been a remarkable phenomenon. It also did more to put home–school work on the educational map and give it 'street cred' amongst teachers, than everything else put together.

Firstly, it combined, to an unusual degree, initiatives at all levels, from formal research projects, through LEA initiatives and networks, to countless home-made, school-based schemes and programmes. The common feature, however, was that 'it worked', often spectacularly!

Secondly, much of this work seemed to embrace and take in its stride the adoption of very different methods and approaches. The combination of two-way communication, the patient monitoring of pupil gains and the recording of changes of attitude and behaviour, still suggests useful lessons to be learned.

Above all, however, such work accelerated the growing conviction amongst ordinary parents and teachers, often rooted in a positive experience of working together, that parents and other carers have a crucial role to play in their children's education and development.

All of this was very successfully captured in the earlier version of this book. As with everything else, the world has changed. The consensus amongst teachers, parents and pupils, however, that early literacy is of key significance in children's education, remains the same.

So this entirely new collection of contributions that sets out to review and interpret our continuing experience, to identify significant areas of growth and development, and to make what we have learned more explicit, is both welcome and overdue. I am delighted to introduce a book which so successfully locates the main concerns within the range, diversity and positive achievements of contemporary home–school work, in Britain and further afield.

More than anything, I am delighted to endorse a range of widely differing accounts which acknowledge the skill and importance of ordinary parents as both prime educators and major partners in their children's education and development.

Dr John Bastiani

Contributors to the Book

The Editors

Sheila Wolfendale has been a primary school teacher, remedial reading teacher and educational psychologist in several local education authorities and is currently Director of a postgraduate professional Masters' and Doctoral level training course for educational psychologists in the Psychology Department of the University of East London. She has authored and edited many books, booklets and articles on particular interests and specialisms, such as reading and learning difficulties, special needs, early years and parental involvement. In 1988 she was awarded a Professorship in the Department of Psychology, Polytechnic of East London, now University of East London.

Dr Keith Topping has been a teacher and educational psychologist. He is currently Director of the Centre for Paired Learning in the Department of Psychology at the University of Dundee in Scotland. Here he develops and researches the effectiveness of methods for non-teachers to tutor others in fundamental skills and higher order learning across a wide range of ages and contexts. He is also Director of a school psychology training programme at Dundee University and Director of the Higher Education Effective Learning Project. He is the author of several books and more than 100 other publications including multi-media distance learning packages, and conducts training workshops around the world.

Chapter Contributors

Peter Branston taught in a primary school in Leeds and after qualifying as an educational psychologist worked in South Wales for a number of years, finally as Principal Educational Psychologist for the County of West Glamorgan. He is currently operating as a consultant psychologist to educational institutions in England and abroad.

Professor **Trevor Cairney** is Director of Research at the University of Western Sydney Nepean. He is an English educator with over 25 years' experience as a teacher, educational consultant, lecturer in three institutions, faculty Dean and head of a research centre. He is currently President of the Australian Reading Association, Director of the NSW Children's Literacy and ESL Research Network, and a member of the Australian Language and Literacy Council. He has conducted 20 funded research projects in Australia and the USA, and has published the results of his work in seven books and more than 100 articles and book chapters. His most recent books are *Beyond Tokenism: Parents as Partners in Literacy Learning* (Australian Reading Association and Heinemann, USA) and *Pathways to Literacy* (Cassell).

Lori J. Connors is Associate Research Scientist at the Center on Families, Communities, Schools and Children's Learning at the Johns Hopkins University. She holds a BS, MS and a PhD from Boston College. Lori Connors was a post-doctoral Research Fellow at Johns Hopkins University and an Early Childhood Specialist at the Massachusetts Department of Education. She is the Director of Partners in Learning: Family Literacy Programs Project and Co-Director of the High School and Families Partnership Project.

Sarah Gale is the Parent Partnership Project Manager in the London Borough of Tower Hamlets, but until recently she job-shared the PACT Co-ordinator's post with Roger Hancock in neighbouring Hackney. Prior to joining PACT, she was involved in a variety of home–school reading initiatives as a language co-ordinator and as a peripatetic specialist teacher, but also, and most importantly, as a parent!

Dr Ted Glynn is a former primary teacher who is currently Professor of Education at the University of Otago and a board member of the New Zealand Council for Educational Research. He completed his postgraduate training at the University of Auckland and the University of Toronto and has been teaching and researching in the field of applied behaviour analysis in education for over 25 years. He has contributed to the training of education psychologists at the universities of Auckland and Otago. He has written and published extensively. Ted is currently researching parental involvement in children's learning of literacy skills (oral language, reading and writing), particularly within the context of bilingual education in New Zealand. He is committed to working to improve the quality of education provision for Maori students and their families in both Maori immersion and mainstream settings in New Zealand.

Dr Eve Gregory is Senior Lecturer in Education at Goldsmiths College, University of London, where she works mainly on courses concerned with early literacy and language development. Her particular interests are literacy and bilingualism, involving parents in children's literacy development and links between culture, learning and cognition. She is author of many journal articles and chapters, and has recently completed a book on approaches to reading with young emergent bilinguals, *Learning to Read in a Second Language: Making Sense of a New World* (London: Paul Chapman).

Roger Hancock began teaching in a primary school in the London Borough of Camden in 1969. Since then he has worked in special education, curriculum development and teacher education. At present, he co-ordinates home–school projects in the London Boroughs of Hackney and Tower Hamlets where, increasingly, he is involved in fund-raising to support the existence of such projects. He is an Honorary Research Associate of the University of Greenwich, and has written a number of articles and chapters on parental involvement.

Dr Peter Hannon researches and teaches in the Division of Education at the University of Sheffield, England. Following doctoral research at the University of Manchester and work as a preschool teacher in a community school, he has carried out a number of studies of parents and literacy with colleagues at Sheffield. He directed research in the Belfield Reading Project and the Sheffield Early Literacy Project. He has many publications in the field including *Literacy, Home and School* (Falmer Press, 1995).

Dr Max Kemp retired as foundation Director of the Schools and Community Centre, University of Canberra in 1992 and is now Visiting Fellow at Griffith University, Queensland. In this position he is currently working in Fiji on a long-term teacher education development programme supported jointly by Australian Assistance for International Development (AusAID) and the Fiji government. Max is a Past President of the Australian Reading Association and has published extensively with particular emphasis on literacy for children with special needs, assessment in literacy, and evidence from parents-as-tutors programmes. Further information about the Canberra project can be obtained from Max's successor as Director, Brian Gray, University of Canberra, PO Box 1 Belconnen, ACT 2611, Australia.

Ray Phillips read Social Sciences at Birmingham University. He served for two years on the executive of the National Union of Students and was later appointed Project Director on the pilot Student Community Action Programme. He has been a member of two national Working Parties of the Calouste Gulbenkian Foundation on Community Support and Local Employment Initiatives. From 1980 to 1982, Ray was Chair of the National Federation of Voluntary Literacy Schemes. More recently he was involved in the setting up of the European Anti-Poverty Network by the European Commission. He has worked since 1975 at the Newham Parents' Centre, where he was appointed Director in 1980. In the course of his work, he has written many discussion papers and several chapters on aspects of education and community action.

Chapter 1

Editors' Introduction

Sheila Wolfendale and Keith Topping

PURPOSE AND SCOPE OF THE BOOK

This book reviews a decade or so of rapid developments in parental involvement in reading and provides a compendium of current UK and international practice in the wider area of family literacy. It considers the evidence for the effectiveness of new and established approaches within their broader social and political contexts. Organizational guidelines for implementation are coupled with details of practical resources available, and the book points the way towards anticipated further developments.

The contributors have all had demonstrable long-term engagement in parental involvement in reading/family literacy, as researchers and practitioners in education and community initiatives. They each provide their own distinctive perspective on their experience of operating parent- and family-focused literacy work, much of which has been replicated and adopted in many other settings.

Rationale for this book

The pace of educational change is rapid. Practitioners feel that it has accelerated in recent years, with the bombardment of educational legislation which has significantly and irrevocably altered the landscape for teachers, children and their parents.

There is seldom time to revisit educational practices, which at the time of their inception were regarded as innovative. Nor do educational researchers and practitioners have time and opportunity to ponder and reflect upon the longer-term effects of their own and others' practice.

We decided to return to the domain first known as 'parental involvement in reading' for a number of reasons:

- The precursor to this book (Topping and Wolfendale, 1985) was positively received. In that book the chapter authors described their own trail-blazing work in the area and provided inspiration and stimulus to countless teachers, educational psychologists and others to follow in their footsteps and initiate similar projects themselves.

- There has been a profound change of attitudes towards parental involvement in education on the part of legislators and practitioners. Education legislation in the UK from the early 1980s onwards almost without exception has contained provision for the extension of parents' rights in education (Mansfield, 1994). The 'parental involvement in reading' movement chimes well with these developments.
- Parental involvement in reading has moved on. A number of earlier seminal projects have maintained many of their original features, have adapted to changing circumstances and demands and have been able to sustain, in the face of financial retrenchment within education. A record of the enduring and changing features of these successful projects should inform and guide efforts to achieve maximum cost-effectiveness as we enter the new millennium.
- We wanted, also, to explore and record related developments in the domain now labelled as 'family literacy'. There has been a shift in perceptions of home–school links in reading. From linkage with the extension of parental involvement in other areas of education (Bastiani, 1993), the conception of 'parents as educators' (Topping, 1986) has broadened beyond the original narrow pedagogical focus (helping parents to help their child with reading) towards the notion of a home–school alliance that promotes the wider interests of children as learners in the community. Thus *family literacy* embraces a much wider range of activities and is often concerned with the needs of parents and carers as much as with the learning needs of children. It is concerned, too, to value and incorporate into formal education the cultural and linguistic heritage each child possesses.

This book is thus not exactly a *sequel* to the 1985 Topping and Wolfendale book, yet its point of departure is indeed that earlier volume. Intentionally, we have set out to demonstrate *continuity* and *transition*: to depict the enduring and evidently successful features of parental involvement in reading; to highlight adaptive features of the earlier projects; and to portray the evolution towards the broader connotation of family literacy.

On the theme of 'lessons learned' we attempt to assess *effectiveness* – each author considers the effectiveness evidence from his/her own work, and the final chapter provides an overview of effectiveness in this area of work.

The book attempts to marry retrospect with prospect. A number of the authors consider the way forward for their own area of work and the final chapter speculates and predicts future directions. It also includes some thoughts on the potential for family literacy to incorporate the 'new literacy', that is, exploiting and harnessing information technology within the home–school learning alliance.

Readers familiar with the earlier book will note that this new volume takes a wider international perspective. This reflects the following:

- There is much exciting and informative parallel work in this area in other predominantly English-speaking countries, and to be aware of this is now imperative.
- The inclusion of an international dimension is consistent with the forging of European and international links in many other areas of education (Dombey and Meek Spencer, 1994; Macbeth and Ravn, 1994).

● Fast-developing technology now guarantees us more or less instant electronic access to each other across the globe.

Organization of the book

The contents of the book have been organized for ease of access. Inevitably, given the complexity of the area, there are overlaps between sections and chapters. After this introduction, the book consists of three parts, with an appended Resource Directory.

Part 1 reviews a decade of parental involvement in reading: three of the contributions describe the longer-term effects and take-up of work that was first described in Topping and Wolfendale (1985), namely, Hackney PACT (Roger Hancock and Sarah Gale), Pause Prompt Praise (Ted Glynn, who describes work in UK and New Zealand), and Paired Reading (Keith Topping). Although the CAPER project (Peter Branston) did not appear in that earlier book, we are delighted to include this chapter, since the work has been ongoing throughout most of the 1980s.

Part 2 charts the evolution towards family literacy, and encompasses a kaleidoscopic view of innovative practice from the UK, Australia and North America. Peter Hannon contributed to the earlier book, but here he describes a venture which focused on the early, preschool years and the precursors to later literacy. Eve Gregory discusses bilingual dimensions, and Ray Phillips emphasizes the community context to family literacy. Trevor Cairney and Max Kemp bring their considerable Australian experience to our attention and Lori Connors provides a valuable window into the substantial work in family literacy in the United States.

Part 3 seeks to provide a unifying schema for the rich array of contemporary work described in the previous two parts. Keith Topping, in his chapter on effectiveness, critically appraises the data from established and more recent projects, looks at process issues and outcome measures, and indicates areas where further action research is most urgently needed. Sheila Wolfendale's final chapter considers the continuities and transitions from parental involvement in reading towards family literacy. Then, picking up on the themes expounded by chapter authors, she explores the dimensions of contemporary family literacy work, finishing with a peep into the crystal ball.

The Resource Directory will, we hope, provide a treasury for readers in their own endeavours to establish and sustain family literacy projects.

NOTE TO READERS

Since July 1995 the Department for Education is known as the Department for Education and Employment.

REFERENCES

Bastiani, J. (1993) *UK Directory of Home–School Initiatives*, 2nd edn. London: Royal Society of Arts.

Dombey, H. and Meek Spencer, M. (eds) (1994) *First Steps Together: Home–School Early Literacy in European Contexts*. Stoke on Trent: Trentham Books.

Macbeth, A. and Ravn, B. (eds) (1994) *Expectations about Parents in Education: European Perspectives*. Glasgow: Computing Services, University of Glasgow.

Mansfield, M. (1994) *Home and School Links: Practice Makes Perfect*. London: Campaign for State Education.

Topping, K. (1986) *Parents as Educators*. Beckenham: Croom Helm/Cambridge, MA: Brookline.

Topping, K. and Wolfendale, S. (eds) (1985) *Parental Involvement in Children's Reading*. Beckenham: Croom Helm/New York: Nichols.

Part 1

A Decade of Parental Involvement in Reading

Chapter 2

Hackney PACT: Reflecting on the experience of promoting home reading programmes

Roger Hancock and Sarah Gale

'PACT' (standing for 'Parents and Children and Teachers') is the arrangement whereby children regularly take school books home to read to their parents and other family members, and teachers and parents communicate about the children's reading progress on some form of record card. This home reading model was first tested out by Hewison and Tizard (1980).

PACT attracted interest in the early 1980s when the London Borough of Hackney appointed a small project team to promote the idea of parental involvement and home–school reading programmes. PACT, as a centrally funded service, was established at this time and has continued to operate (with a two-year break following the disbanding of the Inner London Education Authority in 1990) to the present day.

In recent years, PACT (the service) has continued promoting parental involvement in children's reading through various means including home reading programmes and family literacy initiatives. Currently, in addition to its traditional home reading and literacy focus, PACT works with schools to establish other forms of parent–teacher collaboration. Examples include school policy-making about behaviour and discipline, home and community activities related to various school–industry links, and shared maths homework (IMPACT).

Some early development work on Maths PACT (King and Puttock, 1986) has been superseded by IMPACT (Inventing Maths, Parents and Children and Teachers) (Merttens and Vass, 1990). Anyone who is familiar with the rich variety of take-home maths activities and tasks that support IMPACT will readily agree that, as well as learning maths *per se*, children and their families become involved in a lot of language development, reading and writing. Family numeracy develops family literacy.

A guiding principle underpinning all initiatives set up by PACT is the importance of providing parents with an opportunity to share their ideas, skills and knowledge (see Hancock, 1994). This is easier said than done as there is a tendency for all professionals to take a firm lead (if not control) when they meet their clients. In education, this can easily result in parents being viewed as passive recipients of school ideas which produces a reluctance to reveal their own feelings, insights and expertise (Wolfendale, 1983).

The term 'family literacy' refers to the natural forms of literacy that are generated within the family and thus distinguishable from 'schooled literacy' (Meek, 1991), a more organized, systematic literacy which is very much based on the reading of books and the writing of continuous prose.

The professionals know quite a lot about literacy at school but very little about literacy in the home. Families are highly individual groups of adults and children with differing social class, religious and cultural affiliations. Some writers, however, have given us illuminating glimpses of the sort of family practices that are supportive of children's literacy learning (e.g. Bissex, 1980; Taylor, 1983; Tizard and Hughes, 1984; Goelman et al., 1984; Minns, 1993). What seems to be coming out of such studies is firstly, the message that there is considerable literacy learning in many homes, and secondly, that much of it is embedded in the social processes and cultural traditions of family life. For instance Taylor, in her study of six white, middle-class, American families, writes:

> Within the context of the family, the transmission of literary styles and values is a diffuse experience, often occurring at the margins of awareness. Even when parents quite consciously introduced their children to print, the words were locked into the context of the situation. The label on the shampoo bottle, the recipe for carrot bread, and the neon signs in the street were not constructed to specifically teach reading; they were part of the child's world, and the child learned of their purpose as well as their meaning. (Taylor, 1983, p. 20)

Literacy in the family can be momentary and, like a lot of human learning, it can be difficult to see, difficult for a professional researcher or home-visiting teacher to notice and capture. Indeed, Taylor found that the parents in her study were often unaware of the way in which literacy learning was being supported in their own homes. Literacy learning in the family is inextricably woven into the social life of its members, wherever they might be (e.g. Hancock, 1995). Families thus mediate literacy through a wide variety of social situations and environmental contexts.

This natural view may be compared with the more professionalized conceptions of family literacy. The search is on for effective family literacy models and programmes and, in many ways, this echoes an earlier search which resulted in home reading programmes. The great danger, of course, is that the resultant programmes will be conceptualized and defined only by one party. This certainly happened (and still happens) in the case of home reading when some programmes were set up with no real consultation with the parents carrying out the programme. Similarly, with family literacy, there is a possibility that families will play little part in formulating what takes place.

Educational innovations experience a testing journey in order to move from the status of a good idea to becoming firmly and safely integrated into classroom practice. It is probably true that the great majority fall by the wayside. PACT, however, resulted in tangible changes to classroom practice. For instance, within the London area, surveys of primary schools in Brent (Hancock, 1988), Tower Hamlets (Hancock, 1991, 1992) and Hackney (Hancock and Gale, 1992) all revealed high teacher enthusiasm for the idea of involving parents in children's reading and also interest in the specific professional practice of home reading programmes. Given government changes experienced by schools and the build-up of teacher workloads, it is truly surprising that many teachers remain committed to an idea that must make further demands on their time.

The appearance of other influential home reading projects in various parts of the country (e.g. Pritchard and Rennie, 1978; Jackson and Hannon, 1981; Weinberger, 1983) suggested that there had been similar high take-up elsewhere in the United Kingdom. However, one or two studies have cast doubt on this (e.g. Hannon and Cuckle, 1984).

PACT ACTIVITY: ORGANIZATIONAL FEATURES

The basic PACT model involving children taking school books home and parent–teacher communication through reading record cards seems, on the face of it, to be very straightforward. However, this would be an underestimation of what is actually required to support the practice. The original PACT team was very aware of the importance of attending to the essential human infrastructure that would support the model. For instance, they stressed the need for teachers to work closely with parents in order to set up the intended reading partnership and defined their respective roles. They underlined the importance of professionals sharing their knowledge with parents but also recognized the need for teachers to link with parents' knowledge about their children and reading. They also emphasized the establishment of reliable communication systems to maintain the new home–school dialogue about reading (Griffiths and King, 1985). The two main publications that were written at the time (i.e. Griffiths and Hamilton, 1984; Pitfield Project, 1984) looked at the finer details of operating programmes and were generally very thorough and realistic in their approach to what was needed in order to launch and sustain them.

A centralized project team can offer guidance through staff in-service, conferences, videos, newsletters and publications, but they cannot ensure that such considerations will be taken on in practical terms by individual schools and teachers who are attracted to the idea of home reading. When large numbers of teachers are involved in the adoption of an innovation there tends to be considerable variation in the way in which it is interpreted.

An innovation enters a tight weave of educational settings where it endeavours to take some sort of hold. There have, consequently, been a variety of school responses to the home reading idea. Some schools regularly send books home but do not maintain any regular written communication with parents about children's reading. Instead, they rely on the face-to-face discussion that takes place during the various times when parents come to school – e.g. Primary Learning Record meetings, reading evenings, individualized parent sessions and so on. In areas where parents are not confident in English some schools recommend the use of mother tongue materials (from home and school) to enable parental involvement and also encourage the involvement of other family members who may be more literate in English. Some schools operate programmes on a purely voluntary basis. With older, more able primary children, some schools have devised homework tasks which require discussion with a parent about the chosen book and then a written response which comes back to the teacher.

Such variations and adaptations are inevitable when an innovation touches down in the real world of the classroom where there are no researchers or project team members to give extra support or provide a reminder of the original model. Demonstration projects (like the Haringey and Belfield Projects) often have the benefit of extra resources which are not usually available to schools when tested approaches are further disseminated. In fact, the dissemination process can be seen as another testing phase when project ideas and practices are operationalized by classroom teachers. In the end, it is only that which works and that which can be successfully integrated into classroom life that survives in education.

Like many things in life, home reading can be set up well or otherwise. In Hackney, during the early phases of interest and in the rush to implement a good idea, some schools quickly arranged programmes. Parents were not always given a proper opportunity to discuss what was intended and a chance to contribute to its formulation. Additionally, there were sometimes inadequate arrangements to allow parents to feed back how they and their children were experiencing a programme. What ensued, in some situations, was a professionally directed liaison in which parents felt put upon and organized – a one-way programme. This difficulty remains an issue to the present day. Given that most contact with parents often comes at the end of the school day when teachers are, understandably, losing their energies, there is a temptation to concentrate only on getting the school's message across and to give inadequate time to parents for discussion and response.

PACT has come to expect, indeed promote, a degree of variation and adaptation when home reading is set up. In offering support and advice to schools, PACT has evolved a framework that identifies the key elements that need consideration when home reading programmes are being planned and implemented.

A SUGGESTED FRAMEWORK FOR PLANNING AND CONSIDERING HOME READING PROGRAMMES

Before moving towards parents with any proposal, it is important for teachers to:

- feel committed to the notion of parental involvement in children's education and recognize the importance of working closely with parents;
- recognize that parents and families have much to contribute to children's reading development and that professionals stand to develop improved practice by gaining insights into this.

Reading record cards

As already indicated, some schools send books home with children without record cards. However, such records should be seen as an important feature of home reading programmes. They offer a simple, yet effective system for the development of a parent–teacher dialogue about children and their reading progress. Even a cursory analysis of the written responses made by teachers and parents reveals a shared process of interpretation and judgement about children's reading progress. Parents begin to understand what teachers see as significant and important in reading and teachers are able to tap into parents' ideas, approaches and concerns. To a large extent, meaning is thus being negotiated, ideas about reading are being shared, and possible ways forward are identified (see, for instance, Hannon *et al.*, 1986; Woods and Merttens, 1994).

Traditionally, teachers and parents have not had this form of specifically focused, ongoing exchange about a key area of learning. For many years, like so much of education, the school's approach to reading has been largely invisible to parents. The movement of books between home and school serves to show parents what sorts of reading materials are valued at school and the record cards help parents to understand professional approaches to the teaching of reading.

Book resources

Schools have different approaches to the selection of books that children take home. In Hackney, fiction continues to be popular and there is often a mixture of reading schemes (basal readers) and 'real' books. Some schools have deliberately introduced non-fiction and information books to ensure that all children feel motivated. There is reason to think that sending books home has provided teachers with an increased impetus to scrutinize stocks for unacceptable bias in terms of words, pictures and themes.

Damage and loss are constant problems when books are in transit. One school has reluctantly stopped sending books home as its budget cannot cover the high losses sustained. Another has decided to make a small termly charge to all parents to help cover replacements. Many schools take steps to protect books in some way and the most popular arrangement is some form of book bag, often with the school's name or personalized logo. Some schools have successfully attracted a local business sponsor with the offer of putting its name alongside the school's.

Selecting the classes

PACT is generally very successful with children in the first four years of formal schooling. More time and effort is needed to initiate it with nursery (kindergarten) and the later primary (elementary) school years. For instance, with preschool children, parents need to be ready to take a very active and imaginative role in terms of the variety of things that can usefully be done with inexperienced readers when working with a book. There may, for instance, be a need for drama, discussion and singing rather than reading as such.

Where the whole school is involved in a programme, there may be considerable differentiation of the way in which parental roles are interpreted through the age range. When a school is about to launch or relaunch a programme, it is wise to begin where implementation is easiest and then move onto the more challenging age groups, thus working from a firm base of parent contact and teacher experience.

Achieving parent participation

The initial contact with parents is crucial and experience suggests that efforts made at this stage pay off. Timing is a key factor in getting parents into school. Government and media claims that reading standards have fallen make parents quite anxious; consequently, school-based meetings to discuss reading can be quite well attended. However, if a home reading programme is to be successful, it is important that all parents are reached and PACT has learnt from its sister project, IMPACT, on this front. If parents are given the choice of three meetings on one day (the first early in the morning just after school starts, the second just after school ends, and the third early in the evening) then a very high percentage will be able to come. This will be greatly enabled if the letters inviting the parents are written (or at least decorated and addressed) by the children who are to be used as post persons.

It is important that the child's role in enlisting parental involvement is not neglected. Children are the intermediaries so their agreement and enthusiasm are essential. It is well worth spending preparation time talking to them and sharing the reasons why the programme is a good idea. Once it is underway, it is also important to give them opportunities for feedback about their experiences.

The parent meetings themselves should be quite short (say 40 minutes) with as much time given to parent questions and discussion as to teacher explanation and talk. To maintain a feeling of informality and individuality, a day's meetings should ideally involve only one class of parents and not more than two. If possible, parents should be given the opportunity to talk in small groups. Like teachers and children, parents can learn a lot from each other. The meeting should focus very tightly on the structure and requirements of the programme and the respective roles (and responsibilities) of teachers, parents and children. Consideration should be given to the needs of parents who are not confident in English, and it may be necessary to involve an interpreter(s) during the main meeting, separately or maybe at another time.

Managing the programme and the workload

The programme should always be shaped around class teachers' workloads. Schools may feel it is desirable that children read to their parents every night. However, it might be better to tailor the frequency of reading to what is felt to be manageable, say, for example, three official times each week – Monday, Wednesday and Friday. At the initial parent meeting it is important for teachers to specify their involvement in the record cards, e.g. I will read and initial everything that you write but will only write a comment when I feel it is necessary. A major criticism that continues to come from parents is that some teachers fail to read or acknowledge what the parents write.

As with other areas of work related to children's learning in school, it is helpful to have a designated member of staff who agrees to provide support and back-up to new teachers and to those who find themselves running into time-consuming difficulties. This makes a lot of sense in terms of drawing upon and rationalizing the skills and interests of staff with experience and expertise, but it is also a statement about the importance of the programme.

Monitoring and evaluating the programme

PACT takes the view that some kinds of evaluation data are very important, not so much to prove the value of the programme but to inform and guide the way in which it develops and responds to the experiences of the three parties who are responsible for its operation. This might involve reflecting on:

- children's comments and behaviour (enabling an assessment of the degree to which they are co-operating, wanting to read with their parents and enjoying the experience of the programme);
- parents' feedback (e.g. derived from day-to-day doorstep contact with them; from their writing on the record card, from interviews linked to the Primary Learning Record and from meetings arranged specifically to discuss the programme);
- teachers' experiences of operating and managing the initiative.

Children who are not able to get home reading support

There will always be some children who find themselves without regular support at home. First, there are the not insignificant number of children and parents who really find it difficult to work together. Working with one's own child in a learning and 'teaching' context can give rise to high emotions (on both sides). Children sense that the parent is being different in some way and sometimes react to this by being defensive and un-cooperative. Parents can invest too much in the situation and express this by making high and sometimes unrealistic demands. For most parents and children the difficulties can be overcome when parents are reminded that the occasion must be enjoyable for both parties. The event should be 'frequent, fun and friendly'.

Secondly, some parents will need help in order to help their children in the way that schools suggest. Ideas which are straightforward to teachers (e.g. 'sharing' a book, telling the story from the pictures, intelligent guessing of words) are not always familiar to parents with little experience of helping children to become readers. There may therefore be a need for sensitive professional engagement with parents' existing experiences and then careful explanation of what is meant by these professional practices.

Thirdly, there are the needs of parents who are not literate in English. One way round this problem is to recruit someone else from the family, perhaps an older sibling or a relative, or to have back-up arrangements at school. However, there is reason to think that parents can feel very inadequate when they are unable to help their children as other parents are. It is therefore important to seek ways of including them. There is a need here for individualized guidance from teachers about an appropriate parent role and related activities. PACT has found that it is possible to define an effective listening, talking and encouraging role for parents, even though they may not be as able at reading as their young children. Parents (the great majority mothers) actually provide, not so much support for reading as such, but a more general enabling climate of positive encouragement which serves to motivate and support the child's efforts and progress.

Boosting a flagging programme

Once a home reading programme is up and running, it will be necessary to renew everyone's interest and involvement each year. To some extent, this can be seen as part of the cyclical requirement for a successful and thriving programme. However, in addition to this, it will sometimes be necessary to give it a special boost.

The entry of education into a market culture has put teachers in touch with a new range of presentational and packaging skills which were traditionally used by those advertising and selling commercial products and ideas. The good side of this development is that schools are becoming better at representing themselves and promoting their interests to parents and the wider community – better at getting messages across. These new marketing skills can be used effectively in the service of home reading, particularly if they are used to create an event and surround this with excitement and energy.

One way of highlighting the value of a programme is to work at livening up its appearance. Everybody responds to bright, new materials. New reading record cards and children's PACT folders can be produced in the school's corporate colours and all communications about the programme can reflect this colour scheme. Some schools have enlisted the help of local sponsors in meeting the cost of this. Another idea is to draw attention to the importance of the programme within a bigger event like a book week, literacy week or home–school partnership fair: this could include parents reading stories and telling others about how they go about helping their children. A regular newsletter aimed specifically at highlighting the importance of home and school working together would also have its advantages.

THE ADVANTAGES OF HOME READING PROGRAMMES

We tend to think of schools as places where there is a degree of stability and permanence and sometimes forget that they are places where there is considerable periodic change – of teachers (changing classes, resigning, redundancy, retiring and being newly appointed), of children (moving through the educational system, changing schools), and of parents (accompanying the children through the system). This movement means that innovations like home reading programmes are repeatedly put to the test by teachers who find themselves in new situations, by new classes of children, and by new parents. The question: Why should teachers set up home reading programmes? is therefore always very relevant.

Four main reasons can be given

1. It would seem logical to expect that extra practice at home with a sympathetic, encouraging and supportive adult will result in children showing an increased ability to read.
2. If teachers and parents work closely together to support children in a key area of learning, there is the expectation that children will experience a sense of security

and benefit psychologically from the feeling that both their teacher and their parents are working together to help them.

3. If parents and teachers get to know each other as people and develop shared expectations and practices in terms of reading development, then children will not be expected to handle a separate set of attitudes and expectations from home and school respectively.
4. Home reading programmes provide teachers with an opportunity to learn about family and community literacy practices and to incorporate this understanding into the school curriculum.

These then are the potential benefits; but it would be unfair to teachers if promoters of home reading programmes like PACT held back on the problems and difficulties associated with the idea. It may be useful to summarize them here. Home reading programmes:

- are particularly demanding of teacher time during the initial setting-up period, although this is reduced once a programme is up and running;
- are demanding of teacher skills and ingenuity in multicultural areas where parents are not confident at reading English or helping children with reading in the way that schools suggest;
- are demanding of teacher time and creativity when parents and children find it difficult to work together.

Although one would hope that children's reading attainments would improve (measured or otherwise) as a result of a programme of parent help, clearly this cannot be seen as the only indicator of worth and success.

The benefits of a programme may be diffuse, delayed or unforeseen and thus illusive to evaluation. In Hackney, teachers are recognizing a range of benefits, such as: more time spent reading books; increased interest in books; greater care taken of books; more discussion about books, authors and illustrations; greater use of local libraries; the wish to buy books to own and to give as presents; more siblings choosing to look at books together; increased parent understanding of how children learn to read; increased parent interest in books and reading; heightened awareness of unacceptable bias in children's books.

There can be no doubt that many schools are committed to the idea. It seems that teachers have a strong innate feeling that asking children to read school books to their parents is a good thing, almost along the lines of an act of faith. To what extent does intuition and faith eliminate the need for clear scientific evidence? We live in a period when budget holders are asking us to provide measurable outcomes for an ever increasing number of things that we do. However, there is still much that is done in school that cannot be measured by performance indicators. In school, a great deal of what is done is done because it is guided by the informed opinions of experienced and reflecting professionals. 'We do these things because they are good things to do' (Stake, 1980).

Experience in Hackney and elsewhere suggests that few schools have either the motivation or the time to evaluate their home reading programmes in terms of measured reading attainment gains. PACT therefore supports the collection of qualitative impressionistic language data from the parents, children and teachers who are carrying out the programmes. This gives invaluable feedback about the difficulties and benefits of the programme in action which can be used to inform and shape its development. Formative evaluation is generally more useful than summative.

SUMMARY AND CONCLUSION

A distinction has been made between literacy at home and literacy at school. At home, literacy tends to be embedded in social, relational and activity contexts, and generally lacks the obvious formal organization of schooled literacy. Home reading programmes are devised primarily to support children's literacy in school; however, there is always the possibility that they will influence and support literacy at home. In addition, if teachers listen and respond to parents' ideas about literacy then natural family literacy practices can influence home reading programmes.

In Hackney and surrounding areas, school interest in home reading programmes remains high. Many teachers have tested out the basic home reading model in their own classrooms and this has led to a degree of interpretation and modification. PACT views this as an important and desirable development as it is only that which works in classrooms that can survive. Some schools are tempted to rush their programmes through and give parents very little chance to contribute. With regard to the current interest in family literacy programmes, it does seem important that this professional pitfall is avoided and that such programmes are not defined and owned only by teachers.

Interestingly, few schools feel the need to evaluate the worth (especially in terms of children's reading progress) of their programmes. To a large extent it is assumed that children's reading will benefit if their parents help them.

In its current approach to supporting schools, PACT tries to be realistic and honest about the idea of home reading programmes. This is done through clearly specifying the benefits – particularly in terms of teachers and parents talking to each other and working together for children – and the demands that are made on teacher time, workloads and energy.

PACT's framework for home reading programmes has arisen from teachers who have experience of running successful (and not so successful) programmes. Such programmes can be seen not only as a very worthwhile form of extra support for children's reading and literacy development, but also as a highly significant point of entry for the development of closer home–school understanding.

REFERENCES

Bissex, G.L. (1980) *GYNS AT WORK: A Child Learns to Write and Read.* Cambridge; MA: Harvard University Press.

Goelman, H., Oberg, A. and Smith, F. (eds) (1984) *Awakening to Literacy.* London: Heinemann.

Griffiths, A. and Hamilton, D. (1984) *Parent, Teacher, Child: Working Together in Children's Learning.* London: Methuen.

Griffiths, A. and King, A. (1985) PACT: Development of home-reading schemes in the ILEA.

In K. Topping and S. Wolfendale (eds), *Parental Involvement in Children's Reading*. Beckenham: Croom Helm/New York: Nichols.

Hancock, R. (1988) Parental involvement in children's reading: results of a survey of Brent primary school headteachers. *Reading* (Journal of UKRA), **22**(3), 168–74.

Hancock, R. (1991) Parental involvement in children's reading in Tower Hamlets. *Reading* (Journal of UKRA), **25**(1), 4–6.

Hancock, R. (1992) Parental involvement in children's education in Tower Hamlets. In *Learning by Design*. London: Tower Hamlets Professional Development Centre.

Hancock, R. (1994) Professional language, literacy and parents. *Language Matters*, **3**, 16–19.

Hancock, R. (1995) Family literacy – a French connection. *Primary Teaching Studies*, **9**(1) (Spring).

Hancock, R. and Gale, S. (1992) *The 1991 PACT Survey*. London: PACT.

Hannon, P.W. and Cuckle, P. (1984) Involving parents in the teaching of reading: a study of current school practice. *Educational Research*, **26**(1), 7–13.

Hannon, P., Weinberger, J., Page, B. and Jackson, A. (1986) Home–school communication by means of reading cards. *British Educational Research Journal*, **12**(3), 269–80.

Hewison, J. and Tizard, J. (1980) Parental involvement and reading attainment. *British Journal of Educational Psychology*, **50**, 209–15.

Jackson, A. and Hannon, P. (1981) *The Belfield Reading Project*. Rochdale: The Belfield Community Council.

King, A. and Puttock, S. (1986) *Maths PACT Report*. London: PACT.

Meek, M. (1991) *On Being Literate*. London: The Bodley Head.

Merttens, R. and Vass, J. (1990) *Sharing Maths Cultures: Inventing Maths for Parents And Children and Teachers*. London: Falmer Press.

Minns, H. (1993) 'Don't tell them daddy taught you': the place of parents or putting parents in their place? *Cambridge Journal of Education*, **23**(1), 25–32.

Pitfield Project (1984) *Home–School Reading Partnerships in Hackney: A Handbook for Teachers*. London: PACT.

Pritchard, D. and Rennie, J. (1978) *Reading: Involving Parents*. Coventry: Community Education Project.

Stake, R.E. (1980) Programme evaluation, particularly responsive evaluation. In W.B. Dockrell and D. Hamilton, *Rethinking Educational Research*. London: Hodder & Stoughton.

Taylor, D. (1983) *Family Literacy: Young Children Learning to Read and Write*. New Hampshire: Heinemann.

Tizard, B. and Hughes, M. (1984) *Young Children Learning: Talking and Thinking at Home and School*. London: Fontana.

Wolfendale, S. (1983) *Parental Participation in Children's Development and Education*. London: Gordon & Breach.

Woods, P. and Merttens, R. (1994) Parents' and children's assessments of maths in the home. In R. Merttens and P. Woods (eds) *AERA 1994*, New Orleans. Papers presented at the annual meeting of the American Educational Research Association, The IMPACT Project, University of North London Press, London.

Weinberger, J. (1983) *Fox Hill Reading Workshop*. London: Family Service Units.

Chapter 3

Children and Parents Enjoying Reading (CAPER): Promoting parent support in reading

Peter Branston

INTRODUCTION

Children and Parents Enjoying Reading (CAPER) began in the county of West Glamorgan in South Wales when an educational psychologist, a special needs teacher and a deputy headteacher began to look at ways in which parental support for promoting children's reading skills could be encouraged. In-service teacher training running in the county (Edwards and Branston, 1979) was leading schools and educational psychologists to the conclusion that a scheme or project might provide the necessary focus to bring together and systematize the efforts that individual teachers and schools were making.

The deputy headteacher had attended one of the in-service courses and decided to introduce a home–school reading programme in Year 3 for 8- to 9-year-olds. The school's remedial reading teacher took responsibility for organizing the scheme. Parents were invited to a meeting to discuss the 'important subject of children's reading'. The turn-out for that meeting came as a surprise to the school, because parent meetings were not generally well attended.

> Parents proved to be eager to help, anxious for advice and ready to follow suggested guidelines for encouraging their children's reading. (Branston and Provis, 1986, p. 3)

The school was not slow to see the potential of harnessing this support and was keen to extend the project to other classes in school. Parents discussed the project widely and also pressed for it to include their children's class. The project eventually involved all the 7- to 11-year-old pupils in the school. This school was not the only one to respond to the in-service course but the particular approach it adopted led directly to the development of the CAPER project.

In-service training was held in the project school with invited headteachers and in September 1983 the CAPER scheme (as it had then become) was introduced to four schools in the county with 6- to 8-year-olds. Teachers met termly to develop and pool effective strategies for maintaining and extending the project. This in-service activity generated a great deal of teacher materials and resources which were collected together and distributed as a Resource Pack for Schools (Branston and Provis, 1984a). The pack aimed at providing schools with a *structured programme*, explaining the *scope* of the project and the *demands* it would place upon the school.

The Resource Pack broke new ground in that it spelt out for schools what were the key requirements in initiating and sustaining a home–school reading programme. It was of critical importance that the pack was also supported by external support in the shape of a *CAPER Organizer*.

THE RESEARCH BACKGROUND

Probably the most important impetus for our initiative was *A Language for Life*, the report of the Bullock Committee (DES (Bullock Report), 1975), set up by the government in the light of evidence that the post-war rise in reading standards in England and Wales was not being maintained.

From the evidence set before them, the Bullock Committee drew the conclusion that reading standards were declining, not overall, but amongst the:

> children of unskilled and semi-skilled workers. Moreover, the national averages almost certainly mask falling reading standards in areas with severe social and educational problems. (para. 2.29)

We were impressed with Hewison's (1979) finding of a significant correlation between children's reading attainment and whether or not parents listened to them read on a regular basis. Firm evidence for such a connection was further reinforced by Tizard *et al.* (1981), who were able to conclude that parental help both reduced the proportion of failing readers and increased the proportion of able readers.

A FOUR-STEP MODEL FOR CHANGE

The central players in establishing CAPER had learnt some important lessons from their involvement in other government funded projects. The philosophy of earlier projects seemed to be that all that was required were good ideas and resources which by an almost magical process would be welcomed by and used enthusiastically by schools. Shipman points to the 'commendable conservatism' schools actually showed in response to such projects and remarks on the fact that new practice usually leaves the school at the same time as the researchers (Shipman, 1978).

We were helped immensely by *Knowledge Utilization Systems in Education* (Paisley and Butler, 1983), which describes in depth the features of successful state-level dissemination policies and strategies in the USA. Their findings supported the notion of a four-stage model of introducing changes in practice in schools, a model which was employed with CAPER. The stages were as follows:

Initiation stage: the first part of the project comprising all those activities designed to inform and to prepare interested schools.

Implementation stage: all the practical aspects required to get the project up and running.

Maintenance stage: helping to overcome difficulties an individual school may be having. Support at a moment when enthusiasm is faltering may be critical in sustaining the project.

Incorporation stage: signs that a school is incorporating a successful scheme into everyday operations.

The four-stage model guided our thinking about the project and helped considerably with planning. The stages worked as follows:

Initiation stage

Schools wishing to participate in the project were given a pack of materials (Branston and Provis, 1984a) to get the project underway. The pack included the essential kit shown in Table 3.1.

Table 3.1   *The essential CAPER kit*

Invitations to parents to meetings in school.
Model talks for use at parents' meetings.
A handout for parents to be distributed at the meeting summarizing the points made.
The CAPER Comment Booklet passed between home and school.
The parent questionnaires and various review sheets.
The materials for parent training: 'The Parent Workshops'.
The 'Clinic Pack' for work with individual parents.
Guidelines for schools intending to develop within school Parent Listening Groups.

All of this material was subsequently gathered together (Branston and Provis, 1986).

Implementation

It is a common misconception that people simply need to hear about a good idea to put it into practice. The truth is that we are all committed to the ways we behave. Implementation in the CAPER project was about securing time and a certain kind of practice from teachers, parents and children. To maximize take-up one had to point to other sites where success was occurring, to be crystal clear about what parents, children and teachers were expected to do in the project, to provide the materials and to work with senior management in the school to persuade them of the project's worth. The importance of the external support that this required cannot be exaggerated.

A common starting point with each school was to develop teacher participation by holding initial teacher meetings in school. At these the required commitment from teachers was stressed and the suggestion made that the project should be undertaken in not more than two classes to start with. This gave all staff the opportunity to see what the project would involve for them. What teachers especially wanted to know was what extra work would be required of them and the outcomes they might expect.

Schools, in conjunction with the project facilitators, drew up operational plans. One school's plan can be seen in Table 3.2.

Table 3.2 *One school's operational plan*

Parents, children and teachers all commit themselves to their part in the project.

For parents this commitment is:
- to read with their children each evening for not more than 15 minutes;
- to fill in an appropriate comment about their children's reading;
- to return the comment booklet each day to school.

For teachers the commitment is:
- to share a belief in the potential of the project;
- to present CAPER as fun not homework;
- to adjust classroom routines to accommodate the project;
- to maintain the home–school link through the comment booklet;
- to help ensure a fresh supply of good children's literature is always available.

For children the commitment is:
- to read every day with their parents;
- to take care of the books they take home;
- to bring the comment booklet back to school each day.

This plan of action was then shared with parents. As the project developed, parents were more directly involved in drawing up plans.

Maintaining the scheme

Early experience with parents and teachers in encouraging home–school collaboration had shown an initial and genuine enthusiasm and a real desire to promote reading through parental involvement. This enthusiasm tended to be short-lived and when the CAPER project began a great deal of thought was given to ways of sustaining interest and support. We rapidly saw that most of the work of the project would have to be directed at maintenance activity. Table 3.3 demonstrates this point well.

Table 3.3 *Developmental relevance of CAPER activities*

Project activities	Introductory	Maintenance	Development
First meeting with school	*		
First meeting with parents	*		
CAPER comment booklet		*	
Parent booklet		*	
Parent workshops		*	
CAPER clinics		*	*
Inset with teachers	*	*	
Poster competitions		*	
Parent questionnaires		*	
Parent newsletters		*	
Publicity	*	*	
Conferences/exhibitions	*	*	*
Research		*	*
Committee reports	*	*	

Thus a whole range of activities was undertaken to maintain the CAPER scheme. These included regular calendared visits to participating schools; meetings with head-teachers to review progress and plan for the future; competitions for participating schools; the systematic change of books through the school's library service to ensure a constant stock of suitable children's fiction; exhibitions in teachers' centres and local stores of school and home produced materials.

Incorporation stage

Evidence from other projects (Paisley and Butler, 1983) suggested that schools require external support to sustain new initiatives and that this support needs to be more intensive at the outset then tapering off. Paisley and Butler's detailed review indicated that the incorporation of new practice into the life of a school appears to take approximately two years; therefore CAPER adopted a two-year support calendar for schools entering the scheme.

CAPER became part of the day-to-day life of a large number of schools. This was evidenced in reports by headteachers to their school's governing bodies and in advertisements for teaching vacancies which mentioned an interest or experience in the scheme as desirable and a range of school-initiated activities. The scheme met with overwhelming support from parents and in all schools the Parent–Teachers' Association made generous contributions towards books and materials. Parental enthusiasm played an important part in establishing the scheme in participating schools.

In spite of the insistence in the Bullock Report (1975) that parents did not really need to concern themselves about the nature of the reading process, it was evident very early on in the project that this was an area of keen interest for them and therefore something which we felt the CAPER project had to address. Since the project required close co-operation between schools and parents, the roles of teachers and of parents had to be precisely defined.

Teachers needed to be reassured that parents were not being groomed to take on a responsibility that was rightfully theirs, and indeed some parents also insisted on that distinction before they would agree to participate. Schools were, in addition, apprehensive that the project might be inconsistent with their own reading policy. With this in mind CAPER spelt out two broad principles:

- The focus in the project would be *real books*. While schools might continue to send home reading scheme primers, the CAPER book stock would consist solely of children's fiction.
- Parents would aim to have fun with books.

Teachers responded readily to the notion that children were turned off by reading and that methods of teaching reading in school which had emphasized mechanics at the expense of pleasure might play an important part in this. Children needed to be taught the basics, but reading ought to be much more fun.

PARENT WORKSHOPS AND CLINICS

The Parent Workshops (Branston and Provis, 1984b) and the Clinic Pack (Branston and Provis, 1984c) delivered to schools through meetings with teachers detailed the

Table 3.4   *Workshop 4: Insight into reading*

We guess at print.	It is acceptable for children to guess.
We needed several attempts to get the unknown word.	Children may not get it right first time.
We leave out words and guess back at them.	Children may need to be shown how to do this.
We change our guesses in the light of further reading.	Children need to be encouraged to read for meaning.
For us the right word makes sense.	We shouldn't worry too much if the child sometimes sacrifices precision for flow.

approach to helping with reading which CAPER espoused. Much of the material is reproduced in *Children and Parents Enjoy Reading* (Branston and Provis, 1986), but underpinning it all is that reading together can be fun.

The workshops consisted of structured activities within school for groups of parents aimed at improving their skills in promoting reading. The Workshop Pack was not only a guide to parents, it also required schools to 'outline their approach to reading'. Learning to read was seen as a *process* which took time and required patient support. If a parent could tap into the narrative impulse which children appear, seemingly without exception, to possess then they would maximize the child's potential for literacy development.

It became clear that the anxiety felt by some parents arose because of a misunderstanding about their role. By stressing the importance of enjoyment as a valid and an educational objective, much of this anxiety was dissipated. The workshops aimed to acquaint parents with our view of the reading process and to maintain the distinction between the parent and teacher role.

An underlying assumption in the workshops was that children are like adults when it comes to learning and therefore a good way of understanding their learning processes is to consider our own. Using a cloze procedure in Parent Workshop 4 (Branston and Provis, 1986, p. 74) the points shown in Table 3.4 could be drawn out.

Reading clinics provided parents with the opportunity to demonstrate their listening skills and to raise any issues about reading which were causing them concern. Attendance rates at clinics were in excess of 80 per cent. Some parents needed a number of invitations and considerable notice so that they could attend. It was very noticeable that parents unable to make the first meeting were just as committed to their children's education as parents who came straightaway.

Where parents failed to attend, advice was provided in the Resource Pack. For example, did parents feel intimidated by school? Perhaps their experiences as pupils had not been particularly fruitful or happy. What did schools do to make parents positively welcome? Experience of running the scheme challenged commonly held assumptions about parents. It became clear just how busy parents were and that the main objective in the project was to *secure time for reading at home* in a context where there were numerous other and equally valid competing priorities. An example of this was where, early on in the project, parents questioned the suggestion one or two of us made that bedtime was the best time to read with children. Our assumption that this was a peaceful and free time of the day for most parents was just plain wrong. Our advice then became: *read with your child at any time which is convenient for you.* Schools in the project modified their advice to parents accordingly.

CHILDREN'S BOOKS

An essential requirement for the success of CAPER in schools was a plentiful supply of good children's literature. Experience had shown that each class required about 50 books each half term to sustain the reading programme and substantial effort was centred on generating collections of appropriate reading material. Very considerable support for the project came from the Children's Library Service, which set up a CAPER book Swap Scheme where project schools were allowed a box of books per class per term. This was precisely the kind of support which pulled schools towards the project. Book fairs were held in schools, advice given on books that worked with particular age groups, moneys sought from a range of central and school budgets and from local and national parent support groups.

Our experience on examining the book stock in schools about to begin the scheme was that often it was not up to sustaining the project. Non-fiction predominated and the fiction collection did not accord with any particular reading principle. Books had been gathered through a process of accretion over the years. There was, therefore, a need to promote debate about the books in school, to part with books that nobody read and to develop book collections according to an agreed plan.

We gave wholehearted endorsement to the call in the Bullock Report (1975) for each school to have a *book policy*, the essentials of which would be:

- a *'conscious design'* in acquiring books;
- a record of all books the school possesses;
- every classroom should have its book corner (including fiction) changed from week to week;
- one teacher to have responsibility for enacting the policy.

The book policy was a key prerequisite for the successful implementation of the CAPER scheme and all CAPER schools were encouraged to develop one. Teacher 'readers groups' were established and materials they produced included book reviews, lists of fiction popular with particular age groups and books which challenged stereotypical gender prejudice. These lists were circulated to project schools.

EVALUATING CAPER

In 1987 funding was obtained from the Welsh Office for a small-scale research project into the effectiveness of parental support for reading with children in nursery classes in selected West Glamorgan schools (Welsh Office, 1987).

It was felt at the outset that the CAPER methodology, when suitably modified, might prove particularly effective with children of nursery school age, that is between 3 and 4 years of age. A pilot project had already been undertaken by Curran (1985) using an experimental group of 20 children randomly drawn from the nursery population of one primary school and a control group drawn from the nearest neighbourhood school. The project ran for two and a half terms. Parent participation was fostered by a series of workshops and individual clinics where parents were given the opportunity to discuss their children's progress and any problems encountered in using books. The emphasis in the work with parents was how the enjoyment to be

Table 3.5   *Research hypotheses from the Welsh Office Nursery Project*

The Nursery Project would:

- extend children's oral language skills by improving their language comprehension, augmenting their vocabulary and increasing their picture recognition skills;
- promote children's interest in both picture and story books by changing children's book use behaviour, by increasing the frequency of book usage and the amount of time spent in using books, and by changing children's attitudes towards the use and care of books;
- develop children's concepts about print by increasing their 'pre-reading skills';
- change parental behaviour by increasing the time they spend in sharing books with their very young children;
- improve home–school links by increasing parent–teacher contact and thus developing positive parent attitudes towards their children's schools;
- effect change in terms of teacher attitude towards the use of fiction with young children and their willingness to engage parents in supporting children's education.

found in books could be fostered. At the end of the intervention Curran was able to report that the experimental group had made significantly greater gains than the control group on all four evaluation instruments: the British Picture Vocabulary Scale, the Verbal Comprehension and Naming Vocabulary Scales from the British Ability Scales, and Clay's 'Concepts of Print' Test (Clay, 1979). Subjective reporting by parents, children and their teachers endorsed the view of the project's success. Curran suggests caution in interpreting the results in view of the small numbers involved and the need for further research.

The Welsh Office (1987) project, which again used CAPER materials and methodology, was a larger scale study involving 80 children in four nursery classes and matched controls. A small team, set up to oversee the project, generated hypotheses which were felt to be possible outcomes of the planned intervention. These are set out in Table 3.5.

The detailed results of the project are written up elsewhere (Calvert, 1987; Jones, 1987; Welsh Office, 1987), but the main findings can be summarized as follows. Two sorts of data were collected: objective test findings and 'softer' data (questionnaire, critical incident diaries kept by teachers, a child observation schedule and interview).

Little if any difference in favour of experimental schools was found on the objective tests, much in line with Hannon's (1987) finding in his study of the effects of parental support. What did emerge was that in the experimental schools, children's 'book behaviour' changed substantially. They spent a significantly greater time with books, they took greater care of books and they were handling books 'more confidently'. No such change was registered amongst the controls. Children in experimental schools were asking for books far more frequently at the end of the project than at the beginning. Again this was not the case with the controls.

Parents and children in the experimental schools came to spend more time together with books; not so in the controls. At the end of the project parents report a significant increase in the number of books at home. No significant change was registered in control group homes.

Parents in the project schools reported, through questionnaire, a greater eagerness in their children to read and greater contact with the school. The project gave them greater confidence in helping their child with reading and they were firmly of the view that the reading project would have a beneficial effect on their child's future reading progress.

One interesting and unexpected finding was that by the end of the study a much wider group of people had been drawn in to help with reading in the project schools. In all schools Mum was by far the one who helped most, but in the experimental schools the network had been extended to include grandparents, uncles and aunts and other siblings. Dad's involvement had also measurably increased.

An interesting finding to emerge was that the rate of participation amongst parents varied very considerably, even amongst schools which appeared to have similar catchment areas. It appeared that the level of commitment within a school and by participating teachers to the project was a significant factor in the project's success. The more enthusiastic the school the greater the level of parental participation.

Teachers in the project schools kept 'critical incident diaries' in which they recorded events they thought important. It was interesting to note from these that the scope of parental involvement widened considerably beyond the original objectives of the project. For example, schools devised CAPER competitions and exhibitions, further 'at home' activities for parents and children, and visits from poets and authors. One school invited 'interesting people' to come in and read their favourite children's story. In two schools parents were encouraged through the project to come in to school as helpers. Guidance to schools included advice on promoting the effectiveness of parent-helpers.

It was instructive looking through the critical incident diaries to note teachers and parents developing common interests and the increasing references to 'we' rather than 'I'. One teacher's diary entry illustrated this co-operation well:

> Parents and I discussed what could be done to encourage the 8–10 children who were not involved in the scheme . . . parents felt that if the children were to visit the library as part of the school day they could choose their books and take them home. (Welsh Office, 1987)

One also notes that teachers were learning from parents. One mother had been discouraging her child from interrupting during 'story-time'. The teacher concerned reports:

> Following her comments I questioned my own approach. We tend to discourage interruption . . . . (Welsh Office, 1987)

The diversity of response in schools was remarkable. The project had quite narrow objectives but appeared to generate an enormous enthusiasm in each school. Activities included exhibitions of work in local shops, newspaper articles, prizes and competitions, 'home fun' for parents and children, coffee mornings, book swaps, visits by children's librarians and local bookshops, book sales in schools, video productions, 'CAPER character' parades and many other home–school activities. CAPER T-shirts and jumpers, badges and a host of other promotional activities were produced by parents. It seemed as though the project had helped to realize and harness the energy of a large number of parents eager to support their local school.

Headteachers in the Nursery Project were asked what they thought the project had achieved and to rank these achievements in order of importance. Their ranking is given in Table 3.6.

Table 3.6 *Headteachers' ranking of achievements of Nursery CAPER Project*

Ranking	Achievement
1.	Encouraged the view in teachers, parents and children that reading is fun.
2.	Promoted mutually beneficial links between school and home.
3.	Encouraged a parental contribution to children's development.
4.	Broadened the school's view on how children learn to read.
5.	Helped in the development of children's reading skills.
6.	Provided a focus for language and communication work in the nursery.
7.	Made teachers more aware of the range of good children's literature.

Headteachers' principal criticism of the scheme was that:

the organisers had underestimated the voracious demand for books that the project would generate and more guidance would have engaged diffident parents earlier in the project. (Welsh Office, 1987)

The headteachers' view ran counter to that of the project organizer for whom the critical value of the project was that it had *significantly deepened teachers' awareness of the range of children's books available.*

A parent questionnaire used in the project asked them to name their three favourite children's authors. This was a task both parents and teachers often had difficulty with at the start of the project. It certainly was not the case when the Nursery project finished. (Welsh Office, 1987)

Evidence from the Children's Library Service strongly supported the view that the project vastly increased their turnover of stock. Local bookshops also reported an increase in the sale of children's books.

READING ADVISORY CENTRE

One development which grew directly from the CAPER project was the Reading Advisory Centre. CAPER gave detailed advice on an individual basis to parents through the CAPER Clinic Pack and the clinics attracted a number of parents whose children's progress gave their parents more than usual concern.

The Reading Advisory Centre was established specifically for those parents and their children. It was staffed on a part-time basis by an educational psychologist who had worked closely with the CAPER project and particularly in setting up the CAPER clinics. Parents and children came in regularly for advice and guidance. Teachers were invited to accompany parents and in-service training was held for teachers at the centre over a five-year period.

Children could only be seen after assessment by teacher and psychologist and where school had 'given it their best shot'. The assessment which was requested reflected the view the RAC had about the reading process and how to help. Stress was laid upon what literacy skills a child had and included the following elements:

- a pen portrait of the child indicating any strengths or interests in whatever area;
- an analysis of the child's concepts of print using the Sand and Stones materials (Clay, 1979);

- the child's knowledge of the language of books, i.e. words like chapter, contents, dedication, etc.;
- an account of the child's understanding of how written language works;
- the child's knowledge of how stories work;
- the assessment also referred to a reading age, to the child's level of intellectual development and phonological awareness.

Because children were never seen without their parents, wider but related issues could also be addressed. For example, it was found that some children were using their reading difficulty to control interaction or as a bargaining tool within the family. The reading difficulty had some functional purpose for the child as well as the parent. Sometimes the unsettled child could be observed testing out parental attitudes and feelings during a reading session. Most commonly, we saw parents coming to terms with their feeling that someone, the school, or more threateningly, themselves, was to be blamed for the child's 'lack of progress'.

Children were seen with parents initially on a fortnightly then on a monthly basis for half an hour. Parents found their own way to the centre, so the set-up was one which favoured those with their own transport and/or with high motivation. These were parents who had experienced long-term and high levels of anxiety about their child's reading and it was almost always the case that parents were desperate for help.

The half-hour session with parent and child focused upon the way in which the parent helped with the child's reading. The session aimed to promote the confidence of both the parent and child. A careful record was kept of the progress the child had made since the previous appointment. Progress was gauged in terms of the child's increased decoding skills, the new words the child had learnt and the number of books the child and parent had read together.

The parent and child were encouraged to have fun with books and the parent advised to give as much help as possible to enjoy the book. The method used to learn words was suggested by Warner (1963). The child selects the word which is then written as a flash card. The chosen words are checked at the end of the week and any words the child doesn't know are discarded on the basis that the child 'didn't really want them'. This method proved successful time and time again in building up a bank of words which children recognized with ease.

In order to reinforce the guidance given at the centre a range of materials was produced. Perhaps the most effective was the *Ready For Reading* video which was lent to parents and schools. The video is aimed at parents giving detailed guidance of effective ways of promoting children's reading. It has been used to great effect with groups of parents in school.

A study of the effectiveness of the Reading Advisory Centre was undertaken by Rathmell (1991) which used New Paradigm Research (Reason, 1988) in which interviews and meetings were held with service users over a period of twelve months.

Rathmell identified the key features of the RAC as:

- individual, consultant-style appointments;
- master–apprentice interaction style during appointments;
- treats all children as readers/builds confidence;
- shows parents how they can help between appointments;
- emphasizes reading for meaning and enjoyment;

- uses a range of techniques such as miscue analysis depending on difficulty;
- emphasizes choice of books.

Parents were 'extremely positive' about the attention their children received, the guidance and support given and the progress in written language skills their children made.

CONCLUSIONS

As indicated above, considerable thought had been put into ensuring that home–school reading links were sufficiently rooted in the life of the school to ensure their continuation after external support was withdrawn. The growth of the scheme was impressive so that by 1987, three years after its inception, CAPER had extended to 105 primary schools and eight comprehensive schools. At this time the scheme had its own organizer with her own staff and an annual budget for books and equipment.

In September 1987 the funding from central government which had sustained the project finished. From 1987 until 1993 the project was funded by the Local Education Authority. During that period the project continued to thrive. As experience was built up in particular schools, external support was transferred to new schools coming into the project. By 1993 it was felt that all schools in the LEA had the necessary knowledge and materials to mount and maintain schemes from their own resources.

Any evaluation of CAPER should be made against the scheme's aims, which were:

- to promote reading standards;
- to extend children's experience of good literature;
- to promote purposeful parental involvement;
- to stimulate debate on the ways children learn to read.

Comments on these follow:

The promotion of reading standards

CAPER developed in a climate where concern had been expressed about reading standards and it was unsurprising that most schools were attracted to the project by the possibility that CAPER would accelerate children's reading progress. The support materials provided to schools included guidance on 'before and after' evaluation of children's reading ability, narrowly defined as improvement in reading scores. Reports from schools provided some evidence that CAPER helped to promote children's reading ages, but the evidence was anecdotal since no school undertook the kind of evaluation which would withstand rigorous examination. But CAPER did not stand or fall on that issue; indeed the Welsh Office (1987) evaluation did not demonstrate any such effect. Headteachers in that project ranked improvement in reading skills only fifth out of seven achievements. While gains in reading ages were obviously to be welcomed, the main thrust of CAPER had been to promote children's enjoyment of books.

Children's experience of good literature

There can be little doubt that this aim was fully achieved. Schools and parents reported a growth in the use of books quite unforeseen in the original prospectus for CAPER. This increased book awareness was achieved by the class-teacher creating opportunities for children to select their own books, to offer their own opinions about books and to recommend them to their friends.

The peripatetic children's librarians gave enthusiastic support for the scheme both in helping to select appropriate titles and in visits to participating schools. They reported a remarkable increase in the circulation of their book stock directly attributable to the development of CAPER. There was strong evidence that the project had a significant effect on children's 'book behaviour'. This was a major finding in the Welsh Office research project and was invariably noted in CAPER schools. Children were more confident in the way they handled books and treated them with 'greater respect'.

Purposeful parental involvement

Throughout the project parent feedback was consistently encouraged. Questionnaires were used extensively and provided an impressive testimony to the commitment and response to the scheme by parents. The following comments are typical.

> Cathy seemed to be falling behind until the scheme began: her reading now has greatly improved.

> Helped Erin become a confident reader and helped her appreciate the pleasure of reading: in short, CAPER has turned Erin into a very happy 'bookworm'.

> Kathy has a small speech problem, I feel that the scheme is helping her to improve her speech.

> They have a very large selection of books as you cannot buy books every week.

> I think Christopher's reading flow has improved but I do not know if this is due to the scheme or not; it's certainly disciplined our reading sessions.

> It has taught my daughter to enjoy reading immensely – previous to this scheme it was always a big effort to get her to read. Both my husband and I are very grateful to the teachers for operating this scheme.

The theme that occurs again and again is that parents respond strongly and positively to the opportunity to participate in collaborative projects with schools.

Stimulating debate on how children learn to read

CAPER both encouraged and influenced the debate on how children come to be readers. CAPER did not directly challenge any orthodoxy but it did stress the enjoyment and fun to be had from books. Fun is quite a subversive notion in education. It is hard to package and challenges the ethic implicit in a lot of what happens in school. Some legitimation, it seemed, was needed for reading for pleasure *in school* to be supported by teachers. CAPER provided that legitimation. It was, after all, sponsored by the LEA and by government grant. The notion, too, that teachers should model the enjoyment to be had from reading, by reading for pleasure in class, while children did the same, also needed to be encouraged. The debate about reading as process or task was considerably sharpened by the project. Teachers involved in the scheme inevitably broadened their views on how reading should be taught and generally could be seen to be using methods which encompassed both 'real books' and 'objectives teaching'.

Throughout its operation CAPER was run on campaign lines and like all campaigns there comes a time when the campaign runs out of steam or the organizers feel that its objectives had been achieved. CAPER began in 1984 and ended formally when funding by the LEA finished in 1993. In that time all schools in the county knew of the scheme and the majority participated. The scheme spawned other projects outside the Authority and outside the UK. Staff who inspired its development have moved on and taken the principles of the project with them. The experience of the project has been recorded in research papers and guidance handbooks and is available to schools and teachers who believe in the critical role parents play in developing their children's reading skills.

REFERENCES

Branston, P. and Provis, M. (1984a) *Caper: A Resource Pack for West Glamorgan Schools*. Swansea: West Glamorgan County Council.

Branston, P. and Provis, M. (1984b) *Caper Workshop Pack*. Swansea: West Glamorgan County Council.

Branston, P. and Provis, M. (1984c) *Caper Clinic Pack*. Swansea: West Glamorgan County Council.

Branston, P. and Provis, M. (1986) *Children and Parents Enjoy Reading (CAPER)*. London: Hodder & Stoughton.

Calvert, D.A. (1987) The effects of parental involvement in the development of reading and language skills of nursery aged children. Unpublished MSc thesis, University College Swansea.

Clay, M.M. (1979) *The Early Detection of Reading Difficulties: A Diagnostic Survey with Recovery Procedures*. Auckland: Heinemann Education Books.

Curran, P. (1985) Parental involvement with nursery aged pupils. Unpublished MEd thesis, University College Swansea.

Department of Education and Science (1975) *A Language for Life* (The Bullock Report). London: HMSO.

Edwards, L. and Branston, P. (1979) *Reading: How Parents Can Help*. Swansea: West Glamorgan County Council.

Hannon, P. (1987) A study of the effects of parental involvement in the teaching of reading on children's reading test performance. *British Journal of Educational Psychology*, **57**, 56–72.

Hewison, J. (1979) Home environment and reading attainment: A study of children in a working-class community. Unpublished PhD thesis, University of London.

Jones, R.D. (1987) Promoting reading and language skills of nursery aged children through parental involvement. Unpublished MSc thesis, University College Swansea.

Paisley, W. and Butler, M. (1983) *Knowledge Utilization Systems in Education*. Beverly Hills/London/New Delhi: Sage Publications.

Rathmell, N. (1991) The use of new paradigm research in the development of a Local Education Authority reading advisory service. Unpublished MEd thesis, University College Swansea.

Reason, P. (1988) *Human Enquiry in Action; Developments in New Paradigm Research.* Beverly Hills/London/New Delhi: Sage Publications.

Shipman, M.D. (1978) *In-School Evaluation.* London: Heinemann.

Smith, F. (1986) *Reading.* Cambridge University Press.

Tizard, J. *et al.* (1981) Collaboration between teachers and parents in assisting children's reading. *British Journal of Educational Psychology,* **52**, 1–15.

Warner, S.A. (1963) *Teacher.* Virago.

Wells, G. (1987) *The Meaning Makers.* London: Hodder & Stoughton.

Welsh Office (1987) *The Effects of Parental Involvement in the Development of Reading and Language Skills of Nursery Aged Children.* Cardiff: HMSO.

Chapter 4

Pause Prompt Praise: Reading tutoring procedures for home and school partnership

Ted Glynn

HOME AND SCHOOL PARTNERSHIP

Children spend the first five or six years of their lives living at home with parents or caregivers. In this powerful, yet responsive, social context (Glynn, 1985) children typically acquire their first language and learn to use that language to enhance social and cultural relationships with adults and peers, and to develop important academic skills. Parents have typically played a major role in providing learning opportunities, and in providing a structured but supportive environment for their children's learning. Most children are already competent learners by the time they enter pre-school or school contexts. Further, after children have entered preschool or school, they still participate concurrently in responsive, social learning contexts at home.

Educators have long argued for a closer involvement of parents in their children's education. Involvement, however, has been vaguely and inconsistently defined. It has been taken to mean anything from having parents raise funds for their local school, to becoming members of school Boards of Trustees, and participating in all decision-making, from school maintenance to staff appointments and appraisal of principals. Parent involvement in education has also been taken to mean anything, from passive reception of teacher comments on their children's progress at parent–teacher meetings or participation in Individual Educational Plans (IEPs) with a range of educational professionals, to active engagement in teaching activities in their children's classrooms or active engagement in teaching activities with their children at home.

This shared responsibility for the same children presents strong arguments for parents and teachers to share common academic learning objectives for the children with whom they each interact, for example in the learning of oral language, reading, and writing skills. Skills acquired in one context (home or school) may or may not generalize to the other. Facilitating learning in one context may depend on knowing what behaviours are being acquired and reinforced in the other. Successful perform-ance in one context may be precluded by the performance of incompatible behaviours in the other. The regular and reliable exchange of information between home and school about children's learning and behaviour, and a co-operative partnership (or working relationship) between parents and teachers, appear essential. Only by working together and freely sharing information data can parents and teachers enhance the generalization of skills learned at school to the home setting, and the reverse.

Research on generalization of literacy skills across home and school contexts is relatively rare. However, studies involving parents implementing a set of reading tutoring procedures, now known as Pause Prompt Praise, have demonstrated clear gains in children's reading at school resulting from parental intervention at home. Pause Prompt and Praise comprises a set of behavioural tutoring procedures designed to provide additional support for older low-progress readers. Tutoring is carried out by parents, peers, or community members in the context of reading meaningful stories, rather than with words and sounds taken out of context.

WHAT IS PAUSE PROMPT PRAISE?

The Pause Prompt Praise reading tutoring procedures were developed in South Auckland in 1977. A team of researchers worked intensively with parents of a group of 10- to 12-year-old low-progress readers to produce a training booklet and video: *Remedial Reading at Home: Helping You to Help Your Child*. The booklet and accompanying research monograph were first published by the New Zealand Council for Educational Research (Glynn *et al.*, 1979; McNaughton *et al.*, 1981).

The initial research work with Pause Prompt Praise involved intensive observation and training in home settings with a group of older (10- to 12-year-old) readers and their parents, and resulted in the production of a parent training package (booklet and video). The project required close involvement of the researcher in both home and school settings, allowing access to information not readily accessible to teachers. Teachers of children in the original South Auckland project (Glynn *et al.*, 1979) and in a subsequent parallel study in Birmingham, UK (McNaughton *et al.*, 1987) perceived parents as apathetic towards their children's learning at school. Yet there was little evidence that teachers had had contact with their children's homes. The researchers in these studies found otherwise – that parents cared deeply about their children's reading difficulties at school, and were highly motivated to do something about it, to the extent of learning to implement the Pause Prompt Praise procedures. The strength of parents' motivation to help their children learning to read at home is illustrated in a study by Glynn and Glynn (1986) who established that Khmer-speaking mothers of 6- to 7-year-old migrant children were able to improve their children's rate of reading progress at school over and above that of children's participation in the school programme alone. This was achieved despite the mothers having only a few words of English and having little or no schooling in Cambodia. In this study mothers and children were invited to work together, using either Khmer or English to 'work out' the meaning of the stories sent home from the school following usual classroom practice. Mothers appeared to use children's new knowledge and recall of English words learnt at school, and children appeared to use the mother's first-language skills (Khmer) to discuss the pictures and events portrayed in the stories. Important additional outcomes from this study were clear gains in English reading skills for mothers as well as children.

Subsequent research with the Pause Prompt Praise procedures (Glynn and McNaughton, 1985; Wheldall and Glynn, 1989; Wheldall and Mettem, 1985) led to the Research Monograph being published in the UK under the title *Pause Prompt Praise* (McNaughton *et al.*, 1987). Widespread and continuing interest in these procedures has resulted in an updated version of Pause Prompt Praise (Glynn *et al.*, 1992; Dick *et al.*, 1992). A Maori language version, Tatari Tautoko Tauawhi, has been developed and trialled by Maori staff of the New Zealand Special Education Service, and teachers, students and family members in several different schools in which children are being taught in Maori language immersion classes (Atvars and Glynn, 1992; Harawira *et al.*, 1993; Glynn *et al.*, 1993).

The Pause Prompt Praise strategies are derived from the theoretical perspective on reading developed by Clay (1979, 1991) and McNaughton (1987). This perspective views proficient reading as learning to use all the sources of information within and around a text to understand the particular message being conveyed. Differences between high-progress and low-progress readers are thought to lie not so much in their success at identifying letters and letter–sound combinations, but in the flexibility and fluency with which they use this information together with contextual information.

High rates of self-correction are associated with high progress during early reading (Clay, 1969, 1979, 1991). However, the reading contexts available to low-progress readers may be unhelpful in two ways. First, low-progress readers may be given fewer opportunities to read meaningful text material of appropriate difficulty. Second, the type of instruction they receive may prevent them from learning to integrate contextual and letter–sound information and to self-correct. This may lead to a state of 'instructional dependence' on over-intrusive remedial help (McNaughton, 1981).

Pause Prompt Praise is designed for use in a one-to-one oral reading context so that low-progress readers can receive more opportunities to self-correct errors and to practise problem-solving strategies. Assisting readers to learn these strategies requires tutors to learn to implement a set of specific tutoring skills.

Tutoring involves first *pausing* when a reader makes an error (to allow opportunity for reader self-correction without tutor help). Where the error is not self-corrected, tutors offer different types of *prompt* to assist the reader with the meaning of the work or with the letter or sounds in the word *when* the error indicates the reader has already understood the meaning of the word. Tutors also employ specific *praise* to reinforce readers' use of independent strategies such as self-corrections and corrections following tutor prompts. Extensive descriptive data reported by Wheldall *et al.* (1992) demonstrate that even trained practising teachers do not 'naturally' implement these strategies when hearing children read.

The majority of readers who have access to competent reading programmes learn these independent strategies from their regular engagement with texts, as part of their classroom reading activities. Indeed, applying Pause Prompt Praise to readers who are not experiencing difficulties, or who are making better than average progress may be superfluous (Wheldall and Glynn, 1989).

Pause Prompt Praise aims to break into the cycle of dependence, in which low-progress readers encountering an unknown word may 'cue' the teacher to tell them the correct word immediately. The Pause Prompt Praise tutor behaviours cue the readers instead to use all available information to solve unknown words. Such information includes background knowledge of the story topic, familiarity with the language structure of the text, the meaning contained within the context of each sentence or paragraph, and the letter–sound information within words. Tutors are trained to give priority to the reader's understanding of the meaning of words, before attempting to focus reader attention onto letter and sound information. Tutors tell the reader the correct word only as a last resort and after two prompts have been tried. Tutors are not required to respond to every error a reader makes. Given the priority on helping readers understand the meaning of words, tutors may ignore minor errors which do not greatly alter the meaning of the text.

Successful use of Pause Prompt Praise requires readers to practise the skills needed to correct their errors. Successful use of Pause Prompt Praise, therefore, requires regular monitoring of the reader's accuracy level. Levels of text difficulty need to be adjusted (upwards or downwards) to maintain an optimal difficulty level for reader and tutor to work together.

HOW DO YOU USE PAUSE PROMPT PRAISE?

Figure 4.1 outlines the use of Pause Prompt Praise. This figure has been modified from the original tutoring chart (Glynn *et al.*, 1979), as experience over the years has suggested the present layout is more helpful. In Figure 4.1 *Correct Reading* is linked directly to *Praise*. When a reader correctly reads a phrase, a sentence, a whole page of a beginning text, or perhaps a paragraph from a more advanced text, the tutor should praise this specifically. Experienced tutors will praise frequently enough to let the reader know things are going well, but not so frequently as to interrupt the flow of reading. In the figure *Incorrect Reading* refers to errors of omission (no response) as well as to incorrect words substituted or extra words added, whether they 'make sense' or not. Errors which are corrected by the reader *without any help from the tutor* are classed as self-corrections.

When an error occurs, the tutor's first task is to *Pause*. The pause prevents the tutor from interrupting too soon. This may allow readers to notice for themselves that what they have read may not quite make sense, and, possibly, to correct themselves. The pause also allows the tutor time to decide what kind of error has occurred – whether it is a non-attempt or a substitution which does not make sense or one which does make sense. Tutors should pause for up to five seconds, during which a self-correction may occur, or, alternatively, pause until the reader has reached the end of the phrase or sentence containing the error.

After the tutor has paused, and if the reader has not self-corrected, the tutor offers a prompt to help the reader with the word (see *Prompt* in Figure 4.1). Here tutors learn to select one of three kinds of prompt, according to the type of error the reader has made. Moving from left to right in the Figure, these three kinds of prompt line up with the three types of error. Hence, for a 'non-attempt' error (which has not been self-corrected after a pause), the tutor prompts the reader either to 'read on' or 'read again'. 'Read on' prompts are used if the error is at the beginning or middle of a sentence or clause, and 'read again' prompts are used if the error is near the end.

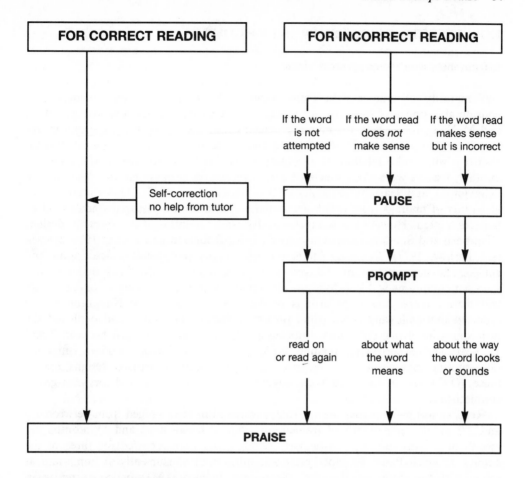

Figure 4.1 *Pause Prompt Praise*
Adapted from Glynn et al. *(1979)*

Sometimes this kind of prompt is sufficient for the reader to 'pick up' the meaning of the word from the context of the sentence or story. If this happens, the reader has made a 'prompted correction', and the tutor should provide specific praise. When the error is a word which does *not* make sense the tutor uses a 'meaning prompt' directing the reader's attention to what the word means (e.g. a question referring to the picture, the context of the sentence, the page, the whole story, or to the reader's prior knowledge and experience). When the error is a word which *does* make sense the tutor may then use a 'letter–sound prompt', directing the reader's attention to what the word looks or sounds like. Note that this kind of prompt is offered only when the error suggest that the reader has already understood something of the meaning of the word.

When readers read the correct word after a tutor prompt, these prompted corrections should be praised. Tutors should give no more than two prompts. After the second prompt, the tutor should tell the reader the correct word. This is the 'bottom line' which tutors try not to reach.

HOW EFFECTIVE IS PAUSE PROMPT PRAISE?

Effectiveness with low-progress readers

The majority of studies with Pause Prompt Praise have involved readers with considerable underachievement in reading. In five of the studies reviewed by Glynn and McNaughton (1985), the minimum underachievement was two years, and in one case this was three years. Readers in one study were all members of a special class for children with mild intellectual disability (Love and VanBiervliet, 1984), and in another, readers were all members of a semi-residential programme for children with behavioural and learning difficulties (O'Connor *et al.*, 1987). Unfortunately, the generality of findings from small-scale intensive intra-subject research studies is often underestimated. However, a number of advocates for intra-subject research designs (Campbell and Stanley, 1966; Kratochwill, 1978; Robinson and Foster, 1979; Hersen and Barlow, 1977), following Sidman (1960), argue that detailed description and continuous measurement of changes in the behaviour of individuals under clearly specified conditions will lead to a greater confidence in the generality of findings than will merely employing large groups of subjects. Glynn and McNaughton (1985) reported that following the original project, a further 11 studies had deployed the procedures involving 118 tutors, tutoring a total of 98 children aged between 7 and 12 years, all experiencing reading difficulties. Nine of those studies employed intra-subject research designs, and three employed group-comparison designs, one of these (O'Connor *et al.*, 1987) employing both intra-subject and between-group comparisons.

Reading age gains across the 12 studies reviewed in 1985 ranged from between 1.5 and 2.0 months per month of trained tutoring, to between 10 and 11 months per month of trained tutoring. Particularly strong gains were reported for three of the studies in which Pause Prompt Praise was introduced concurrently at home and at school (McNaughton *et al.*, 1981; Scott and Ballard, 1983) or concurrently in residential and school settings (O'Connor *et al.*, 1987). Scott and Ballard (1983) implemented the Pause Prompt Praise remedial reading procedures concurrently with parents and teachers of children with severe reading difficulties. Parents and teachers learned the procedures together. Both parties were involved in the same intervention and monitoring of their own and children's behaviour – parents in the home setting, teachers in the school setting. Implementing this study itself increased the amount of parent–teacher contact and exchange of information about children's behaviour. Perhaps the shared control over the reading intervention contributed to the mutual respect parents and teachers had for each other's role. Data from the Scott and Ballard study showed a far higher rate of reading gain for these children than for children in similar studies where the same procedures were implemented by parents or teachers alone (Glynn and McNaughton, 1985).

Two later studies in the UK reported by Wheldall and Glynn (1989) investigated the effects of Pause Prompt Praise with children who were only slightly under-achieving, or who had advanced reading achievement. In the first of these studies, which involved 13-year-old peer tutors tutoring 9- to 10-year-old readers, there was only small advantage for readers tutored with Pause Prompt Praise over readers tutored by untrained tutors (12 months gain in reading comprehension compared with 9 months). The second study involved parent tutors tutoring readers whose achievement was up to 2.5 years in advance of their chronological age. Readers tutored with Pause Prompt Praise made no greater gains than readers given untrained tutoring. In these two studies readers of near average to above average achievement, in contrast with the low-progress readers in other studies, would likely have already learned strategies of self-correction and using contextual information from their school reading programmes and their experience with books. Additional input from Pause Prompt Praise tutoring would have been superfluous.

Range of successful tutors

Glynn and McNaughton (1985) reported successful implementation of Pause Prompt Praise procedures by the 118 tutors across the 12 studies reviewed. Successful implementation required major gains by tutors in their rate of pausing, in their rate of prompting (including their rate of successful prompts), and in their rate of praise. In the studies reviewed 62 tutors were parents tutoring their own children, 31 were teachers, parents of residential staff tutoring children other than their own, and 15 were older students tutoring younger students.

Subsequent to the Glynn and McNaughton review, Henderson and Glynn (1986) reported a study in which four parent tutors were trained by trainee teachers to implement Pause Prompt Praise successfully with their own children at home. Wheldall and Glynn (1989) summarized successful implementation of the Pause Prompt Praise procedures by the 26 junior high school and high school student tutors, who were tutoring younger, low-progress readers. Medcalf and Glynn (1987) carried out a study in which three 11- to 12-year-old, low-progress tutors successfully tutored three similar-age, low-progress readers, and Houghton and Glynn (1993) report successful tutoring by five low-progress, 13-year-old tutors tutoring similar-age, low-progress readers.

Reading benefits for tutors

One important trend emerging from research with Pause Prompt Praise is the finding of reading gains for tutors as well as readers. Peer tutoring of reading provides an important learning context for demonstrating reciprocal gains for tutors and tutees. By attending carefully to tutees' reading in order to implement Pause Prompt Praise correctly, tutors themselves stand to gain from the process. Hence it may be more appropriate to select, as tutors, readers who are themselves experiencing reading difficulties albeit at higher levels than those read by tutees. In the study by Medcalf and Glynn (1987) an educational psychologist assisted three primary teachers to teach Pause Prompt Praise to three 11- to 12-year-old tutors who had reading deficits of between one and three years. These tutors in turn tutored three 11- to 12-year-old readers who were underachieving in reading by between four and six years. After eight weeks of tutoring, there were substantial gains for both tutors and tutees on an informal prose reading inventory, and on the number of successive book levels read to criterion.

Medcalf (1989) carried out another study with 10 9- to 11-year-old readers. Underachievement in reading ranged from between 0.7 and 1.7 years to between 4.3 and 4.9 years. Three readers who were slightly underachieving (between 0.7 and 2.5 years) were randomly assigned to tutor three other readers whose underachievement ranged from 2.0 to 6.3 years using Pause Prompt Praise. The four remaining readers were assigned to an individual tape-assisted reading programme. The mean gains from the six children in the Pause Prompt Praise programme (tutors and tutees) were 2.5 years on the informal prose inventory contrasted with gains of 1.4 years for children assigned to the tape-assisted programme. Among the children in the Pause Prompt Praise programme, tutors gained an average of 3.5 years, whereas tutees gained 1.6 years. Six months after the completion of the programme, the gains for children peer-tutored with Pause Prompt Praise and for children in the tape-assisted programme ranged from two to five years. The three children who had acted as Pause Prompt Praise tutors made the greatest reading gain (4.0 years). Houghton and Glynn (1993) also introduced Pause Prompt Praise tutoring to five pairs of 13-year-old readers. Both tutor and tutee children were below-average readers. Both groups made major gains in reading accuracy and comprehension.

It is interesting to speculate whether studies reporting gains for peer tutors employing Pause Prompt Praise might hold good also for parent tutors and sibling tutors. One study which offers some support for this claim is a study previously referred to (Glynn and Glynn, 1986). In this study, parallel reading gains were reported for Cambodian refugee mothers and their own children. These mothers were invited to tutor their own children using reading books sent home from school, in the medium of their own Khmer language. However, because these Khmer-speaking women had minimal English at the time, only a modified version of Pause Prompt Praise could be attempted. Further, the then limited availability of Khmer translators precluded establishing how closely the procedures were implemented.

However, with the current revitalization of the Maori language in New Zealand, in which both Maori children and many of their parent generation concurrently are learning to read in Maori, an opportunity is available to assess the impact of Tatari Tautoko Tauawhi (Pause Prompt Praise) tutoring on the Maori language reading skills of the parent generation.

Tutor training

Given the growing evidence of the effectiveness of Pause Prompt Praise when implemented by both parent and peer tutors, attention has begun to focus on strategies for training tutors. Henderson and Glynn (1986) explored the effectiveness of feedback provided to parent tutors by trainers when the parents were learning the procedures. Four third-year College of Education students were observed as they provided feedback to parents who were tutoring their own children with Pause Prompt Praise. The study examined the type of feedback these students provided the parents, and then intervened to improve the effectiveness of that feedback. There were clear changes in trainee feedback behaviour from baseline (their 'natural' feedback style) to trained feedback conditions. In almost every instance, student trainees assumed a high level of control over the learning of parent tutors, allowing little opportunity for parents to recall or to self-correct their own tutoring behaviour. Following training, the student trainees showed a marked shift from their baseline feedback patterns. They allowed parents much more opportunity to recall and explain their own use of the procedures with individual errors. They provided parents with prompts or cues about tutoring procedures that were far less intrusive than those used as baseline. Concern over excessive dependence of some readers on over-intensive 'help' from tutors may be paralleled by concern over excessive dependence of some tutors on over-intrusive trainers.

From Pause Prompt Praise to Tatari Tautoko Tauawhi

Pause Prompt Praise has recently been reconstructed in the Maori language, and presented at a hui (formal gathering or meeting conducted according to Maori protocol) for Maori staff of the New Zealand Special Education Service. Together with people of the Ngai Te Rangi and Ngāti Ranginui groups in Tauranga, the author and Maori staff of the New Zealand Special Education Service introduced the procedures (known in Maori as Tatari Tautoko Tauawhi) to assist children who are learning to read in Maori. Tatari Tautoko Tauawhi was trialled within a tuakana–teina (peer tutoring) context. Glynn *et al.* (1993) report that tuakana (tutors) were quite successful in using the procedures in Maori. Following training with Tatari Tautoko Tauawhi they responded to four times more teina (tutee) errors, doubled their rate of pausing and doubled their use of 'read on' and 'read again' prompts. They also doubled their use of praise for prompted corrections. Although this initial study was brief, data indicated a lower error rate and a slightly higher correct rate for teina (tutee) children, in contrast with non-tutored children. The tuakana children also benefited from decreased error rates, consistent with gains reported from peer tutors using Pause Prompt Praise (Medcalf, 1989; Medcalf and Glynn, 1987; Houghton and Glynn, 1993).

Delivery of tutor training

Training in the delivery of the Pause Prompt Praise and the Tatari Tautoko Tauawhi version of the procedures is currently delivered through two separate workshop sessions. Full details of the content covered in each session are described in the bilingual *Resource Manual for Staff* (Atvars *et al.*, 1994).

The first workshop trains tutors to implement the procedures with tutees. It consists of six components:

1. A brief introduction, locating Pause Prompt Praise in the context of learning to read as a process of learning to 'make sense' of continuous text material, by drawing on whatever information is available (whether from the story context, the illustrations, the reader's prior experience, or from knowledge of letters and sounds).
2. A brief discussion of how to prepare for a successful tutoring session, including choosing a suitable time and place and selecting appropriate books (taking into account both reader interest and difficulty level).

3. A brief discussion of the different kinds of errors readers can make (omissions, insertions, substitutions which do not make sense, and substitutions which do make sense).
4. An examination of the process of reader self-correction of errors, and the importance of this as an indicator of the learning of independent reading skills.
5. An examination of all the specific tutoring behaviours involved in implementing Pause Prompt Praise.
6. Opportunities to role play both tutor and reader behaviour and to receive feedback on programme.

Throughout this training workshop, participants are shown the relevant sections of the training video, and the session ends with a series of role plays in which each participant experiences both the reader and tutor role under supervision of a trainer.

The second workshop prepares trainers to train new Pause Prompt Praise tutors. Intending trainers must have participated in the first workshop session. They then supply a brief audio tape of their own implementation of the procedures, which demonstrates their use of all tutoring behaviours in response to a range of reader errors. This tape is scored by a member of the National Delivery Team comprising Special Education Service staff, teachers skilled and experienced in delivering the procedures, and the present author. Following this, intending trainers are invited to plan and implement their own local tutor training workshop for a group of parents or community members. National Delivery Team members attend this workshop to assess trainers' knowledge and skill in implementing the procedures, and their conduct of the workshop from the point of view of coverage of items (1) to (6) above, and (in the case of the Maori language version of the processes), from the point of view of trainers' use of culturally appropriate activities and learning styles.

Blackstone (1979) advanced three types of argument in support of parental involvement in education. The first embodied the rights of citizenship and the rights of parents to have a say in controlling agencies and social services which affect their lives. This argument supports parent representation on school Boards of Trustees, and on ethical and research committees. Blackstone's second argument is based on the belief that parents (or their behaviour) 'must be changed so that their children's learning needs can be met more adequately'. Woods (1988) cautions of the dangers of such a pathological or deficit model. Professional input at home, following such a model, may lead to undue dependent behaviour on the part of parents. Parental roles in such model, Woods claims, can be demeaning or insulting, and can even deskill rather than enskill parents. Furthermore, parental assertiveness in challenging professionals can be interpreted as an additional indication of pathology.

Blackstone also describes a third argument, a 'utility' argument, in which a greater extent of overlap between teacher and parent roles is desired for its own sake. The degree of overlap between parent and teacher roles in preschool education is seen as a positive model for parent–teacher partnership higher up in the education system. This model, Blackstone argues, is likely to result in increased parent–professional contact, exchange of information between settings, and an enhanced respect for the knowledge, status, and competence of each party with regard to facilitating children's learning.

There are clear arguments supporting the use of parent–teacher partnership programmes such as Pause Prompt Praise within the context of parental involvement in their children's learning. Further research studies need to be designed to capitalize on the strengths of parental input into children's literacy skills at home, and to combine those strengths with those of teacher input into children's literacy skills at school. A longer-term follow-up study of the effects of Pause Prompt Praise is currently in progress with 11- to 12-year-old Maori readers in several classrooms in an intermediate school in Mount Maunganui, NZ. Such studies need to be designed so that they can embody elements of parent–professional partnership and shared control. After seventeen years since the original study began, and more than fifteen years since the first training booklet and video, Pause Prompt Praise continues to be implemented successfully by both parent and peer tutors to assist readers who are experiencing difficulties.

REFERENCES

Atvars, K., Berryman, M. and Glynn, T. (1994) *Tatari Tautoko Tauawhi: A Resource Manual for Staff*. Tauranga: Bay of Plenty East, Special Education Service.

Atvars, K. and Glynn, T. (1992) *Tatari Tautoko Tauawhi: Hei Awhina Tamariki ki te Pānui Pukapuka*. Videotape, produced by Audiovisual Section, Higher Education Development Centre, University of Otago.

Blackstone, T. (1979) Parental involvement in education. *Educational Policy Bulletin*, 7(1), 81–98.

Campbell, D.T. and Stanley, J.C. (1966) *Experimental and Quasi-experimental Designs for Research*. Chicago: Rand McNally.

Clay, M.M. (1969) Reading errors and self-correction behaviour. *British Journal of Educational Psychology*, 89, 47–56.

Clay, M.M. (1979) *Reading: The Patterning of Complex Behaviour*, 2nd edn. Auckland: Heinemann Educational Books.

Clay, M. (1991) *Becoming Literate: The Construction of Inner Control*. Auckland: Heinemann Educational Books.

Dick, M., Glynn, T. and Flower, D. (1992) *Pause Prompt and Praise Reading Tutoring Procedures: Tutor training video*. Audiovisual Unit, Higher Education Development Centre, University of Otago.

Glynn, T. (1985) Contexts for independent learning. *Educational Psychology*, 5, 5–15.

Glynn, T., Atvars, K., Furlong, M., Davies, M., Rogers, S. and Teddy, N. (1993) Tatari Tautoko, Tauawhi: Hei Awhina Tamariki ki te Pānui Pukapuka. *Cultural Justice and Ethics Symposium Report*. Wellington: New Zealand Psychological Society.

Glynn, T., Dick, M. and Flower, D. (1992) *Pause Prompt and Praise Reading Tutoring Procedures: Tutor's booklet*. Department of Education, University of Otago.

Glynn, T. and Glynn, V. (1986) Shared reading by Cambodian mothers and children learning English as a second language: Reciprocal gains. *The Exceptional Child*, 33(3), 159–72.

Glynn, T. and McNaughton, S. (1985) The Mangere Home and School Remedial Reading Procedures: continuing research on their effectiveness. *New Zealand Journal of Psychology*, 66–77.

Glynn, T., McNaughton, S., Robinson, V. and Quinn, M. (1979) *Remedial Reading at Home: Helping You to Help Your Child*. Wellington: New Zealand Council for Education Research.

Harawira, W., Glynn, T. and Durning, C. (1993) *Tatari, Tautoko, Tauawhi: Hei Awhina Tamariki ki te Pānui Pukapuka*. Tauranga: Bay of Plenty East, Special Education Service.

Henderson, W. and Glynn, T. (1986) A feedback procedure for teacher trainees working with parent tutors of reading. *Educational Psychology*, 62, 159–77.

Hersen, M. and Barlow, D.H. (1977) *Single Case Experimental Designs: Strategies for Studying Behaviour Change*. New York: Pergamon Press.

Houghton, S. and Glynn, T. (1993) Peer tutoring of below-average secondary school readers with Pause, Prompt, Praise: successive introduction of tutoring components. *Behaviour Change*, **10**, 75–85.

Kratochwill, T.R. (ed.) (1978) *Single Subject Research: Strategies for Evaluating Change*. New York: Academic Press.

Love, J. and VanBiervliet, A. (1984) Training parents to be home reading tutors: generalization of children's reading skills from home to school. *The Exceptional Child*, **31**, 114–27.

McNaughton, S. (1981) Low-progress readers and teacher instructional behaviour during oral reading: the risk of maintaining instructional dependence. *The Exceptional Child*, **28**, 167–76.

McNaughton, S. (1987) *Being Skilled: The Socializations of Learning to Read*. London: Methuen.

McNaughton, S., Glynn, T. and Robinson, V. (1981) *Parents as Remedial Reading Tutors: Issues for Home and School. Studies in Education No. 2*. Wellington: New Zealand Council for Educational Research.

McNaughton, S., Glynn, T. and Robinson, V. (1987) *Pause, Prompt and Praise: Effective Remedial Reading Tutoring*. Birmingham: Positive Products.

Medcalf, J. (1989) Comparison of peer tutored remedial reading using the Pause, Prompt and Praise procedures with an individualised tape-assisted reading programme. *Educational Psychology*, **9**(3), 253–62.

Medcalf, J. and Glynn, T. (1987) Assisting teachers to implement peer-tutored remedial reading using pause, prompt and praise procedures. *Queensland Journal of Guidance and Counselling*, **1**, 11–23.

O'Connor, G., Glynn, T. and Tuck, B. (1987) Contexts for remedial reading: practice reading and pause, prompt and praise tutoring. *Educational Psychology*, **7**, 207–23.

Robinson, P.W. and Foster, D.F. (1979) *Experimental Psychology: A Small-N Approach*. New York: Harper & Row.

Scott, J. and Ballard, K. (1983) Training parents and teachers in remedial reading procedures for children with learning difficulties. *Educational Psychology*, **3**, 15–31.

Sidman, M. (1960) *Tactics for Scientific Research*. New York: Basic Books.

Wheldall, K. and Glynn, T. (1989) *Effective Classroom Learning*. Oxford: Basil Blackwell.

Wheldall, K. and Mettem, P. (1985) Behavioural peer tutoring: training 16-year-old tutors to employ the 'pause, prompt and praise' method with 12-year-old remedial readers. *Educational Psychology*, **5**, 27–44.

Wheldall, K., Wenban-Smith, J., Morgan, A. and Quance, B. (1992) Reading: how do teachers typically tutor? *Educational Psychology*, **12**, 177–94.

Woods, S. (1988) Parents: whose partners? In L. Barton (ed.) *The Politics of Special Education Needs*, 190–207. London: The Falmer Press.

Chapter 5

Tutoring Systems for Family Literacy

Keith Topping

It took some teachers a little while to accept the value of really involving parents in children's learning. As parents progressed from the role of teacher's aide with menial tasks in school to that of home-based partner in helping children overcome learning difficulties, doubts were voiced. What could parents offer that teachers could not?

The answer, of course, is – many things – in many areas of the curriculum. The first of these is simply the availability of extra practice. The second is the luxury of one-to-one immediate feedback, preventing the compounding of error upon error. Thirdly, parental praise is very potent – more powerful in general than that of a teacher. The fourth advantage that a parent has is greater scope for modelling or demonstration of the desired behaviour. Thus, compared to teacher input, parental modelling is more powerful, parental reinforcement is more valuable and can be more frequent, parental feedback is more immediate, and practice is more regular.

Parents have many strengths on which contextually appropriate tutoring systems can be designed to capitalize. Any attempt to get by in family literacy programmes by handing out restricted and watered down aspects of traditional teacher practice is doomed to failure in the long run. Structured tutoring systems are intended to ensure parents' early experiences are successful, to give them the confidence to go on to customize and design approaches ideally suited to their own family.

Such tutoring systems must be extremely flexible and capable of wide application at the initiative of family members. In disadvantaged families, neighbourhoods, countries and continents, family literacy methods must be free of great cost, specialist materials, complex technology and exotic training requirements. The real challenge is to design tutoring systems which can be used by anyone, anywhere, with any material which is to hand and is of interest.

All kinds of tutoring constellations can spring up once a family has been empowered. For instance, father might tutor son who then tutors mother who then feels able to tutor younger daughter except on the hard bits where son takes over.

In this chapter three tutoring systems will be reviewed: Paired Reading, Cued Spelling and Paired Writing. In each case the method will be discussed, its organization in practice detailed and research evidence on effectiveness summarized. Further information about all three methods will be found in Topping (1995).

PAIRED READING

Method

The Paired Reading method is now known around the world. However, like many educational innovations, it has been subject to considerable dilution. Paired Reading is *not* any old thing that two people do with a book. It is not uncommon to hear the assertion 'Yes, we do Paired Reading', when subsequent observation of practice shows that the pair are actually not following the 'rules' of the method.

For a full description of the proper method, see Topping and Wolfendale (1985) and Topping (1995). The framework of the technique is outlined in Figure 5.1.

Paired Reading is characterized by the child choosing high interest reading material irrespective of its readability level (provided it is within that of the *helper*) from any source.

Families commit themselves to an initial trial period in which they agree to do at least five minutes Paired Reading on five days each week for about eight weeks. Grandparents, siblings, friends and neighbours can be encouraged to help, but must all use the same technique – the target child is deliberately asked to quality control the tutoring they receive.

In Paired Reading the child is likely to want to talk about a book *they* have chosen, and talk is also more necessary given the (probably) greater difficulty of the text, as a check on comprehension.

A very simple and ubiquitously applicable correction procedure is prescribed. After pausing for 4 to 5 seconds to allow self-correction, the tutor just models the correct way to read the word, the child repeats it correctly and the pair carry on.

Much verbal praise and non-verbal approval for specific reading behaviours is incorporated. Undesirable behaviours are engineered out of the system by engineering in incompatible positive behaviours.

Tutors support children through difficult text by Reading Together – both members of the pair read all the words out loud together, the tutor modulating speed to match that of the child, while giving a good model of competent reading.

On an easier section of text, the child may wish to read a little without support. The child signals for the tutor to stop Reading Together, by a knock or a touch. The tutor goes quiet, while continuing to monitor any errors, praise and pause for discussion. Sooner or later while Reading Alone the child will make an error which they cannot self-correct within 4 or 5 seconds. Then the tutor applies the usual correction procedure and joins back in Reading Together.

The pair go on like this, switching from Reading Together to Reading Alone to give the child just as much help as is needed at any moment, according to the difficulty of the text, how tired the tutee is, and so on. Children should never 'grow out of' Reading Together; they should always be ready to use it as they move on to harder and harder books.

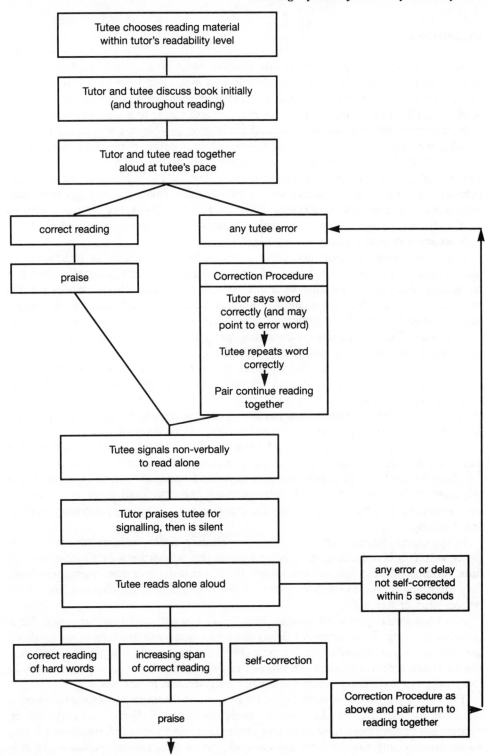

Figure 5.1 *Paired Reading method*

Organization

Paired Reading (PR) is widely used with children of all reading abilities. This helps to avoid stigmatization. A small group of fairly well motivated families is a good choice for a first effort, but not so small or scattered that there is no sense of group solidarity. The children must have easy and frequent access to a wide range of books.

Parents (and all other potential tutors) are invited to a launch or training meeting, together with the children who will be the tutees, since pairs are trained together from the outset. Training should include information about the technique *and* a demonstration of how to do it. The demonstration can be on video, live by role play between teachers or by a teacher with a user-friendly child, or by a graduate pair from a previous programme. Reading Together and Reading Alone are demonstrated separately to start with, then in normal alternation. The correction procedure, the 4 to 5 second pause and praise are also highlighted.

Given the necessary space and privacy, the pairs now practise the technique. To practise Reading Together the pair need a book above the child's current independent readability level, so it is highly desirable to have the tutees choose books for the practice in school before the meeting. As the pairs practise, circulating professionals can diplomatically check on technique, offer further advice, coach or re-demonstrate as necessary. Before advising or coaching, professionals should have practised the technique themselves on a variety of children.

After practice, there is time for feedback and questions, an outline of the day-to-day organization of the project, and refreshments if appropriate. Pairs keep a PR diary, noting the date, what was read, for how long, with whom and any comments about how well the child did. Some parents have trouble thinking what to write in the last column, so some schools provide them with a 'dictionary of praise'.

The diary is taken into school each week by the child to show the teacher, who adds their own positive comment and signs the card officially, also issuing a new one for the next week. Pairs should have an easy read handout to remind them of the technique and to show to other family members (this may need to be in more than one language). You may wish to have the pairs contract into the programme more or less formally.

In discussing diaries with children in the ensuing weeks, teachers check if all is going well. If it is not, the family may be called into school for a brief conference. If time permits, a home visit is even better. In all cases the pair are asked show 'how they are doing it' and the difficulty level of the books chosen are checked (these may be too hard or too easy).

After the initial period of commitment, pairs are gathered together again for a feedback meeting. Some present will say little and some will not attend, so feedback questionnaires can be useful (see Topping (1995) for examples). The children's reading can be tested before and after the project, enabling overall results to be fed back to the group, but individual scores should not be given out to parents.

The main purpose of the meeting is to regenerate enthusiasm and group cohesion – reference to 'the end' of the project should be avoided. Each family should be encouraged to say where they want to go from here: go on with PR five days a week, go on but for only two to three days a week, go on with reading at home but in a different way, or stop for a rest and perhaps start again later. Children may wish to go on keeping the diary and teachers will have to decide how often they can find time to see this in the longer run.

Effectiveness

Paired Reading has been the subject of a very large amount of research, starting in the UK and now internationally, and this has recently been reviewed by Topping and Lindsay (1992).

Much of the evaluation has been in terms of gains on norm-referenced tests of reading before and after the initial intensive period of involvement. Published studies do not always reflect the reality of ordinary life in the classroom, but with PR it is possible to compare the results of 60 published (and therefore selected) studies of projects with outcome data from 155 unselected projects operated in one school district.

In the published studies, involving a total of 1012 children, for each month of time passed the average Paired Reader gained 4.2 months in reading age for accuracy and 5.4 months for comprehension. In the 155 unselected projects, involving 2372 children, for each month of time passed the average Paired Reader gained 3.3 months in reading age for accuracy and 4.4 months for comprehension.

Of the published studies, 19 included control or comparison groups, while of the unselected projects, 37 included control groups. Although the control groups often also made gains greater than would normally be expected, the PR groups on aggregate did far better, although the differential was greater in the selected projects.

But do these gains last? Published reports on five projects with follow-up data are available, but of the unselected projects 17 included such evidence. In the latter, up to 17 weeks after the initial project intensive period, 102 children in seven projects were still gaining over two months of reading age per chronological month elapsed for both accuracy and comprehension.

At longer-term follow-up, 170 children in 10 projects were still gaining well over one month of reading age per month elapsed in both accuracy and comprehension. Thus it seems that while the initial starting acceleration does not continue indefinitely, the gains certainly do not 'wash out' subsequently, and follow-up data from control group projects confirm this (Topping, 1992).

The data from the unselected projects further suggested that well-organized projects yielded better test results, that participant children from lower socio-economic classes tended to show higher gains, that home visiting by teachers increased test scores and that boys tended to accelerate more than girls. Also, second language Paired Readers accelerated more than first language Paired Readers in accuracy but less in comprehension (while of course accelerating a great deal more than non-Paired Readers of either type).

Taking another approach to evaluation, the subjective views of parents, children and teachers in the unselected projects have also been gathered, by structured questionnaire enabling responses to be summarized (Topping and Whiteley, 1990). In a sample of over 1000 parents, after PR 70 per cent considered their child was now reading more accurately, more fluently and with better comprehension. Greater confidence in reading was noted by 78 per cent of parents. Teachers reported better reading in the classroom in a somewhat smaller proportion of cases (about 8 per cent less). Of a sample of 964 children, 95 per cent felt that after PR they were better at reading, and 92 per cent liked reading more. Eighty-seven per cent found it easy to learn to do, 83 per cent liked doing it, and 70 per cent said they would go on doing it.

Paired Reading has also been used in an Adult Literacy context, with spouses, friends, neighbours and workmates acting as tutors. The advantages of being able to use more appropriate and more readily available reading material and receive tutoring on a little and often basis closely linked to everyday life are extremely important, especially for the majority of adults with literacy difficulties who cannot or will not attend a class.

Scoble *et al.* (1988) reported the evaluation of a six-week project of this type, noting average gains of 10.4 months in reading age for accuracy and 13 months for comprehension for those students who could register on the scale at pre-test. On miscue analysis, most tutees showed a striking increase in self-correction. Once PR is applied in a more complex Family Literacy context, it soon becomes very difficult to evaluate, since there are problems establishing who is doing what and with which and to whom.

CUED SPELLING

Method

The basic structure of the technique comprises 10 Steps, four Points to Remember and two Reviews, as illustrated in Figure 5.2 and described in greater detail in Topping (1995).

The 10 Steps and four Points apply to every individual target word worked upon by the pair, while the 'Speed Review' covers all target words for a particular session and the 'Mastery Review' covers all the target words for one week or a longer period if desired.

The child chooses high interest and utility target words irrespective of complexity (Step 1). The pair check the spelling of the word and put a master version in their Cued Spelling Diary (Step 2). The pair read the word out loud synchronously, then the child reads the word aloud alone (3).

The child (*not* the parent) then chooses Cues (prompts or reminders) to enable him or her to remember the written structure of the word (4). These Cues may be phonic sounds, letter names, syllables or other fragments or 'chunks' of words, or wholly idiosyncratic mnemonic devices.

The pair then say the Cues out loud simultaneously (5). The child then says the Cues out loud while the parent models writing the word down on scrap paper to this 'dictation' (6). Roles then reverse, the parent saying the Cues out loud while the child writes the word down (7). The child then says the Cues and writes the word simultaneously (8). At Step 9, the child is asked to write the word as fast as possible. Finally (10), the child again reads the word out loud.

The four Points cover aspects of the technique relevant to its practical application. At every attempt at writing a target word, the parent covers up previous attempts on the work paper, to avoid the possibility of direct copying (some children prefer to do

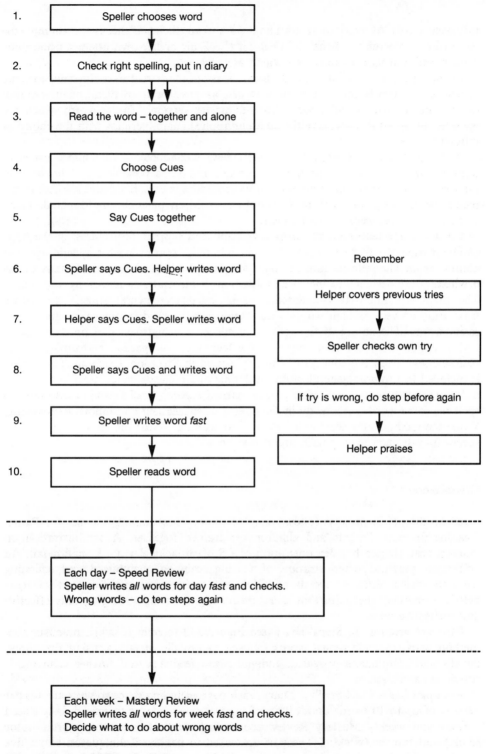

Figure 5.2 *Cued Spelling: the 10 Steps*

this themselves). At every written attempt on a word, the *child* checks the attempt, the parent only intervening if the child cannot check his or her own attempt accurately. Tutors praise at various junctures which are specified.

In the 'Speed Review' at the end of each session, the parent asks the child to write all the target words for that session as fast as possible from dictation in random order. The child then self-checks with the 'master version'. Target words which are incorrect at Speed Review have the 10 Steps applied again, perhaps with the choice of different Cues.

At the end of each week, a 'Mastery Review' is conducted – the child is asked to write all the target words for the whole week as fast as possible from dictation in random order. No specific error correction procedure is prescribed and it is left to the pair to decide what they wish to do about errors. Many pairs choose to include failed words in the next week's target words.

Cued Spelling features swift error correction and support procedures, in the hope of eliminating the fear of failure. It is flexible and appropriate for a wide age and ability range. The self-selection of target words and self-management of many of the procedures are designed to increase motivation. It incorporates modelling and praise. The Steps are finely task-analysed (are in small incremental stages), to reduce frustration on very difficult words – but they can be worked through very quickly on easier words. The nature of the activity should ensure high levels of time on task.

The emphasis in the later stages of the technique on speeded performance is of course drawn from the concept of 'fluency' found in Precision Teaching. This aspect is included to promote generalization over time and contexts, since otherwise there is a danger that the tutee will merely have learned spelling 'tricks' while continuing to spell the same words incorrectly in the course of subsequent continuous free writing. While the method may seem complex on first reading, 7-year-old children have been successfully trained in its use in about one hour.

Organization

Cued Spelling (CS) projects follow many of the organizational guidelines for Paired Reading projects. Parents and children are trained together. A demonstration on video is best, since a live demonstration of CS often lacks clarity of small detail. An additional practical demonstration of Cueing, using a chalkboard and soliciting from the group different words and different cueing strategies for each word, is helpful in making the point that there are no 'right' cueing strategies, only effective and ineffective ones.

Pairs are given a '10 Steps' chart (see Figure 5.2) to refer to while practising the method with the child's own words (chosen before the meeting), using the paper, pencils and dictionaries provided. Individualized feedback and further coaching is provided as necessary.

Each pair has a Cued Spelling Diary, each page including space to write the master version of up to 10 words on all days of the week, with boxes to record daily Speed Review and weekly Mastery Review scores and spaces for comments from tutor (daily) and teacher (weekly). The pair are asked to use the technique on about five words per day (implying a minimum time of 15 minutes) for three days per week for the next six weeks. The children are encouraged to choose words from their school spelling books, graded free writing, relevant project work or special Cued Spelling displays of common problem words, and collect these (in a CS 'collecting book'), so they always have a pool of suitable words from which to choose.

Children bring their CS Diaries into school once each week for the class teacher to view. The words chosen need to be monitored, since some children choose words they already know while others choose extremely difficult words of very doubtful utility – in this a formula of 'three for everyday use and two just for fun' is usual.

As Cued Spelling has been much used in a reciprocal peer tutoring format, its use in family literacy in situations where both members of the pair are of equal spelling ability is entirely possible, although it is then especially important that the master version of the word is looked up in the dictionary *and* copied correctly into the CS Diary. Thus a parent who is of limited spelling ability could work with their child of similar spelling ability or sibling tutoring could operate between children of similar or different ages. In reciprocal tutoring, the fact that everyone gets to be a tutor is good for the self-esteem of both members of the pair, who of course end up learning their partner's words as well as their own.

Effectiveness

The initial reports on Cued Spelling were of a descriptive nature. Emerson (1988) reported on a brief project using the technique with four parents who tutored their own children at home. Results at Mastery Review were excellent. Scoble (1988) reported a detailed case study of an Adult Literacy student tutored by his wife using the technique. After 10 weeks of Cued Spelling, a Mastery Review of all words covered in the preceding weeks yielded a success rate of 78 per cent. Subsequently, Scoble (1989) reported on the progress of 14 similar pairs, most of whom had done Paired Reading together first. The most long-standing student had used the method for over a year and usually achieved Speed Review scores of 100 per cent and Mastery Review scores of 90 per cent. Harrison (1989) reported on a similar project and its extension to peer tutoring between Adult Literacy students in a class situation.

In the event, however, the most popular application of Cued Spelling then proved to be in a peer tutoring format. Oxley and Topping (1990) reported on a project in which eight 7- and 8-year-old pupils were tutored by eight 9-year-old pupils in the same vertically grouped class in a small rural school. This cross-age, cross-ability peer tutoring project was found to yield striking social benefits and the children spontaneously generalized peer tutoring to other curricular areas. Subjective feedback from both tutors and tutees was very positive.

The self-concept as a speller of both tutees and tutors showed a marked positive shift compared to that of non-participant children, especially so for the tutees. After six weeks, a total Mastery Review of all target words yielded average scores of 66 per cent correct, but a test session of up to 92 items for such young children was considered of doubtful reliability. Results on two norm-referenced tests of spelling were equivocal, since although the scores of both tutees and tutors were strikingly improved at post-test, so were those of non-participant children in the same class.

Peer-tutored Cued Spelling in a class-wide, same-age, same-ability reciprocal tutoring format was reported by Brierley *et al.* (1989). All pupils in the three first-year mixed ability classes (aged 9 to 10 years) in a middle school participated. Tutor and tutee roles changed each week. All the children were trained in a single group meeting. After six weeks, a total Mastery Review of all words covered yielded average scores of 80 per cent.

On a norm-referenced test of spelling, the average gain for all children was 0.65 years of spelling age during the six-week project, certainly many times more than normal expectations. Subjective feedback from the children was very positive, 84 per cent of the children reporting feeling they were better spellers after the project. Subsequently, peer-tutored Cued Spelling was initiated by a number of schools, especially in the reciprocal tutoring format, but few found time to evaluate it.

A study of parent-tutored Cued Spelling with children of 8 years of age and of the normal range of spelling ability (France *et al.*, 1992) indicated that the intervention appeared to be effective in differentially raising the spelling attainments of participants as compared to non-participants who were more able spellers, at least in the short term. Children felt Cued Spelling was easy to learn to do and that it improved their spelling along a number of dimensions. However, they said they tended to become bored with it and had difficulty finding enough words with which to use the technique.

It can be argued that any method involving extra time on task at spelling and extra valuable parental attention and approval related to spelling might be likely to yield differential gains. A study by Watt and Topping (1992) compared Cued Spelling with traditional spelling homework (an alternative intervention involving equal tutor attention and equal time on spelling tasks), compared the relative effectiveness of parent and peer tutored Cued Spelling and assessed the generalization of the effect of Cued Spelling into subsequent continuous free writing.

On a norm-referenced spelling test, Cued Spellers gained over two months of spelling age for each chronological month elapsed, while the traditional spelling homework comparison group of more able spellers gained only half a month of spelling age per month. The average score for parent-tutored children at final Mastery Review of words used in the programme was 93 per cent correct. Parent and peer tutoring seemed equally effective.

Participating children returned questionnaires identical to those used by Oxley and Topping (1990). Of these, 56 per cent found it easy to think up good Cues while the rest thought it hard, but 87 per cent now felt happier about spelling in general and that their spelling was better when writing, while 83 per cent felt they now did better at spelling tests. Ninety-one per cent reported a higher rate of self-correction after doing Cued Spelling and the same proportion said they liked doing Cued Spelling, while 87 per cent said they wished to go on doing Cued Spelling. Parents returned feedback questionnaires and 88 per cent reported a higher rate of self-correction, confirming the feedback from the children, while 58 per cent reported noticing their children spontaneously generalize the use of Cued Spelling techniques to other words. Three of the four teachers involved noted higher rates of self-correction of spelling in classwork and a general improvement in free writing.

Pre–post analysis of written work was based on samples of writing from Cued Spellers and comparison children. The average number of spelling errors per page reduced from 8.5 to 4.62 for the Cued Spellers and from 3.7 to 2.1 for the comparison children, who clearly had a lower error rate to start with and thus had less room for improvement. Generally, all but one of the participants and all but one of the comparison children were adjudged to have improved in quality of written work (one would of course expect children in school to improve over time), but the CS group recorded an average of 1.7 specific improvements per child while the comparison group averaged 1.25.

PAIRED WRITING

Method

Writing can be a lonely business and a blank piece of paper strangely daunting. Paired Writing is a framework for a pair working together to generate (or co-compose) a piece of writing – for any purpose they wish. The guidelines are designed to structure interaction between the pair so that a higher proportion of time is spent on task.

There is great emphasis on continuity – the pair stimulating each other to keep going. There is also constant in-built feedback and cross-checking – what is written must make sense to both members of the pair. The system is designed to be supportive and eliminate the fear of failure. Anxiety about peripheral aspects of writing such as spelling or punctuation should be reduced and dealt with in an orderly way. The 'best copy' is a joint effort of the pair and can be signed by both.

Peer evaluation is incorporated, relieving the supervising professional of the burden of grading innumerable scripts (sometimes returned so much later that the feedback is totally ineffective). Research shows that peer evaluation is at least as effective as teacher evaluation.

Paired Writing usually operates with a more able writer (the Helper) and a less able one (the Writer), but can work with a pair of equal ability so long as they edit carefully and use a dictionary to check spellings. In this latter case, it is possible to reciprocate roles from time to time to add variety.

The system may be used in creative writing or English composition, or in descriptive or technical writing, or as part of cross-curricular work, employment or other life needs. A Paired Writing project may be designed to mesh in with, or follow on from, direct instruction from a professional teacher on structural aspects of the writing process or a Paired Reading or Cued Spelling project, but the method may equally be used on an *ad hoc* basis as the need arises.

The structure of the system consists of six Steps, 10 Questions (for Ideas), five Stages (for Drafting) and four Levels (for Editing) (see Figure 5.3). Further details will be found in Topping (1995).

Step 1 is Ideas Generation. The Helper stimulates ideas by using given Questions and inventing other relevant ones, making one-word notes on the Writer's responses.

Step 2 is Drafting. The notes then form the basis for Drafting, which ignores spelling and punctuation. Lined paper and double spaced writing is recommended. The Writer dictates the text and scribing occurs in whichever of the five Stages of Support has been chosen by the pair. If there is a hitch, the Helper gives more support.

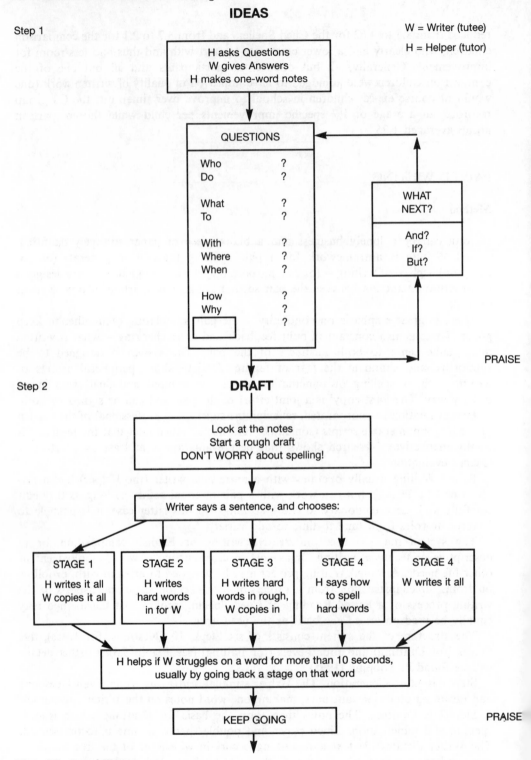

Figure 5.3   *Paired Writing*

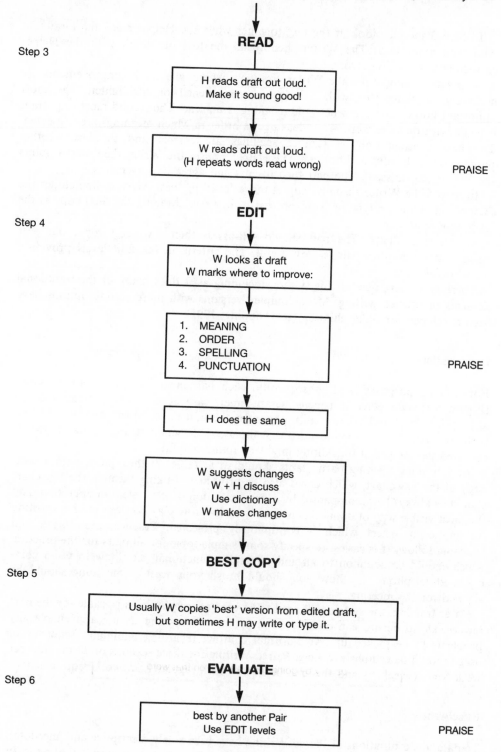

Step 3

READ

> H reads draft out loud.
> Make it sound good!

> W reads draft out loud.
> (H repeats words read wrong)

PRAISE

EDIT

Step 4

> W looks at draft
> W marks where to improve:

> 1. MEANING
> 2. ORDER
> 3. SPELLING
> 4. PUNCTUATION

PRAISE

> H does the same

> W suggests changes
> W + H discuss
> Use dictionary
> W makes changes

BEST COPY

Step 5

> Usually W copies 'best' version from edited draft,
> but sometimes H may write or type it.

EVALUATE

Step 6

> best by another Pair
> Use EDIT levels

PRAISE

In Step 3 the pair look at the text together while the Helper reads the Draft out loud with expression. The Writer then reads the text out loud, with the Helper correcting any reading errors.

Step 4 is Editing. First the Writer considers where s/he thinks improvements are necessary, marking this with a coloured pen, pencil or highlighter. The most important improvement is where the meaning is unclear. The second most important is to do with the organization of ideas or the order in which meanings are presented. The next consideration is whether spellings are correct and the last whether punctuation is helpful and correct. The Helper praises the Writer then marks points the Writer has 'missed'. The pair then discuss and agree improvements.

In Step 5 the Writer (usually) copies out a 'neat' or 'best' version. Sometimes the Helper may write or type or word-process it, however. Making the final copy is the least important step.

Step 6 is Evaluate. The pair should self-assess their own best copy, but peer assessment by another pair is very useful. The criteria in the Edit levels provide a checklist for this.

There is nothing new in this system, including as it does many of the traditional elements of process writing. More complex versions with more editing options have been developed for older children (see Topping, 1995).

Organization

For training purposes (and subsequently) each pair must have a system flowchart (Figure 5.3), two pens or pencils, scrap paper, easy access to a dictionary of an appropriate level and good quality paper for the best copy. Most pairs will do best with lined paper. It is recommended that the use of erasers is strongly discouraged. A coloured pen or pencil for editing might be found helpful.

At a training meeting participants should sit at tables in their pairs, with a hard copy of the flowchart, which could also be projected. Talking through the flowchart should as always be accompanied by a demonstration of the system in operation, and the most visible way of doing this is usually by live role play between teachers writing on an acetate sheet which is continuously projected. Practice, monitoring and coaching follow. It is easiest to specify some simple topic for all pairs for the practice, which should be common to all and preferably functional, e.g. 'how to use a coin-operated telephone' or 'how you should brush your teeth'. One hour should be allowed for the meeting.

After training, the system will need to be used as frequently as possible for the next few weeks, to ensure consolidation and promote fluency in its use and enable any problems to be picked up. An informal contract regarding minimum frequency of usage should be established – e.g. Paired Writing for three sessions of 20 minutes per week for six weeks – and this can be tied in with regular homework requirements.

Effectiveness

To date, the evaluations of Paired Writing have been solely descriptive and anecdotal. The task of evaluating quantitative and qualitative change in children's writing is an enormously time-consuming undertaking from a research point of view, and the difficulty of checking if any changes endure in the longer term even greater.

The objective of Paired Writing is to produce an increase in the quality and quantity of written output which generalizes to the solo writing situation and endures over time. Along the way, parent writing skills may also improve. Where tutors are siblings, a more complex issue arises – is the final product better than if the members of the pair worked separately? If the abilities of the two are very disparate, this may not be the case, and the altruism of brothers and sisters is rarely infinite.

Most of the usage of Paired Writing since its inception has been on a same-age cross-ability peer tutoring basis in schools with classes of mixed ability students. Parent-tutored Paired Writing has often been undertaken by parents worried about their child's learning difficulties, although the interpretation of learning difficulty has been wide, so that the method has been used with University students by parents worried about upcoming examination performances, for instance.

THE FUTURE – WIDER ALTERNATIVES

This chapter has focused on literacy, but the possibilities are endless. A great deal of work has been done on parent and peer tutoring of mathematics, and interest is spreading rapidly into other areas of the curriculum such as science (see, for example, the Paired Science pack by Croft and Topping, 1992).

Of course, some families will remain unreachable, at least for now. Paradoxically, a school operating a successful family literacy programme can place the most disadvantaged children who are left out in a still worse position relative to their peers who are participating in the programme. In this situation, many teachers feel compelled to arrange alternative extra support for the most needy non-participant children, perhaps via volunteer adults coming into school or by giving up their own recess times to act as surrogate parents. Where any non-professionals are deployed as tutors the methods described above will be useful. However, the organizational complexity of fixing up a reliable rota of substitute parents who are available often enough actually to make a difference to the child's attainment should not be underestimated.

Other children are a human resource ready at hand. Well-engineered systems for tutoring by non-professionals are often highly suitable for peer tutoring with only minor modification. If appropriate methods are deployed, both tutees and tutors gain in attainment – the tutors 'learning by teaching'. Further guidance on organizing peer tutoring successfully will be found in Topping (1988).

However, the use of volunteer, surrogate parent and peer tutors carries with it an insidious danger. It may prove so successful in raising motivation and capability in literacy in the school environment that it reduces teacher motivation to keep struggling to involve those parents who are most difficult to involve. Volunteer and peer tutoring will never be as good as true family literacy activity taking place out in the community – only that ensures generalization of literacy competence to the 'real life' environment and ensures that the skills gained will be used and so will endure.

Only true family literacy activity genuinely empowers the family, giving them skills they can use to help each other, help their friends and neighbours, help those who will not come to school and help new generations of children in due course. Only true family literacy injects competence, confidence and ownership into communities which may be desperately impoverished in these respects.

NOTE

The *Paired Reading* and *Paired Learning Bulletins* are available on microfiche from ERIC (1985 ED285124, 1986 ED285125, 1987 ED285126, 1988 ED298429, 1989 ED313656), as is the *Ryedale Paired Reading Adult Literacy Training Pack* (ED290845). Details of the *Paired Science Pack* are available from the author at the Centre for Paired Learning, University of Dundee, Dundee DD1 4HN, Scotland.

REFERENCES

Brierley, M., Hutchinson, P., Topping, K. and Walker, C. (1989) Reciprocal peer tutored cued spelling with ten year olds. *Paired Learning*, **5**, 136–40.

Croft, S. and Topping, K. (1992) *Paired Science: A Resource Pack for Parents and Children*. Dundee: Centre for Paired Learning, University of Dundee.

Emerson, P. (1988) Parent tutored cued spelling in a primary school. *Paired Reading Bulletin*, **4**, 91–2.

France, L., Topping, K. and Revell, K. (1992) Parent tutored cued spelling. *Support for Learning*, **8**(1), 11–15.

Harrison, R. (1989) Cued spelling in adult literacy in Kirklees. *Paired Learning*, **5**, 141.

Oxley, L. and Topping, K. (1990) Peer-tutored cued spelling with seven- to nine-year-olds. *British Educational Research Journal*, **16**(1), 63–78.

Scoble, J. (1988) Cued spelling in adult literacy – a case study. *Paired Reading Bulletin*, **4**, 93–6.

Scoble, J. (1989) Cued spelling and paired reading in adult basic education in Ryedale. *Paired Learning*, **5**, 57–62.

Scoble, J., Topping, K. and Wigglesworth, C. (1988) Training family and friends as adult literacy tutors. *Journal of Reading*, **31**(5), 410–17.

Topping, K.J. (1988) *The peer tutoring handbook: promoting co-operative learning*. Beckenham: Croom Helm/Cambridge, MA: Brookline.

Topping, K.J. (1992) Short- and long-term follow-up of parental involvement in reading projects. *British Educational Research Journal*, **18**(4), 369–79.

Topping, K.J. (1995) *Paired Reading, Spelling and Writing: The Handbook for Parents and Teachers*. London: Cassell.

Topping, K.J. and Lindsay, G. (1992) Paired reading: a review of the literature. *Research Papers in Education* **7**(3), 1–50.

Topping, K.J. and Whiteley, M. (1990) Participant evaluation of parent-tutored and peer-tutored projects in reading. *Educational Research* **32**(1), 14–32.

Topping, K.J. and Wolfendale, S. (eds) (1985) *Parental Involvement in Children's Reading*. Beckenham: Croom Helm/New York: Nichols.

Watt, J.M. and Topping, K.J. (1992) Cued spelling: a comparative study of parent and peer tutoring. *Educational Psychology in Practice*, **9**(2), 95–103.

Part 2

Towards Family Literacy

Chapter 6

School Is Too Late: Preschool work with parents

Peter Hannon

INTRODUCTION

Parental involvement in the teaching of literacy is not just for families whose children are in school. Waiting until children enter school is too late if we want the full benefits of involvement. In this chapter I argue that preschool work with parents should be given more attention and I offer a theoretical framework to underpin practice. To illustrate what can be done I draw on projects from the UK, the USA and Australia. I think we can identify practical implications from recent work but there are some crucial research questions still to be addressed.

Ten years ago, when I contributed to the forerunner to this book (Topping and Wolfendale, 1985), I was exploring parental involvement in hearing children read at home in the early school years. My concern has since shifted to the preschool years because I came to see school programmes, despite their value in some respects, as somewhat limited in often being based on a narrow conception of literacy (reading – specifically children's oral reading with an adult – to the neglect of writing) and in having a relatively modest impact on school attainment (mostly confined to short-duration programmes). Not everyone, I realize, will share my view and I do not have space to develop it fully here (instead, see Hannon, 1995). Nevertheless, it led me to wonder whether, by waiting until children start school, we might be missing an opportunity to work with parents at the time it is likely to be most beneficial – just as the foundations of literacy are being laid.

Importance of the preschool period for literacy development

One difficulty in thinking about preschool work with parents is that until recently we have not had a particular clear idea of what is involved in preschool literacy development and therefore of what we might change. However, over the last ten to fifteen years several lines of research have given us a better view of the importance of preschool development, the nature of that development, and the role of parents in it.

We now know that what children learn about literacy in the preschool years is extremely important. Quite simple measures of literacy development at school entry (e.g. ability to recognize or form letters, book handling skills) are powerful predictors of later attainment – better, arguably, than other measures of ability or oral language development (Wells, 1987; Tizard *et al.*, 1988). Other predictors from as early as 3 years of age include knowledge of nursery rhymes (Maclean *et al.*, 1987) and having favourite books (Weinberger, 1993). The teaching implications of these findings are not straightforward (for it does not follow that concentrating directly on any of these things will, in itself, improve later literacy attainment) but it is clear that preschool literacy experiences *of some kind* are important. If we are serious about raising school attainment we cannot afford to wait until children start school.

Research has also given us a fuller appreciation of the nature of literacy development in the preschool period – what Yetta Goodman has termed the 'roots of literacy' which, she argues, often go unnoticed (Goodman, 1980, 1986). Particularly interesting is what children learn from environmental print – a major feature of the print-rich cultures of the Western world – which for some children may be more influential than books. Children's early writing development can also be traced back into the preschool period, especially if one looks at children's understanding of the function of writing as well as its form (Teale and Sulzby, 1986; Hall, 1987). Other aspects of preschool development that have been highlighted by researchers include phonological awareness (Goswami and Bryant, 1990), understanding of narrative and story (Meek, 1982; Wells, 1987), and de-contextualized talk (Snow, 1991). I find it helpful to conceptualize preschool literacy development in terms of various *strands* – children's experiences of *reading* (environmental print as well as books and other texts), of *early writing* (from scribbling and mark making to recognizable forms), and of *oral language* (to include storytelling, phonological awareness, de-contextualized talk).

Obviously, parents and other family members have a central role. Children do not acquire all this knowledge of written language entirely on their own. A survey by Hannon and James (1990) found parents of preschool children, across a wide range of families, to be very active in promoting children's literacy. Most would have appreciated support from nursery teachers but did not get it. Some parents go so far as deliberately to teach their children some aspects of literacy (Farquhar *et al.*, 1986; Hall *et al.*, 1989; Hannon and James, 1990). However, although virtually all parents attempt to assist preschool literacy, they do not all do it in the same way, to the same extent, with the same concept of literacy, or with the same resources (Heath, 1983; Taylor, 1983; Wells, 1987; Taylor and Dorsey-Gaines, 1988; Hannon *et al.*, 1991). Much of the variation in children's abilities at school entry must be due to what parents do, or do not do, in the preschool years. This is an encouragement to think about work with parents but, before considering practicalities, we need to be clearer about the focus of any intervention.

THE *ORIM* FRAMEWORK

Through work at Sheffield University with Jo Weinberger, Cathy Nutbrown and others, I have come to see the importance of parents in terms of their providing the following for developing readers and writers:

● *Opportunities* for learning.
● *Recognition* of the child's achievements.
● *Interaction* around literacy activities.
● *Model* of literacy.

Some parents probably provide these more consciously, more meaningfully and more frequently than others.

In the preschool years, parents can provide vital learning *opportunities*: by resourcing children's drawing or scribbling activities; by encouraging their socio-dramatic play; by exposing them to, and helping them interpret, environmental print; by teaching nursery rhymes which aid speech segmentation and phonological awareness; by sharing story books and other written materials; by having other printed matter such as books, encyclopaedias, newspapers and so on in the home; by creating space for literacy activities by rationing TV viewing; and by enabling children to use libraries and to participate in visits, trips and holidays which provide further literacy demands and opportunities. Parents can provide unique encouragement for children in their *recognition* and valuing of children's early achievements in, for example, handling books, reading, understanding logos, and writing. They need to *interact* with children – supporting, explaining, and challenging them to move on from what they know about literacy to do more. An important way of doing this is to involve children in real literacy tasks in which they can make a meaningful contribution (e.g. adding their 'name' to a greeting card, turning the pages of a book) thereby enabling them to do today with an adult what tomorrow they will be able to do independently. Finally parents act as powerful *models* if and when children see them using literacy, for example, in reading newspapers for information or enjoyment; writing notes or shopping lists; using print to find things out, to follow instructions; or to earn a living, for example, by bringing work home; and generally demonstrating how written language is linked to a wide range of adult purposes in the home, community and workplace.

For any strand of literacy we care to distinguish, parents have the potential to provide opportunities, recognition, interaction, and a model. Figure 6.1 suggests how *ORIM* applies to the three strands of literacy I mentioned earlier. Each cell in this matrix refers to an aspect of parental support for preschool literacy (e.g. providing a reading model, appropriate interaction in writing). It can be used to describe how particular families support children's literacy development, but it is more useful as a *map of intervention possibilities*. One can ask of each cell in the matrix 'What can we do here to support the parent's role?'

DESCRIPTION OF PRACTICE

Some preschool work with parents has come about because there has traditionally been a high level of parental involvement in classroom activities in preschool education and, as nursery teachers have now begun to include more literacy activities in their classrooms, parents have been drawn into them. Parents can be found with children sharing books, cutting/sticking, adding captions, making books, helping at drawing/writing tables, adding to classroom print displays, writing or reading with a computer, supporting literacy related socio-dramatic play, teaching nursery rhymes,

**STRANDS OF
PRESCHOOL LITERACY**

	Reading	Writing	Oral language
Opportunities			
Recognition			
Interaction			
Model			

PARENTS PROVIDE

Figure 6.1   *A map of intervention possibilities*

identifying/collecting logos and signs on 'print walks', and occasionally providing a model of reading or writing themselves. This kind of involvement is valuable but distinctly limited because it is often about parents providing opportunities rather than recognition, interaction or a model of literacy. It is also limited because only a minority of parents come into school – often not those whose children would benefit most. Parents in school may not work with their own children and, even if they do, they are not in their most powerful teaching situation (the home) shaping children's home learning. It is better to play to parents' strengths.

Involvement focused on children's home learning does not suffer from the same limitations. It means playing to parents' strengths and, in principle, all parents can be involved.

In terms of the map of intervention possibilities in Figure 6.1, the territory which has been best explored is the top left cell, increasing children's opportunities for early reading experiences. The opportunities in question have usually been book sharing. Other strands of early reading experience, particularly environmental print, have been relatively neglected.

In a British project described by Swinson (1985), parents of preschool children (aged 3 to 4 years) were encouraged to read to their children from books made available from a school. There were two initial meetings for parents to discuss home reading to children and to provide general advice on 'good practice'. The project ran for most of a school year. In the Calderdale Pre-School Parent Book Project, parents of nursery children were systematically encouraged to borrow books from project schools over an eight-month period (Griffiths and Edmonds, 1986). In the United States, McCormick and Mason (1986) have described a programme in which children had 'little books' mailed to them in the months before they started kindergarten. The Pittsburgh Beginning with Books Project has provided packs of books for much younger children, without parent–teacher interaction, but on a very much larger scale with thousands of children (Locke, 1988; Segel and Friedberg, 1991). There has since been a similar initiative on a smaller scale in Britain (Wade and Moore, 1993). In the Australian West Heidelberg Early Literacy Project a home visiting initiative led to a programme in which preschools sent books home and supported parents, through meetings in school and other means, in reading to their children (Toomey and Sloane, 1994).

Most initiatives have sought simply to increase children's opportunities by providing books via parents although, in the United States, Edwards (1989), Goldsmith and Handel (1990) and Arnold and Whitehurst (1994) have, from different theoretical orientations, attempted also to influence parent–child interaction in book sharing.

Parental involvement in the teaching of writing has received as little attention in the preschool period as it has in the school period. One initiative has been reported by Green (1987) who describes a US project in which parents of kindergarten children were shown three ways to help them at home (by acting as a scribe, by writing to children, and by encouraging children to write themselves).

The oral language strand of early literacy development has also been neglected, although Wade (1984) has reported an initiative in which there was an attempt to enhance young children's storytelling ability. It included some preschool children and involved parents at home.

Overall, then, most practice has concentrated on reading (usually of books), generally with the aim of increasing *opportunities*. There has been less work on environmental print, writing and oral language. There have been some attempts to change parents' *interaction* with children but very little explicit concern with parents' *recognition* of preschool literacy achievements or how they provide a *model* of literacy.

THE SHEFFIELD EARLY LITERACY DEVELOPMENT PROJECT

One initiative with a reasonably broad focus was the Sheffield Early Literacy Development Project which I undertook with Jo Weinberger and Cathy Nutbrown. We aimed to find practical ways of working with parents to promote preschool literacy development in the home (Hannon et al., 1991). The project focused on children's home learning and developed methods of work with parents which could be carried out in both home and school locations. It concentrated on children in the middle of the preschool period – around 2½ to 3 years of age. In reading, the emphasis was on children's experiences of environmental print as well as books. There was, however, little direct attempt to influence the oral language strand.

There was no selection of families except that those invited to take part in the project lived in a defined area and had children in the target age range. Several parents admitted to difficulties themselves in reading or writing, but all children had English as a first language.

We devised three main methods of work with parents: provision of literacy materials, home visiting and meetings. These are outlined below but fuller details can be found in Weinberger *et al.* (1990).

Provision of literacy materials

Books for children and parents were made available to borrow for use at home. There was also a bookclub where similar books could be purchased. Other materials provided were intended to encourage recognition of environmental print and the development of writing and included magazines and catalogues, forms, cards and envelopes, plain paper, lined paper, pencil, sharpener, and ball-point pen. The literacy materials (additional to whatever was already in the home) were introduced through a home visit.

Home visits

Some families had a series of six fortnightly home visits from one of the project team. An attempt was made to balance the need for a flexible child-centred approach with the need for coherent coverage of key aspects of preschool literacy development. Visits were planned on the basis of a 'review–input–plan' structure. Each child's literacy activities since the previous visit were *reviewed* with the parent. A new idea of activity was *introduced*, building on the child's previous experiences. A *plan* of what might be done next with the child was agreed with the parent. (This series of visits followed the initial visit at which programme materials had been introduced into the home.) Further books for borrowing and replacement drawing/writing materials were brought by the visitor. Other activities included making books, using photographs, cutting, sticking and labelling, finding print in the home and neighbourhood, matching logos, and trying different kinds of drawing/writing materials. Children's work saved by parents was reviewed to show development (between visits, and over longer periods of time).

Meetings

A series of five meetings was held for parents to give them an opportunity to share experiences in a small group and to have a more formal input from the research team. A crèche was available when necessary. Topics included family literacy; print in the environment; the development of writing from early mark making; how children enjoy books; judging quality in books; sharing books and stories with children; using public libraries; methods of literacy teaching in schools; recognizing and recording aspects of literacy development. Methods used were group discussion, videos, slides, overhead projector transparencies of children's writing, displays of books, handouts, information about research, sharing of observations, and a 'jigsaw' profile of literacy development. Handouts were prepared after each meeting summarizing information given and parents' views. Meetings took place in the school except for a group visit to the local library at which all children were enrolled as library members. Books for borrowing, and additional drawing/writing materials, were made available at the meetings (which followed the initial visit to introduce programme materials into the home).

One simple method of assisting parents' *recognition* of preschool literacy development – which other workers have subsequently found useful – was to represent children's early achievements in reading and writing which many parents might not have recognized as such (e.g. 'knows the letter which begins own name', 'points to print in the environment and asks what it says', 'makes marks left to right') as pieces of a jigsaw. The jigsaw was printed on a sheet of paper and parents were invited to shade in pieces according to whether they had observed their children doing these things (Weinberger *et al.*, 1990). The metaphor of the jigsaw is helpful in conveying the idea that literacy has many different 'pieces' but they do not have to be fitted together in any definite order to make a whole. A further development of this idea (see Hannon, 1995) is to remove the rectangular boundary to the jigsaw and also to have blanks for parents to fill in according to what *they* think are significant achievements, thus suggesting that literacy is not bounded and that parents' views about what it consists of are important too.

ORGANIZATION

In thinking how to work with parents it is helpful to be aware of a distinction between the *focus* and the *location* of such work. The focus may be on children's school learning or their home learning and the work with parents to influence it could be located either in schools (or centres) or in the parents' homes. This means four possible combinations of these options to be considered. It is important not to fall into the trap of thinking that parental involvement means getting parents into a school or preschool to assist children's school learning – that is only one of four possibilities.

Anyone starting preschool work with parents has to decide a series of issues which are listed in the form of questions in Table 6.1. Most of the questions are self-explanatory. Question 4 refers to the possibility of working selectively with certain families where children might be considered 'at risk' in some way. As this involves questionable theoretical assumptions and also some practical difficulties, it is nearly always better to offer a programme to all families. Questions 5 and 6 refer to the intervention possibilities in Figure 6.1 – the particular cells which are to be the focus of the work with parents. Question 7 draws attention to the fact that such work involves time, effort and some other costs. If a school or preschool centre has no additional resources for the work, it may need to reduce other activities. It is important to be able to answer Question 8 since good home–school communication can make or break a programme. All innovation ought to have some degree of evaluation (Question 10) although this has to be fitted to the resources available. I

Table 6.1.   *Starting preschool literacy work with parents*

10 key questions
1. Is the focus to be children's home learning, school learning or both?
2. Is the work with parents to be carried out in school, at home or in both locations?
3. What is to be the target age range of the children?
4. Is the programme to be selective or comprehensive?
5. Which strands of literacy are to be addressed?
6. Which aspects of the parents' role are to be supported?
7. What resources will be needed for the programme and where will they come from?
8. How will the programme be explained to families?
9. What is the timetable for implementation?
10. Will the programme be evaluated? If so, how?

have previously suggested some ways of thinking about 'evaluation by tests' and 'evaluation by participants' (Hannon, 1989). Given the problems of finding suitable tests for preschool literacy development (Nutbrown and Hannon, 1993), and associated research design problems, schools should think carefully before opting for evaluation by tests.

EFFECTIVENESS

There are two basic questions to be asked about effectiveness. First, does preschool literacy work with parents really change families' literacy activities? Second, what difference does it make to children's literacy development?

To answer the first question, we carried out a qualitative evaluation of the Sheffield Early Literacy Development Project (Hannon *et al.*, 1991). We used a range of case study data (field notes, samples of children's work, records of book borrowing, observations and pre-programme and post-programme interviews). We found that take-up and participation levels were high, there was no drop-out, the intervention was welcomed by parents, and both they and the project team experienced it as meaningful. There was some evidence that home-based methods had more impact than school-based ones, particularly in book sharing. Changes in families' literacy activities were assessed in terms of the *ORIM* framework.

There was a dramatic increase in children's *opportunities* for book sharing, which in some families would otherwise have been negligible but, according to parents' interview responses, the project also succeeded in significantly increasing children's opportunities for encounters with environmental print. For example, one parent said:

Before you came I never thought about her reading things like mugs and boxes and signs and things. We read all sorts now from the top of the bus.

In relation to early writing, the range of opportunities broadened to include a greater variety of materials and purposes.

Parents' *recognition* of early literacy development appeared to have been enhanced as these parents' comments indicate:

I noticed his writing more by going to the meetings . . . . One time he was drawing it was all lines. Then after a few weeks he changed and started doing circles.

It's been an eye-opener for me – being told and explained to – that they can understand a lot more than you give them credit for.

It's made me see more in children that I've never seen before. If it wasn't for the project I wouldn't have thought so clearly what children can do.

There was evidence that parents' *interaction* with children had changed too. Almost all parents reported that they now made a point of involving their children in their own (adult) day-to-day literacy activities. Previously only a minority had done so. One parent, for example, explained how when she was ordering from a catalogue, she gave her child a piece of paper so 'she thinks she's doing it too'. The nature of book sharing may have changed too.

I used to just sit and read them a story and then I'd say 'Put it away now, I've read it'. Now I'll sit and read and she tries to read to me and tells me what's going off.

Finally, in relation to parents providing a *model* of literacy, before the intervention all parents had said they had provided a model of reading at least sometimes but not all had provided a model for writing. Afterwards there was only one parent not providing a writing model. One parent provided a reading model in this way:

I'll say to him, 'Mummy's going to read a bit. You get your book and you read.'

In summary, we found that the methods tried in the project were feasible, that they were valued by participants, and that they did change families' literacy activities.

Of course, it is the second question – concerning effectiveness in changing children's literacy development – which is the crucial one. The evaluation of the Sheffield project was not designed to answer that question but there is evidence from other studies that preschool interventions can have an impact on development.

The clearest evidence concerns the effects of increased book sharing. Swinson (1985) found that raising nursery children's level of daily home reading from around 15 per cent to close on 100 per cent in a one-year programme resulted in gains in oral vocabulary and verbal comprehension, and, in a follow-up after school entry, gains on word matching and letter identification, compared to children in a control group. Griffiths and Edmonds (1986) found that take-up over an eight-month period was high, parents and teachers viewed the project positively, and there were some gains in measures of children's literacy development. McCormick and Mason (1986) found that, despite minimal parent–teacher interaction (books were simply mailed to families), there was evidence of some impact on literacy attainment at the end of the kindergarten year. Toomey and Sloane (1994) found a positive effect on measures of emergent literacy (although not on a later school literacy test).

There appears to be no evidence concerning the effectiveness of work focused on other aspects of reading. Neither is much known about the effects of parent involvement intervention in writing development apart from the Green (1987) study which reported a positive response from parents and measurable literacy gains for children.

More evidence of effectiveness is needed. This can only be obtained through controlled experiments as there is really no alternative if we want to find out whether preschool work with parents influences children's literacy development. Such research will probably require fairly large samples, systematic long duration programmes, better ways of measuring preschool literacy development than are currently available (Nutbrown and Hannon, 1993), and a careful measurement of the resources needed for work with parents as well as of any benefits which result.

There are other research issues. First, the *ORIM* framework of *opportunities–*

recognition–interaction–model and *reading/writing/oral language* suggests a research agenda. In future studies, techniques need to be developed to explore all aspects of the parent's role, and to detect changes when they occur. Second, an underlying issue concerns ways in which conditions for literacy development might be less favourable in some families than others. Emergent literacy research has emphasized what *all* children know about reading and writing in the early years, rather than what some may *not* know (Teale and Sulzby, 1986; Hall, 1987). On the other hand, findings from the Sheffield study concerning pre-existing family literacy activity suggest that there is significant variation in children's experiences (Hannon *et al.*, 1991). It would be helpful to have more research comparing specific aspects of preschool literacy experience across a range of family backgrounds. Research in this area has to be sensitive to some fundamental theoretical difficulties in distinguishing between children who have 'less' literacy and those whose literacy is simply different from 'school literacy'. Practice has to be sensitive to the question of whether one is extending family literacy or imposing school literacy. A third research issue is the development and evaluation of programmes focused on other strands of literacy – particularly oral language. For example, there is evidence – both survey and experimental – that the development of phonological awareness in the preschool period aids progress in early reading (Bryant and Bradley, 1985; Maclean *et al.*, 1987; Goswami and Bryant, 1990). There is obvious potential for sharing this information with parents and developing parent–child activities involving letters, sounds, and rhymes which may be both enjoyable in themselves as well as helpful for children's literacy development. There are other aspects of oral language, highlighted by the work of other investigators, which could be the basis of work with parents, e.g. storytelling (Wells, 1987) or de-contextualized talk (Snow, 1991). A final issue of importance is how parents' own literacy might be helped. It would be quite wrong to make it a condition of involvement – as happens in some 'family literacy' programmes – that parents should receive adult literacy tuition but some parents would welcome the opportunity to extend their own education. If this can be linked to their role in helping their children, so much the better. The research issue is whether combined parent and child education is more than the sum of the parts.

CONCLUSION

School *is* too late. There is a compelling case for trying to develop ways of working with parents to promote children's preschool literacy development, and good reason to think that if we were successful this could have substantial benefits for later school attainment. Some promising forms of practice have been developed even if we are still a long way from knowing their full effectiveness.

Preschool work with parents is not enough, however, and cannot be expected to immunize children against having difficulties later in school. It should not be considered in isolation from other forms of involvement in the teaching of literacy but rather as the base upon which a comprehensive, continuous, home-focused approach should be built throughout the school years. The transition to school should not involve any discontinuity in families' relationships with teachers and others concerned with children's literacy development. In some schools this may mean a new attitude to what children bring from home to the learning of literacy and a greater readiness to acknowledge parents as teachers. If schools are not prepared for families where parents are active and knowledgeable about their children's development, and where children's literacy experiences have been rich and varied, then advances in the preschool period might be quickly reversed. The principles underlying good practice with families before children enter school are fundamentally the same as those underlying good practice with families of older children.

REFERENCES

Arnold, D.S. and Whitehurst, G.J. (1994) Accelerating language development through picture book reading: a summary of dialogic reading and its effects. In D.K. Dickinson (ed.) *Bridges to Literacy: Children, Families, and Schools*. Cambridge, MA: Blackwell.

Bryant, P. and Bradley, L. (1985) *Children's Reading Problems*. Oxford: Basil Blackwell.

Edwards, P.A. (1989) Supporting lower SES mothers' attempts to provide scaffolding for book reading. In J. Allen and J.M. Mason (eds) *Risk Makers, Risk Takers, Risk Breakers: Reducing the Risks for Young Literacy Learners*. Portsmouth, NH: Heinemann.

Farquhar, C., Blatchford, P., Burke, J., Plewis, I. and Tizard, B. (1985) A comparison of the views of parents and reception teachers. *Education 3–13*, **13**, 17–22.

Goldsmith, E. and Handel, R. (1990) *Family Reading: An Intergenerational Approach to Literacy*. Syracuse, NY: New Readers Press.

Goodman, Y.M. (1980) The roots of literacy. In M.P. Douglas (ed.) *Claremont Reading Conference Forty-fourth Yearbook*. Claremont, CA: Claremont Reading Conference.

Goodman, Y.M. (1986) Children coming to know literacy. In W.H. Teale and E. Sulzby (eds) *Emergent Literacy: Writing and Reading*. Norwood, NJ: Ablex.

Goswami, U. and Bryant, P. (1990) *Phonological Skills and Learning to Read*. Hove: Lawrence Erlbaum Associates.

Green, C. (1987) Parental facilitation of young children's writing. *Early Child Development and Care*, **28**, 31–7.

Griffiths, A. and Edmonds, M. (1986) *Report on the Calderdale Pre-school Parent Book Project*. Halifax, England: Schools Psychological Service, Calderdale Education Department.

Hall, N. (1987) *The Emergence of Literacy*. London: Hodder & Stoughton.

Hall, N., Herring, G., Henn, H. and Crawford, L. (1989) *Parental Views on Writing and the Teaching of Writing*. Manchester: Manchester Polytechnic School of Education.

Hannon, P. (1987) A study of the effects of parental involvement in the teaching of reading on children's reading test performance. *British Journal of Educational Psychology*, **57**, 56–72.

Hannon, P. (1989) How should parental involvement in the teaching of reading be evaluated? *British Educational Research Journal*, **15**(1), 33–40.

Hannon, P. (1995) *Literacy, Home and School: Research and Practice in Teaching Literacy with Parents*. London: Falmer Press.

Hannon, P. and Jackson, A. (1987) *The Belfield Reading Project Final Report*. London/Rochdale: National Children's Bureau/Belfield Community Council.

Hannon, P. and James, S. (1990) Parents' and teachers' perspectives on preschool literacy development. *British Educational Research Journal*, **16**(3), 259–72.

Hannon, P., Weinberger, J. and Nutbrown, C. (1991) A study of work with parents to promote early literacy development. *Research Papers in Education*, **6**(2), 77–97.

Heath, S.B. (1983) *Ways with Words: Language, Life and Work in Communities and Classrooms*. Cambridge: Cambridge University Press.

Locke, J.L. (1988) Pittsburgh's Beginning with Books Project. *School Library Journal*, February, 22–4.

McCormick, C.E. and Mason, J.M. (1986) Intervention procedures for increasing preschool children's interest in and knowledge about reading. In W. Teale and E. Sulzby (eds) *Emergent Literacy: Writing and Reading*. Norwood, NJ: Ablex.

Maclean, M., Bryant, P. and Bradley, L. (1987) Rhymes, nursery rhymes, and reading in early childhood. *Merrill-Palmer Quarterly*, **33**(3), 255–81.

Meek, M. (1982) *Learning to Read*. London: The Bodley Head.

Nutbrown, C. and Hannon, P. (1993) Assessing early literacy: new measures needed. *International Journal of Early Childhood*, **25**(2), 27–30.

Segel, E. and Friedberg, J.B. (1991) 'Is today Liberry Day?' Community support for family literacy. *Language Arts*, **68**, December, 654–7.

Snow, C. (1991) The theoretical basis for relationships between language and literacy in development. *Journal of Research in Childhood Education*, **6**(1), 5–10.

Swinson, J. (1985) A parental involvement project in a nursery school. *Educational Psychology in Practice*, **1**(1), 19–22.

Taylor, D. (1983) *Family Literacy: Young Children Learning to Read and Write*. Exeter, NH: Heinemann.

Taylor, D. and Dorsey-Gaines, C. (1988) *Growing up Literate: Learning from Inner-city Families*. Portsmouth, NH: Heinemann.

Teale, W.H. and Sulzby, E. (eds) (1986) *Emergent Literacy: Writing and Reading*. Norwood, NJ: Ablex.

Tizard, B., Blatchford, P., Burke, J., Farquhar, C. and Plewis, I. (1988) *Young Children at School in the Inner City*. London: Lawrence Erlbaum Associates.

Tizard, J., Schofield, W.N. and Hewison, J. (1982) Collaboration between teachers and parents in assisting children's reading. *British Journal of Educational Psychology*, **52**, 1–15.

Toomey, D. and Sloane, J. (1994) Fostering children's early literacy development through parent involvement: a five-year program. In D.K. Dickinson (ed.) *Bridges to Literacy: Children, Families, and Schools*. Cambridge, MA: Blackwell.

Topping, K. and Wolfendale, S. (eds) (1985) *Parental Involvement in Children's Reading*. Beckenham: Croom Helm.

Wade, B. (1984) *Story at Home and School. Educational Review Publication No. 10*. Birmingham: University of Birmingham, Faculty of Education.

Wade, B. and Moore, M. (1993) *Bookstart in Birmingham. Book Trust Report No. 2*. London: Book Trust.

Weinberger, J. (1993) A longitudinal study of literacy experiences, the role of parents, and children's literacy development. Unpublished PhD thesis, University of Sheffield.

Weinberger, J., Hannon, P. and Nutbrown, C. (1990) *Ways of Working with Parents to Promote Early Literacy Development. USDE Papers in Education No. 14*. Sheffield: University of Sheffield Division of Education.

Wells, G. (1987) *The Meaning Makers: Children Learning Language and Using Language to Learn*. London: Hodder & Stoughton.

Chapter 7

Parents, Teachers, Children: a Whole Literacy Education System

Max Kemp

INTRODUCTION

This chapter describes a programme at the University of Canberra for children and adolescents who have difficulties in dealing with all aspects of literacy. The programme works through the children's parents and also groups of teachers taking postgraduate studies. The current programme has evolved over twenty years, gradually enlarging as a consequence of agreements between the university and the Australian Capital Territory Department of Education, and the attraction of research funding from several sources.

Known as the Parents as Tutors Programme (PTP), the project is run in the Faculty of Education's Schools and Community Centre. The Centre provides a number of educational services but literacy and mathematics support programmes for parents and children are the main ones.

During any year approximately 120 families have access to the various aspects of the PTP. Parents are encouraged to participate as a consequence of counselling by their children's teachers and school guidance personnel. Normally the children have been at school for at least three years and have poor track records despite school-based assistance, and often they are adolescents without much apparent chance of recovery.

The procedures of assistance are quite complex and labour-intensive, but aspects of the programme can and do have application to schools. Many of the participating graduate teachers develop their own systems in schools, replicating some parts of the programme with parents and children but including others only if they have access to support personnel and resources. During their course, the teachers' work with parents and children is constantly monitored by the Centre's three full-time tutors and Director so that the PTP provides the teachers, as well as the families, with practice in methodological and assessment skills.

The descriptions of practices that follow have been chosen because they comprise the initial parent training and can be employed by classroom teachers. The writer assumes that in any school community there is always at least a small group of parents who are interested in and capable of giving support in the literacy curriculum. Such parents may be trained as listeners to oral reading, as readers of stories and 'conferees' at desks during writing sessions, and as assistants in the sensitive and time-consuming tasks of preparing and presenting children's writing for publication.

In all such tasks and others, trained parents may become invaluable. The difficult part for the teacher or the school as a whole is to tap the parental resource, provide a lively training programme, keep the volunteer parents interested and skilled, and ensure the programme's success through good management and tangible results.

This chapter will describe some elements of the PTP in literacy; suggest methods that may be employed; describe some research that supports the idea of PTP; and outline some management procedures that assist the sustainability of in-school projects involving parents.

DESCRIPTIONS OF PRACTICE

When parents contemplate joining the PTP they are interviewed at length regarding their child's history. Both parents, where possible, are asked to participate in all stages of the PTP. Fathers are sometimes diffident during the interview but often become enthusiastic once they understand the nature of the programme and their roles. During this interview the parents are shown one or two skills as listeners to their children's reading, and they practise these with their child in front of the video camera. The videotape becomes the basis of the parents' and child's record of progress. Obviously it is important that everyone is successful in this first task and the process is carefully governed by the tutors so that no one leaves feeling inadequate and disappointed.

The parents then join others in seminar groups that meet for two hours on ten occasions during a university semester. These seminar meetings are lively affairs that involve parents in many activities that demonstrate how literacy skills are acquired and learned. During the activities, explanations are given and issues explored. For example, there are demonstrations of how, during reading, we 'see' many features that do not appear in print but cannot see others that do appear. Self-corrective reading and spelling techniques are demonstrated. Good listening-to-reading techniques are shown on videotapes, and practised. During a coffee break in every session, parents talk to each other about themselves and their children, and also about what they are learning, often making friends and planning mutual help. The ten sessions are well attended. They are a means of giving parents the chance to build a repertoire of knowledge, opinions, attitudes and skills that will help them to understand how errors may be considered as a natural consequence of learning. One major intention is to show constantly that the nature of errors is such that they usually signal corrective strategies.

The structure and content of the ten seminar sessions are shown in Table 7.1.

For the Schools and Community Centre's purposes the content of the seminars is wide ranging and a consistent theory of learning is applied to all conditions and processes – for example, from oral reading to narrative writing, and from reading for research purposes to accuracy in spelling. In schools, teachers usually reduce both the number and duration of the sessions and are likely to concentrate more on one or two

Table 7.1 *Schools and Community Centre Parents-as-Tutors: sample seminar programme*

Session 1 The purposes of the programme: its history and present organization. Introduction to stress management. The reading process: cue systems and strategies. Text and reading.	**Session 2** Error patterns in reading. How to listen to oral reading. To interrupt or not interrupt? Pause and prompt rules. Demonstrating correction strategies.
Session 3 Are reading errors always wrong? The nature of the text. Intervening effectively. Stress management review.	**Session 4** Book orientation. Using paired reading. Transformations.
Session 5 Memory overload – bottlenecks of letters and sounding-out. Using what's in the head during reading.	**Session 6** Looking at early writing. Restarting writing – dictated writing of various texts. Helping without taking over.
Session 7 Solving writing's challenges one at a time. Giving different kinds of assistance at different writing stages. Giving different kinds of assistance with different kinds of text.	**Session 8** What knowledge do we use when we spell? What stages do we go through in our spelling development? Helping strategies in spelling.
Session 9 Reading and writing for specific requirements. 'Whose assignment *is* this?' Supporting independent research and understanding.	**Session 10** Literature for children and adolescents. Parents' reviews of their children's progress. Planning for the IAP.

aspects, such as listening to oral reading, or the writing process, rather than attempt all aspects of the literacy curriculum.

The first three sessions of the PTP must be attended by both parents or one parent and a partner. It seems essential that parents should leave the sessions able to talk to someone about their own child within the context of what the seminars are teaching. Our experience indicates that one cannot afford to hurry through the seminar content, nor to reduce the time parents need to make the content relevant to their own child and family circumstances.

After having completed the seminar series parents are invited to attend the second half, the Individual Assistance Programme (IAP). Not all parents or their children need this. In some cases the improvement in the child's performance has been immediate as a consequence of the change in parents' approaches to assistance. For most, however, the IAP is essential. Regular demonstrations of teaching and management procedures, and supervised practice, are necessary for sustained improvement in the child's literacy development. The IAP lasts for another ten sessions, usually of one hour each, during which a tutor works with a graduate teacher and the parent(s) and child. Each session is carefully structured to maximize the parent's practising of home tutoring procedures. The sessions are videotaped, allowing for a continual review of tutoring techniques and the monitoring of the child's progress.

Although the IAP is labour-intensive, it repeatedly shows the need for parents to have access to demonstrations of and practice in the techniques introduced during the seminar programme. It is often the case that parents believe they are on the right track when, in fact, they are not; and tutors are also able to develop incentives for both parents and child to maintain their efforts. Without the IAP, many parents would stop giving assistance at the first sign of their child's improvement, believing that they have done their job and that further progress would be a consequence only of the child's practising and having the right attitude.

When considering how the IAP may apply in schools, the graduate teachers have seen the need to make their classrooms more open so that parents may see the teacher's demonstrations and also practise their tutoring techniques under supervision. Resource (support) teachers in schools are well placed to follow such a procedure and may find that their efforts in helping parents are, in the long run, more economic than their own individualized 'remedial' teaching of the children. Parents trained in this way by a resource teacher may become, themselves, a resource for the whole classroom, not simply for their own child.

ORGANIZATION

The preceding details about the Parents as Tutors Programme include many aspects of organization, but these are pertinent to a tertiary institution whose job it is to train postgraduate teachers for specialist support teaching in schools. Some adaptations to schools have already been suggested. For teachers who contemplate initiatives in harnessing the support that parents can give, other aspects of the Canberra project have also been adapted in many schools and classrooms.

The summary that follows is designed to give the reader a number of organizational alternatives to think about. School, classroom and community conditions differ immensely. What is suitable in one place may not be possible in another. It needs to be said, however, that neither depressed socio-economic conditions nor high enrolments of children from other-than-English language backgrounds should be considered as factors precluding effective participation by parents. There have been demonstrations of effective work with parents in such places for many years (Hewison, 1979; Glynn, 1980; Builder, 1980, 1982; Jackson and Hannon, 1981; Griffiths and Hamilton, 1984; Hannon *et al.*, 1985; Glynn and McNaughton, 1985; Topping and Wolfendale, 1985; O'Connor *et al.*, 1987; Hannon, 1987).

For ease of dealing with the innumerable possible variables that can affect the way any school or institution may need to organize its own parents-as-tutors programme, a few key phases will be identified and suggestions given about their organization. Some opinions will also be expressed about priorities. These opinions derive from the Canberra project and some of its offshoots elsewhere.

PRELIMINARY CONSIDERATIONS

No programme for parents or peer tutors should commence without thorough preparation of the tutors through training. Leaving such procedures, which may require insight, delicacy and skill, to a prospective tutor's 'common sense' would amount to professional negligence. There is no easy path to effective support teaching, and the sense required for it is not common.

Good parents-as-tutors programmes seem to be easier to manage in primary than secondary schools for a number of reasons. In the latter, peer-tutoring may be more successful but only if the school as a whole is committed to making it so.

If the school is fortunate enough to have a Reading Recovery (RR) (Clay, 1991) programme, it is possible for the RR tutor to build sessions for parents around either the tutoring sessions themselves or videotapes of the sessions. The sessions or videotapes may be used as a succession of demonstrations, provided that they are followed up by both discussion and supervised practice within the classroom.

If there is no RR programme, the parents-as-tutors sessions should be orientated in the first instance to the parents of 'at risk' children in the early grades, or to volunteer tutors who would be pleased to work with teachers at that level. Support for at-risk children is better early than late, and parents tend to be more available for younger than older children. This is not to deny the benefits of assisting the parents of children at any level, but schools may see quicker and longer-lasting returns for their work if they commence in the early grades.

Small initiatives in parents-as-tutors programmes may be better than big ones. Perhaps teachers should begin with just one or two parents on a regular and well-structured basis in their own classrooms. They can then test their own views and methods and closely observe the parents' responses; and they can record what they see and hear while monitoring their own, the parents' and the children's progress. From this small but nevertheless demanding and interesting beginning, teachers may develop the confidence to arrange for larger groups of parents to participate in a more comprehensive programme.

One cannot emphasize too strongly the benefits that teachers will enjoy from having a collection of videotapes that demonstrate all aspects of tutoring that they plan to discuss during seminars. Videotapes provide not only demonstrations of technique but models of behaviour. Suitable videotapes of, for example, a teacher's listening and responding techniques while attending to a child's oral reading, will provide a lasting reference point for parents that talking alone cannot give. Hence, before embarking on a PTP it may be wise to spend several months reflecting on the programme's objectives, what needs to be demonstrated, and how best the demonstrations may be collated and presented.

PHASES OF THE PROGRAMME

The interview

If the Canberra experience is used as a model, the preliminary interview with parents is important to the shaping-up of everyone's success in the programme. The interview should include both parents, if possible, as well as the child. The following elements are focal:

- an atmosphere of partnership and discussion rather than judgement and instruction by the teacher;

- the achievement of success goals in tasks rather than testing for and the recording of deficiencies;
- the teacher as listener and observer rather than talker and teller;
- a book selection activity (see below);
- a book orientation activity (see below);
- a videotape of the child reading aloud from the selected book to one of the parents; and
- a positive review of the child as reader and the parent as listener (see below).

Book selection activity

The purpose of this is to find a book or books that the child is able to read successfully even if support is necessary, and also to explore his or her interests and learning strengths. It should go without saying that nearly every child is able to demonstrate some masteries and positive attitudes: to pets, sport, collecting, experiments, cooking, prehistoric animals, space and space travel, television programmes, for example. The interview will reveal these, and they become the basis for a reading and writing programme. Children lacking confidence at school are often inarticulate about school-related activities, including reading and writing, so they may need to be encouraged to talk about themselves and their out-of-school interests. Parents, too, will reveal more about their child's abilities and interests than teachers are usually able to describe.

The book selection activity (a fuller version is in Kemp, 1987a) comprises the following procedures:

- Before the interview the teacher takes the age and sex of the child into account and selects a wide range of reading material from the library, including (for an older reader in this case) picture-and-text books, wordless books, a magazine, a newspaper, advertising catalogues, factual and story books, model-making instructions, a manual of some kind (for setting a video recorder, for instance) and perhaps a volume of an encyclopedia.
- The reader is asked to look into each book or item and to place it in one of two groups: (1) items that are interesting and that s/he would like to read or listen to; (2) items that are not of interest or are too difficult.

  During the selection the child is asked to give reasons, and the teacher questions to elicit these if the child is not forthcoming. The teacher watches closely to see how the items are handled and how much (and of what kind) interest is shown. This session may be as creative as the teacher wishes to make it. The information gained will generally reflect the care with which the teacher thinks through the possible lines of enquiry beforehand. Additional books and materials may be gathered to supplement those available, whether to feed an expressed interest or to broaden the range of possibilities. For this reason it is wise to conduct the interview in the school library at a time when it is not open to others.
- The first group of books becomes the focus and the second is discarded. The child is asked to look through the first group once more with the purpose of selecting

one that s/he can read for videotaping. If a wordless book is chosen, the teacher and child can compose a text together and record it on a chalkboard or paper. The chosen text becomes the vehicle for book orientation. After the interview, the teacher records his/her observations about the child's interests, attitudes, language (fluidity, vocabulary, ability to exchange), and reading attempts.

Book orientation

Holdaway (1979) described a similar procedure as shared book experience. Clay (1991, ch. 6) uses the term 'book orientation' to describe something different from the procedures summarized here. The purpose is to develop a fail-safe reading activity that will leave the reader and parents with a sense of achievement and a feeling of hope. The teacher demonstrates during the interview, encouraging one of the parents to join in and even take over.

- The book selected in the first activity, preferably a narrative with relevant picture support, is given to the reader to browse through without interruption by the parent, although 'reader-talk' is encouraged. (Reader-talk is any commentary that is relevant to the text's meaning, vocabulary, illustrations or story line. It often provides information about the reader's mastery of the ideas, concepts and even genre of the text.)
- After browsing, the parent and child talk their way through the book together. The child is asked to tell the story as it is revealed through the pictures and/or the text that the child understands. The book is not read aloud; instead, links are drawn between text and pictures by questioning. For example, the parent may say: 'You said that there was a big crowd watching the circus. Can you point to where the text ways that? Can you show me where it says "big crowd" . . . "circus"? Have a look at the picture of the lion. Where does the text tell you about the lion? And the lion-tamer? Tell me what you think happens on this page. What do you think will happen next?' If the text contains few pictures and is about space, for example, the parent encourages the reader to tell what s/he knows, using chapter headings and sub-headings as a lead.

  Once again, the success of this procedure depends in large part on how well the parent is able to tease out from the reader the relationship of the text to pictures or headings, and thence of in-head meaning to text. If the reader is impatient to read, the parent may proceed through the orientation in segments, discussing first then reading one section at a time.
- Once the orientation has been completed the parent decides whether or not the reader is well enough prepared to read alone. If not, the parent reads through the text, the child following perhaps with a transparent plastic strip held under the successive lines of text. If the parent is confident about the child being able to read alone, then s/he does so. The parent provides help when necessary but tries to intervene as little as possible.
- Following the reading, a retelling of the story may be desirable. Another book is then chosen for book orientation and reading at home.

Table 7.2   *Prompting during oral reading*

Before reading:
1. Talk through the text first.
2. Make meaning and understanding the priority.

During reading: *for unknown words or sections*
1. Wait. Give an opportunity for working out.
2. Suggest a strategy: reread, read on,* use picture.
3. Suggest a meaning: 'The word means . . .' or 'What might it be?' or 'The word sounds like . . .' (or rhymes with . . .) or 'What might happen next?'

During reading: *when a 'no-sense' error happens*
1. Wait. Give an opportunity for self-correction after the reader has read on or paused.
2. Say 'You said ". . .". Do you think that what you said sounds right? or . . . makes sense? or . . . looks right?'

During reading: *when a sense-making error happens*
1. Wait. Give an opportunity to self-correct.
2. Let the reading flow. Come back later unless there is a lot of 'inventing' of text. Don't teach.

After reading:
1. Talk about the sequence, meaning and reader's ideas; then focus on the visual structure of words if this helps.
2. Praise particular aspects, such as successfully used recovery techniques and self-correcting.

* 'Reading on' is difficult for early-level readers. If there are too many errors you may need to change the text.

The parent as listener

This is too complex a procedure to describe adequately here but a few basic principles will be given. Table 7.2 indicates these principles.

In the Canberra programme, parents' listening and responding to their children's oral reading has always been one of the most crucial elements of training. Listening to oral reading is something all parents do at homework time and it is regarded as the most straightforward of homework tasks. Yet it is also the source of most frustration for parents, who wonder why oral reading can lead to so many unfortunate family 'scenes' and bickering, often with a child's tantrum to round it off (Kemp, 1987b).

The listening and responding technique (originally called 'Pause–prompt–praise') is adapted from New Zealand work by Glynn (1980) and McNaughton *et al.* (1981). In Canberra, successive videotapes of periodic 'reading together' sessions show that the development of the parents' technique is associated with the child's progress as a reader, and that where such progress is evident, other aspects of literacy development are sure to follow. In that sense, then, the development of the technique is basic to every child's recovery as a school learner, and more so as a self-respecting literate member of the broader community. If that is the case, it is worth putting effort into teaching the procedure well. The first four sessions in the Canberra seminar programme are devoted to that task.

There is little to be gained from training anyone to do a task or follow a set of procedures if the reasons for doing so are not understood. In any kind of crisis the procedures would rightly be discarded because they appear to be unworkable. Children become exposed under these conditions to a variety of tasks that seem to have little relationship to each other and are constantly asked to make a fresh start. If the reasons for a procedure are understood, however, then it is likely to survive momentary crises.

The 'pause–prompt' part of the New Zealand work (the 'praise' part of it is used only sparingly in the Canberra adaptation) produces an instantaneous, positive response amongst parents, who believe that it saves their children from a literacy death as well as the parents themselves from further threats of a broken marriage. What is the procedure and why is it so successful?

The procedure is really quite simple, even if the reasons for employing it are complex, grounded as they are in a tightly structured theory of learning. It is successful because its results are immediate and tangible.

- The chosen text for the child to read to the parent should be one which is readable; that is, it should be within the reader's vocabulary and sentence structure repertoire and, above all, be of interest and meaning to the reader. The listener should be satisfied that the text meets these criteria. A book orientation should precede the reading.
- The child needs to know that s/he will not be interrupted by the listener, even by praise, and that there will be a delay in assistance whenever the reader makes an error or is stumped by unknown words or difficult structures. The delay is to allow the reader to sort out the problem and correct it, if possible. The delay also gives the listener time to think about an appropriate strategy of assistance.
- If the reader is unable to resolve the problem, the listener will provide a series of prompts or questions that are designed to help the reader sort out information that s/he already has and which can be used for self-correction.
- Often the listener will wait until the end of a section (a sentence or paragraph) before pointing out that the reader has made an error affecting the meaning. The listener will not make the correction, but will ask the reader to reconsider what the word or phrase should be.
- Sometimes the reader will get close to a correct pronunciation but not know the meaning of a word; or will lose syntactic rhythm when dealing with a complex sentence structure. The listener will generally wait until the end of the section before assisting the reader in a correction.
- The listener will try always to avoid telling the reader a word or phrase because it is rarely that such telling is of any value. Indeed, the process of oral reading is so complex for a poor reader that any told words are immediately forgotten. (This is often the source of frustration and anger to a parent, who may think and say that the reader is not concentrating.) Rather than telling, the listener tries to assist the reader to identify the word(s) because self-correction is one of the keys to remembering. Of course, there are times when telling is necessary. When this is so, it is important that the reader be asked to reread the sentence immediately with the told words in their context.
- If there are many errors and the reader is unable to self-correct at better than a rate of one-in-three, the listener should read the text aloud with the reader. This may help to engender enough confidence before long for the reader to try reading alone again. Texts often do not function at the same difficulty level throughout and there may be patches where the listener's help is needed.

- The listener may use illustrations or aspects of the story to help the reader recover the meaning at any time.
- The listener should never use reading time to teach word structures. This may be done at the end of the oral reading with one or two words at the most, and only if thought necessary. The focus of reading time must always be on meaning.
- At the end of a paragraph or, better still, at the end of the story, the listener should praise the reader's efforts, particularly self-corrections, in specific terms. Thus it is not enough to say: 'That was very good; you are doing well.' It is more pointed and helpful to say: 'I liked the way you came back to "trainline", here, in this paragraph, and corrected it, because when you read it as "teamline" you knew it didn't make sense.'
- At the end, the reader should be asked to retell and thence respond to a few questions from the listener, or indeed the reader may ask the listener some questions (reciprocal teaching). The retelling is sometimes also used by a reader to ask questions about words, and this may be a good time for the listener to foster such curiosity and give explanations about word structure and spelling/sound relationships.

These three procedures, book selection, book orientation and pause–prompt procedures, mark the start of a support programme of helping parents to be tutors of their own children. It is time now to consider why parents may be seen as effective tutors in their own children's literacy development, and how successful the total programme has been.

EFFECTIVENESS

Why work with parents at all? Are we not really asking them to do the teacher's work?

The Schools and Community Centre has been operating now for twenty years. Originally it functioned as a withdrawal, 'remedial' programme in which only teachers worked. Parents left their children twice each week for an hour and picked them up afterwards. Gradually, however, parents asked if they could stay to observe. This was readily agreed to, and the parents were given explanations along the way about the teachers' reasons for doing things the way they were.

It seemed before long that there were many teachers giving many explanations, all of them consuming limited time. Seminars for all parents, it was suggested, would rationalize this. Also, if the seminars preceded the direct assistance to the children, parents and teachers would be able to use a mutual language and share an understanding of the methods employed in assisting the children. Parents and teachers would work, in effect, in partnership.

Hence the current programme evolved from this beginning to the fulfilling of a genuine need. With the support of the Department of Education it has grown to its current scope and size and with no slowing down of demand. It has proved to be economic, adaptable to needs and successful in achieving its objectives. There is no question that parents who complete the programme are often more successful tutors at home than support or classroom teachers can be at school, provided that two conditions can be met:

1. The parents understand the reasons for using particular tutoring methods with their children.
2. The work of most (not necessarily all) is professionally and regularly monitored.

Of course, any claim of success concerned with human learning must always be tempered by reference to exceptions and varying levels of achievement. The Schools and Community Centre programme is unexceptional in that respect. It has, however, a long history of independent and internal research to show up its strengths and weaknesses as well as give the programme periodic changes in organization, structure and direction.

The evidence

The Schools and Community Centre produces an annual bibliography and a biennial report that detail its publications and reviews of performance.

Two items are selected from the Schools and Community Centre *Report and Bibliography 1992* to illustrate the nature of evidence concerning parents' effectiveness as tutors under the conditions of the Centre's programme, and also to focus on the parents' own perceptions of the Centre's work. The first (Kemp, 1989) is a detailed review of the progress of two sample groups of parents and their children as they progressed through and completed the PTP and IAP. Criterion measures of reading processes on the same text on three spaced occasions were used to assess the children's performance levels and progress; and criterion measures were also used to assess the parents' responses to errors and deviations from text during their children's oral reading on those three occasions.

The children's reading processes were also compared to those of a group of London mainstream children reading the same text on three successive weekly occasions. This was done to assess similarities and differences in the nature of reading processes and performance levels.

Measurements of the children's performances on text were based on fluency, error frequency and self-correction rates; and of their processing of text on substitutions, additions, omissions, hesitations, re-reading, sounding-out, reading ahead and asking for help.

The readers demonstrated improvement in most areas at a significant level, between >0.01 and >0.001. Error reduction, in particular, stood out as the index of improvement; while sounding-out disappeared almost completely as a strategy for recovery from error. These were heartening results but they carried a sting in their tail which will be described shortly.

The parents' responses were measured in the areas of frequency and timing of intervention (whether immediate or delayed), the nature of the instructions they gave to their children for recovering from error or loss of meaning, and the kinds of cues they employed.

As with the children, the parents showed statistically significant improvement in all areas, demonstrating a highly developed repertoire of skills that had been refined to meet all contingencies when listening to their children's oral reading. Of course, group results invariably hide the performances of the weakest and this was true in this instance with some children and some parents making disappointing headway.

Of real concern in this study, however, was the sting in the tail of the children's performances, referred to above. When the children's processing was compared to the London group's, significant differences emerged in the way the latter's better performers dealt with their errors, particularly as they became more familiar with the text's meaning on the third occasion. While the Schools and Community Centre children employed techniques to recover from their errors as they had been taught, and also as their parents had been encouraged to support them to do, their London counterparts increasingly ignored errors that bore no significance to their understanding of the text's meaning. Instead, they hurried to finish, to round off the story, sometimes making up appropriate words or phrases that fitted their understanding thus far.

This study provided a timely reminder that the process of reading is not a mechanical affair, readily contained within a pause–prompt rule system for readers and listeners, but a creative endeavour in which the reader and author together bring meaning to the text. As a consequence of this study, book orientation became a much more important element of tutoring. In short, the more the reader understands the meanings generated by the text before s/he reads it, the fewer breakdowns there will be and the less need there will be for any intervention by a listener.

The second item from the Schools and Community Centre *Report and Bibliography 1992* gives an account of parents' responses to a survey of aspects of the PTP and IAP during preceding semesters. A questionnaire asking for anonymous responses on a seven-point scale to 18 questions about the effectiveness of the programme was mailed to 250 families. A 36 per cent return produced, amongst others, the following indices of parents' views, all of them derived from the two highest points on the scale:

- 75 per cent saw good progress in their children's reading, 54 per cent in writing, and 86 per cent in self-confidence related to school activities;
- 71 per cent described favourable school reports on their children's general progress;
- 80 per cent of children favourably assessed their progress in reading, and 58 per cent in writing;
- 98 per cent of parents rated the PTP seminars as very helpful and 83 per cent believed that they had made good progress as home tutors to their children;
- 96 per cent of parents rated the IAP session as very helpful;
- 95 per cent would strongly recommend the programme to other parents;
- 78 per cent of parents reported that they would not wish to see any changes made to the existing programme.

These positive responses are underscored by the fact that in many cases the parents' expectations, responsibilities and difficulties could be overwhelming. An average age of 10.4 years across a population comprising 73 per cent boys means that there are several adolescent boys and some girls for whom the programme may be too little, too late; and for whom the parents' struggles against entrenched negativism or loss of interest have probably already been lost. Indeed, the open-ended questions contained many parents' expressions of regret that they did not know of the programme's existence until too late, and pleas were also made for its availability to parents of children starting school.

CONCLUSION

Whether viewed from inside a parents-as-tutors programme or at a critical distance, one can only be impressed by the effort that most parents are willing to make for the sake of their children's school success. They recognize that literacy provides their children with greater access to almost everything they may wish to think, to know, to do or to be. Some parents understand this from their own experiences of limitations; some cannot understand why their children are not as they are, and therefore successful; others seek to blame; and a few believe that nothing can be done. Some, regrettably, cannot see past the fault as lying inside their child.

Bringing parents together with the mutual purpose of finding out what the problems are, who has them, what reasons there may be for them, and what some of the solutions are, seems to be a civilized way of meeting the special needs of their children. It is nearly two decades since the Warnock Report (1978) rightly condemned the attitudes of professionals who did not listen to parents speaking about their children. While the professionals may know how to help, for that is their job, their advice can only be validated if parents see its relevance and agree on the actions that they need to take to support their child. School learning, or learning to read and write, may require a parental–professional partnership just as tightly drawn and mutually supportive as physical or emotional care.

One listens with dismay to the arguments put from time to time that involving parents in the school curriculum is merely a cheap way of trying to sustain an education system; and that schools have no business importuning members of their community into doing the tasks that teachers should be doing. Perhaps the argument should be that schools have no business locking the members of their community out, or in any way preventing parents and their children from having the mutual benefits of a three-way learning process from teacher to child to parent in which general community literacy or awareness ultimately becomes the beneficiary.

REFERENCES

Builder, P.W. (1980) Involving parents of poor readers. *Australian Journal of Reading*, 3(4), 212–19.

Builder, P.W. (1982) Parents as partners in the teaching of reading. *Australian Journal of Reading*, 5(4), 216–22.

Clay, M.M. (1991) *Becoming Literate: The Construction of Inner Control*. Auckland: Heinemann Education.

Glynn, T. and McNaughton, S. (1985) The Mangere home and school remedial reading procedures. *New Zealand Journal of Psychology*, 14, 66–77.

Glynn, T. (1980) Parent–child interaction in remedial reading at home. In M.M. Clark and T. Glynn (eds) *Reading and Writing for the Child with Difficulties. Educational Review, Occasional Paper No. 8.* Birmingham, UK: University of Birmingham.

Griffiths, A. and Hamilton, D. (1984) *Parent, Teacher, Child*. London: Methuen.

Hannon, P. (1987) A study of the effects of parental involvement in the teaching of reading on children's reading performance. *British Journal of Educational Psychology*, **57**(1), 56–72.

Hannon, P., Jackson, A. and Page, B. (1985) Implementation and take-up of a project to involve parents in the teaching of reading. In K. Topping and S. Wolfendale (eds) *Parental Involvement in Children's Reading*. Beckenham: Croom Helm/New York: Nichols.

Hewison, J. (1979) Home environment and reading attainment: a study of children in a working class community. Unpublished doctoral thesis, Institute of Education, University of London.

Hewison, J. and Tizard, J. (1980) Parental involvement in reading attainment. *British Journal of Educational Psychology*, **50**, 209–15.

Holdaway, D. (1979) *Foundations of Literacy*. Gosford: Ashton Scholastic.

Jackson, A. and Hannon, P. (1981) *The Bellfield Reading Project*. Rochdale, UK: The Bellfield Community Centre.

Kemp, M. (1987a) *Watching Children Read and Write: Observational Records for Children with Special Needs*. Melbourne: Nelson Education.

Kemp, M. (1987b) Parents as tutors: what more are we learning from them? *Australian Journal of Reading*, **10**(1), 25–31.

Kemp, M. (1989) Parents as tutors: a case study of a special education programme in oral reading. Unpublished doctoral thesis, University of Queensland.

Kemp, M. (1992) *Schools and Community Centre Report and Bibliography 1992: Parents as Tutors of Their Own Children*. Canberra: Faculty of Education, University of Canberra.

McNaughton, S., Glynn, T. and Robinson, V. (1981) *Parents as Remedial Reading Tutors: Issues for Home and School*. Wellington: New Zealand Council for Educational Research.

O'Connor, G., Glynn, T. and Tuck, B. (1987) Contexts for remedial reading: practice reading and pause, prompt and praise tutoring. *Educational Psychology*, **7**(5), 207–23.

Topping, K.J. and Wolfendale, S. (eds) (1985) *Parental Involvement in Children's Reading*. Beckenham: Croom Helm/New York: Nichols.

Warnock, M. (1978) (Chair) *Report of the Committee of Enquiry into the Education of Children with Special Needs*. London: HMSO.

Chapter 8

Learning from the Community: A family literacy project with Bangladeshi-origin children in London

Eve Gregory

INTRODUCTION

> When I receive official letters, like those from the Council, I have to take them to the school because I can't read them. I want my boy to be free of all that ... (Shabbir's father, October 1992)

How can parents with a low proficiency in spoken and written English find ways to integrate learning into their own lives and, at the same time, provide a context for literacy development in the lives of their children? The project described below is an example of one attempt to address this question.

Evidence suggests that links between home and school in multi-ethnic areas in Britain have long been tenuous. Research studies since the 1980s (Ghuman, 1980; Bhachu, 1985; Macleod, 1985; Smith and Tomlinson, 1989; Gregory, 1993a) generally show that problems are due to misunderstandings and the contradictory views of teachers and parents. Parents have high aspirations of their children to be equipped by the school with the skills and qualifications needed for employment with good prospects, but feel that teachers have low expectations and place low academic demands on their children. They also feel that formal discipline in school is low. At the same time, parents recognize their lack of knowledge of the British education and exam system and place inordinate faith in English teachers as far as academic work is concerned.

Teachers, on the other hand, are convinced of the need for parents to assist young children in their learning (especially in reading) at home and that the inability of parents to do this, coupled with their apparent unwillingness to understand English teaching methods, will automatically put children at a disadvantage (Topping and Wolfendale, 1985). There exists, then, a clash in expectations: parents interpret their role as pastoral and place faith in the teachers to take care of children's academic development, especially in English literacy; teachers see the need for parental involvement in their children's academic life, especially in literacy. Macleod (1985) points out that the problems are exacerbated by the existence of very few bilingual and bicultural teachers who are able to mediate between the two groups.

The Bangladeshi community is the most recently arrived larger group of immigrants to Britain and data available show that Bangladeshi pupils' exam performance is lower than that of other large Asian groups (The Select Committee to the House of Commons, 1986/87). The committee concluded that low achievement could largely be understood in terms of a gap between the actual educational needs of the community and provision offered, in particular:

- a gap in basic information offered to parents;
- few strategies available to involve parents in their children's education;
- a tendency to blame the community, marginalize pupils and have low expectations.

In 1991, the University of Lancaster Research Project 'Bangladeshi Parents and Education in Tower Hamlets' (Tomlinson and Hutchinson, 1991) conducted with 53 families came to broadly similar conclusions. In addition, they questioned parents more specifically on their spoken English skills and their literacy ability in both English and Bengali. They found that all the mothers except two had received their education in Bangladesh. About 71 per cent judged their oral English to be either non-existent or poor. Only 33 per cent claimed that they were able to read or write English as opposed to nearly 80 per cent who were literate in Bengali.

We might suppose that the parents' literacy background would be likely to influence their participation in home–school reading projects. Nevertheless, there have been contrasting views on the success of parental involvement in reading schemes in the Bangladeshi community. One study by Hancock (1990) reports that 80 per cent of home–school reading programmes had been 'successful' in establishing partnerships with parents, although Hancock adds that parents lack confidence in their English. Tomlinson and Hutchinson's information throws doubt on these figures, but at the same time explains how they might have been reached. Although 93 per cent of the parents they interviewed reported receiving books home from school, only 40 per cent of mothers and 50 per cent of fathers said they felt able to use these with their children. Their reasons for not doing so fell into two categories:

1. An inability to speak English: 'My English is not good enough . . . We can't do this, it is too difficult.' (p. 21)
2. The belief that it is the teachers' job to teach the children to read in English – especially knowing how little English they spoke and to ask them for help constituted a delegation of responsibilities.

The parents' responses can further be explained in the light of new methods in the teaching of reading which have been adopted in Britain over the past ten years and which have been integrated into home–school reading programmes. Many Infant schools have been influenced by an 'apprenticeship approach' (Waterland, 1985) to early reading. The main points of this approach are: (1) learning to read can be likened to learning to talk. Children take on the role of reader by learning alongside an interested adult with an interesting text; (2) like learning to talk, children learn by experimenting and adult encouragement rather than being corrected; (3) text must make sense so that the child can predict what comes next. The result for home–school reading programmes has been that children may well take books home which depend upon the ability of the parent to read the book to the child. Furthermore, it has often implicitly been assumed that the parent will understand both the theory and practice behind the approach (i.e. what needs to be done, why it is a good idea, etc.). Consequently, with the best of intentions, teachers may well be asking Bangladeshi-origin parents to do the impossible without actually explaining why they should do it. It is, therefore, understandable that parents may feel both disempowered or resentful at what is requested of them (Gregory *et al.*, 1993).

Interestingly, reports on successful parental involvement in reading schemes with monolingual 'non-school-oriented' parents have pointed to the importance of two features: (1) an explicit and structured approach which depends upon parents feeling in control of what they are doing as well as understanding why they are doing it. The Haringey Project (Tizard *et al.*, 1982) involved a number of parents who had difficulty with English literacy. The project featured parental training involving home visits where the task of listening to children reading was modelled. More recently, the Sheffield Reading Project (Hannon and Weinberger, 1994) is based on home visiting and parent discussion groups which are also highly structured. Home visits comprise the format of 'review, input and plan'. Discussion groups are instructional (for example, on one occasion, slides were shown to illustrate print in the environment, hand-outs were given to summarize events of the meeting, etc.); (2) building upon literacy experiences from the home (print in the environment, TV etc.) and linking these with school literacy practices (see also Chapter 6).

If these two features are seen as important in the involvement of monolingual families in their children's literacy, they must surely be vital for families now to the British culture and education system. The problem, however, is this: How can teachers build upon home literacy experiences when they have little idea of the literacy history of parents or the current home and community practices families participate in and the differences which might exist between these and the English school? This question was the starting-point of the project described below.

DESCRIPTION OF THE PROJECT

It was our last visit for that particular day. We had seen Mrs Ahmed a few days earlier and she had agreed to take part in the work. As we expected, she was at home, waiting for the children to return from school. She invited us to sit down and chatted for a few minutes to Nasima, the research officer. The outcome was disappointing.
'Unfortunately, Mrs Ahmed can't talk to us today, because she has to take a bath.'
I picked up my things to go.
'But she asks if we would like a cup of tea.'
I accepted, and whilst she was in the kitchen, whispered:
'If she has enough time to drink tea with us, couldn't she talk about her children's reading as well?'
'But you don't understand', replied Nasima, surprised. 'She's just finished her housework and she feels dirty. Reading is very important for her. She wants to feel properly prepared by washing and changing her clothes.'

This was one of many incidents close to the beginning of the project which jolted us into examining assumptions made of other cultural groups on the basis of our own interpretations and experiences.

The district of Spitalfields in East London where our school is sited has a long tradition of receiving immigrants; the Huguenots during the eighteenth century, followed by Jews from Eastern Europe during the latter half of the nineteenth and early twentieth centuries. Today, their place has been taken by families from Bangladesh and the streets in the area reflect their Muslim religion and culture. The families come almost entirely from the Sylhet region of Bangladesh. They speak Sylheti, a distinctive dialect of Bengali which has no written form. Although many of the men have lived more than twenty years in England, women have usually joined their husbands during the last ten years and the families remain isolated from the English language and culture. The rate of unemployment is high. Those who manage to find work mostly remain together and have jobs as tailors or in restaurants in the immediate vicinity. Consequently, there is little immediate need for the older generation to learn English for everyday necessities. Life revolves around the family, the mosque, neighbours and shops, many of which sell a variety of books and newspapers in Bengali. Even the television – often a powerful medium for cultural integration – has not yet broken through this isolation. Many families prefer to watch videos in Hindi, with the result that young children understand more Hindi than English upon school entry.

We had specific reasons for wanting to begin our own home–school literacy programme. Our situation was exceptional, although by no means unique; the school had 100 per cent Bangladeshi-origin children and, for many, the teacher was the only role model of a native English speaker. Although children were encouraged to speak English to each other in the classroom, most teachers preferred not to prevent children from discussing in their mother tongue. At 7 years of age, both the spoken and written English of many of the children was poor. We knew that the children regularly attended Bengali or Arabic classes in the evening and at weekends. We wondered whether, at these classes, a very different kind of teaching and learning was taking place. As teachers, we were frustrated that parents seemed to place more importance upon these lessons than English school learning. We asked ourselves why this might be and how we could discuss this with parents.

The project began in 1992 and was initiated by the headteacher and myself, a Lecturer in Education with students on Teaching Practice in the school. After two years, we are just beginning to produce materials for use at home and in school. This may seem like very slow progress. However, the reasons lie with our methods of enquiry and should become clear to the reader as the work is outlined below. For simplicity, I have divided the project into six stages: the first three stages took place during Year 1 (1992–93) and the last three during Year 2 (1993–94).

Stage 1: Questioning assumptions and formulating aims

The first step was to unearth our own assumptions on reading which were noted for later discussions. During in-service sessions, we 'brainstormed' our initial concerns: What 'counts' as reading in school and is it different in the children's community schools? What materials do we think should be used for teaching reading? How do we think parents should best prepare their children for 'schooled' literacy? Such an examination of personal and professional beliefs is not easy and demands trust between teachers. Nevertheless, it was an essential first step before beginning to formulate questions and aims for future work. We later recalled remarks such as: 'What reading goes on outside school? Well, they go off to mosque and Bengali classes. There they recite off by heart and get the cane if they misbehave . . . That's why they're so tired when they come to school . . . As for the home, I don't think you'll find much reading going on there.' We then formulated the following questions which were to underpin the project:

- What literacy practices are taking place in the lives of the children outside school?
- How do their families facilitate these?
- What models do we now use to involve families in children's literacy development?
- What assumptions are these based on?
- What are the particular issues that should be addressed in programmes for non-English speaking families?
- What alternatives are there to the predominant models?
- How can we link what we feel to be the best of Infant practices in English and English literacy teaching with both the child's home reading experiences and the families' expectations for school learning?

At this stage, too, we formulated very general aims for our work. These were:

1. To improve the quality of initial reading tuition and the reading performance at Key Stage 1 of the National Curriculum for children who are learning in a second language through building upon home and community learning.
2. To raise teachers' expectations of 'emergent' bilingual children's cognitive and linguistic ability.
3. To produce a home–school reading programme which would be understood and culturally acceptable to both teachers and families and which involves families learning English with their children at home.
4. To build up a bank of approaches and materials for second language literacy teaching which could be disseminated throughout the Infant school, to selected community classes and to the Language 2000 (Parents' Language class in school).

Specific aims were to be formulated as the project progressed, but our immediate task was to investigate and compare what counted as 'reading' in the different worlds of the child; the English school, the home and the community school. How did the children and their families interpret reading and how might this differ from our own view as teachers?

Stage 2: Learning to read in and outside the English school

Close to the beginning of the project, Nasima, the research officer was talking to one of the project children about her work at the English and Bengali school:

Nasima: What do you do at school?
Reshma: I play.
Nasima: Don't you do anything else?
Reshma: Listen to teacher reading story.

Table 8.1 *Learning to read in English and community schools*

English school	Community school
Extent: 2–5 hours per week	6–9 hours per week
Length: 20 mins (often interrupted)	2–3 hours (usually without a break)

Purpose:
  (i)   *Parents*: to improve chances of employment
  (ii) *Teacher*: to gain enjoyment
  (iii) *Child*: to play
	to strengthen cultural identification
	to learn religion
	to learn

Materials: Storybooks
  high quality paper
  coloured illustrations
  complex language
  unstructured
  given to child before able to read
  can be changed when the child pleases
  unfamiliar to parents
  bought by school
	Reading primers
	  low quality paper
	  black and white
	  simple language
	  structured
	  given to child as means of learning
	  must be completed before changing
	  familiar to parents
	  bought by parents

Method: (i) Role of teacher: friend
  reads to child
  implicit
  encourages
  does not correct
  does not test
	Teacher
	  demonstrates
	  explicit
	  instructs
	  corrects
	  tests

(ii) Role of child:
  experiments
  'pretends'
  guesses
	Child
	  repeats
	  practises
	  is tested

Source: Gregory (1994), p. 7

Nasima: What do you do at Bengali school?
Reshma: I read and write.
Nasima: Why do you like your English school?
Reshma: Because I play.
(Gregory, 1993b, p. 4)

For the first year of the project, the Sylheti-speaking research officer/teacher (who had recently completed a Teaching Practice in the school) and I (concurrently teaching the class alongside the class teacher during a term's Sabbatical) spent approximately half a day per week in the children's homes, community or English classes observing the children at work and talking to both children and parents about both their reading histories and current reading activities.

We found that all of our six Year 1 focus children participated in Bengali or Arabic classes; four of the six attended lessons in both. As shown in Table 8.1, the average length of time spent in community classes was between six and nine hours per week which was at least double that spent on directed reading activities in the English classroom. Classes were taking place in very different surroundings; some were in a neighbour's home; others in a formal mobile classroom; yet other children had a private tutor. Parents paid for all types of classes. Table 8.1 contrasts the different types of reading taking place in the community and English class in terms of purpose, materials and participation structures (patterns of interaction).

Stage 3: Making the implicit explicit: refining aims

All the information collected was discussed in in-service (professional development) sessions. Above all, we discussed the very different patterns of interaction between the child and teacher in the English and community classes. The early stages of reading in our English classroom were typified by experimentation. Accuracy or word-for-word reading was not expected at this stage and speech forms were not corrected in order to encourage risk-taking by the child. There was a relaxed atmosphere and children were often allowed to move away from an activity if they did not wish to participate.

This method of teaching was in sharp contrast to both the Bengali and mosque classes we had visited. Here discipline was strict and respect for the teacher was emphasized. Bengali and Arabic lessons had the following pattern: first, a test of what was taught in the preceding lesson (often a spelling test); then, the routine 'Demonstration, Practice, Test'. Children do not experiment by guessing words, but learn step-by-step how to sound out letters, combine letters into syllables, syllables into words, words into phrases. If a child makes a mistake, s/he is corrected with the words 'Not like that, like this'. Paradoxically, it was the teachers of the community classes who stressed the importance of the child as learner and who expressed no doubt for the child's future success in mastering the task at hand, whilst the English teachers emphasized the child's difficulties and potential learning failure. During our visits, we noticed a marked difference in the high level of concentration in the Bengali class in contrast with the apparent lack of ability to remain with a task in the English school.

In the light of our findings, we aimed to design a programme which would build upon the children's learning strategies and show the child to be an important mediator of literacy within the family by providing home–school programmes which both parent and child would understand and see as important.

Stage 4: Deciding upon materials and methods

Our start was disastrous. Encouraged by literacy projects in South America (Freire and Macedo, 1987) and Catalonia (Roc, 1992), we chose a theme which we believed to be essential to the families' lives: rice. We had planned a series of lessons involving growing rice, cooking it, stories and poems, etc. for which children would receive structured work at home. To our initial surprise, parents reacted with considerable hostility and one mother even interrupted the first lesson, to which the children had been asked to bring rice. She made her reason clear: rice is such a menial commodity. It is not worth reading or writing about.

Finally, we decided upon using the Ladybird 'Read-It-Yourself' traditional stories collection. This is a well-known series of inexpensive but hardback and easily available books, divided into different levels with simple vocabulary and colourful illustrations. Ladybird books do not generally enjoy a good reputation with English teachers and it is important to note that the decision could only be made in the light of our findings in Stage 2 and in-service discussions. The task now was to design work for use at home and in school.

Stage 5: Structuring the classroom work

The research officer has worked for one morning per week with the group of project children using the programme. All the sessions have been taped for analysis and in-service discussions. As each story is completed, separate packs are being prepared for class and home use. The aim for classroom work is to link what we see as key out-of-school learning strategies with good second-language language and literacy learning practice in three areas:

1. The interaction between child and teacher.
2. The child's metalinguistic strengths.
3. The high value placed on literacy and the book.

The next section outlines suggested activities in each area.

Stage 6: Using the family literacy packs

This stage of our work has just begun and, at the time of writing, we do not yet know how fast or how far we shall progress; nor, indeed, exactly what progress will look like. What we do know, from observing mothers assisting children with their Bengali primers at home, is that parents can and do help their children when they feel in control of the language. The packs will also be used by the Language 2000 teacher (English language teacher for parents in the school) and, initially, by one community class teacher. We have made a deliberate decision that children take packs home only after they have worked through a story in school, for we have noted the comments of mothers saying: 'S/he can teach me the English now . . .'. We hope that the packs (contents are outlined in the next section) will enable the child to act as a mediator of English literacy and culture (through the English practised in class and the traditional European story) whilst the parent and community class teacher mediate knowledge of Sylheti and Bengali and Bengali culture (through listening to the story, reading the Bengali text and discussing universal morals emerging from the story). In this way, both adult and child are simultaneously 'expert' and 'learner' together.

ORGANIZATION

Below are the main points to bear in mind for a similar project which depends upon work in school as well as in the home. It is important to remember that the whole nature of such a programme means that each school will be different according to the community it serves. After the general organizational points, I shall refer specifically to each stage of the work, as described in the last section.

General organization

1. This type of project demands a long-term view and cannot be rushed. Allow approximately three years before a programme is successfully underway.

2. Be realistic. Focus on a small number of families with whom to set up the project initially. The classroom work can be used with the whole class and the family packs eventually used by all.

3. Choose two colleagues (teachers or one teacher, one assistant or colleagues from Higher Education) to co-ordinate and lead the work, one of whom must obviously be bilingual. Meet regularly (perhaps two or three times per term) with the other Infant staff and once per term with the whole school staff.

4. Start the project with a Year 1 class (age-range 5- to 6-year-olds). This is when many children begin their community classes.

5. Make links with any Adult Language class (e.g. Language 2000 in Tower Hamlets) who can both make and use the packs as part of their curriculum.

6. Enlist as many people as possible in the making of the family project packs (bilingual assistants, Initial Teacher Education students, interested family members, etc.)

Stage 1: Questioning assumptions and formulating aims

Allow two in-service sessions: Session 1: 'Brainstorming' on literacy beliefs (the questions in the last section might be a starting-point). Session 2: Formulating aims (be modest!).

Stage 2: Learning to read in and outside the English school

Choose a sample of families: Suggested approaches:

Method 1: Write to all families in the class, outlining the project and asking those interested to contact the co-ordinator. Visit interested respondents at home and outline the commitment needed. Choose a group from those still interested.

Method 2: Select a group of families (approximately double the final sample number) who fulfil the criteria needed for participating in the project and write saying when the co-ordinator will visit. From these visits, choose a group.

*   Always write to a community class teacher explaining the project and asking for a convenient time to visit a class.
*   Visit the project families as regularly as possible to establish a good relationship.
*   The class teacher records her reading lessons and analyses them with the co-ordinator.

Stage 3: Making the implicit explicit: formulating aims

Be honest in discussions and realistic in aims: the simpler the better!

Stage 4: Deciding upon materials and methods

The choice of books must be acceptable to families and teachers. Invest in a series of books which are cheap, sturdy, have a simple, but well-rounded text and subject-matter which will be seen as important by the family (e.g. Ladybird 'Read-It-Yourself' traditional stories). You will need three copies of each for a single pack: one copy for the Teacher's Pack; one copy to be cut up for magnet-board figurines, and one copy for the Parents' Pack. 'Breakthrough to Literacy' sentence, word makers and project folders are an excellent back-up for families to construct words and sentences (these materials are in the Resources Directory).

Suggested contents of packs are in Table 8.2.

Table 8.2 *Suggested contents of packs*

Teachers' Pack	Parents' Pack
story book figurines for magnet board	story book
Cassette tape (Side 1: story told in English and Sylheti and English) (Side 2: story read in English and Bengali)	
word cards (words from story and additional words) work-cards (Cloze and phonic exercises) card with suggested list and order of activities example of a book made by a child	sentence cards (in English and Bengali on reverse) sentence cards cut up into words in English
Tape with listening activities (see 'Listen, Discuss and Do' materials in 'Resources' Directory)	

Stage 5: Structuring the classroom work

Focus on just a few key aspects of the children's out-of-school learning strategies to build into your programme, e.g. patterns of interaction:

- demonstration, repeat, practice (first as group then individually for intonation, pronunciation, etc.);
- high expectation of teacher: strictness coupled with politeness and longer concentration span, e.g. metalinguistic strengths;
- words with similar/opposite meanings;
- spellings;
- describing words and guessing them;

- using metalinguistic terminology 'sentence', 'word', etc. e.g. high status of reading and the book;
- using the *Talking Pendown* computer program (see Resources Directory);
- having their own lined exercise book, pencil, etc.

Stage 6: Family and community class reading packs

- Either hold a group meeting or visit families individually to discuss using the packs.
- Collaborate with the Adult Language teacher (Language 2000).
- Collaborate with a community class teacher to discuss parallel work.

EFFECTIVENESS

Two comments made by parents were important for the design of our programme:

Researcher: How do you think the teacher goes about teaching your child to read?
Parent: I don't know. It is the teacher's job. She is the expert.
Researcher: But if you had to imagine what she does, what would you say?
Parent: Well, surely, it must be the same as we learned. First, she will teach the names of the letters, then the sounds, then how to put the sounds together into words. . . .

On another occasion:

Researcher: Do you help your child with reading from the English school?
Parent: My child brings home these books (shows 'Mrs Wishy-Washy' from the Story Chest collection, which were the only books allowed home before the project). I cannot understand these words. How can I help my child?

The main advantage of our approach is that we were able to build up a picture of the child and family's literacy world before beginning to design a home–school reading programme. This meant that we understood how parents interpreted 'reading' in their own and their children's lives, what they could and could not do to help their children, and what learning strategies children were bringing with them into the English school from their Community classes. On a small scale, this work emulates projects taking place in the USA (Heath, 1983; Auerbach, 1989). Both these studies argue that a deficit model is easily adopted by teachers if parents are asked to perform school-like activities they are incapable of. Parents' lack of co-operation may be interpreted as lack of interest or even hostility. If, on the other hand, work starts by building upon the families' strengths and literacy activities the families are already familiar with, then the picture looks very different (Gregory, 1996).

Two main principles underpin our work. The first is the belief that learning takes place within the framework of common expectations and interpretations (Bateson, 1979). Longitudinal studies from the USA show us how young Nursery children from 'school-oriented' homes enter school well familiar with the literacy activities of their teachers (story-telling) and that successful teaching can be based upon shared implicit assumptions (Cochran-Smith, 1984). At the same time, studies show us that 'non-mainstream' groups participate in very different reading activities at home and that these children are likely to experience early reading difficulties in school (Heath, 1983; Anderson and Stokes, 1984; Gregory, 1993c). Where special programmes have been designed by teachers to build upon children's existing knowledge and learning strategies, results have improved considerably. Our focus has been to develop the children's metacognitive and metalinguistic awareness which we believe to be their particular strength.

The second principle of our work is that children learn new practices most efficiently when tuition is explicit and structured. A danger in reading instruction based on an 'apprenticeship' and psycholinguistic approaches is that families are assumed to share and understand the reading practices of the mainstream school. Recent studies from the USA (Michaels, 1986), from Australia (Walton, 1993) and from Britain (Gregory, 1993c) argue that teaching methods based upon shared implicit beliefs may buttress low expectations by teachers and low quality tuition for children from 'non-mainstream' groups. Our work takes up Vygotsky's argument that instruction plays a decisive role in leading development and that the role of the adult is to tutor the child explicitly into a 'reflective awareness' (Vygotsky, 1962). We believe that both child and adult are comfortable and familiar with a step-by-step structure which reduces the enormity of the English learning task.

In the short term, of course, the longitudinal nature of this type of project could be seen as a disadvantage; there are no quick results and a high degree of teacher commitment is demanded. Such projects are hypothesized to be cost-effective in the longer term. A programme which can be used by all Infant staff with the whole class can be co-ordinated and managed by one 'home/school liaison' teacher who spends half her time in children's homes and half in the classroom. In contrast, a scheme such as the Reading Recovery programme demands one-to-one tuition and encompasses only the few weakest children in each class.

To develop a similar project, schools need to designate staff who are prepared to work as ethnographers (Heath, 1983) which means studying their own beliefs and practices as well as those of the families they work with. We combined an ethnographic approach with a more careful analysis of discourse and interaction patterns (Gregory, 1993c) and phenomenographic interviews with the children (Francis, 1993). It was through these interviews that we learned about the child's perceptions of reading in the different schools, as well as their important role as mediator of literacy to the family. Although this work is being used as a research as well as an action project, it could be incorporated without difficulty into any staff development work.

CONCLUSION

One also hears the claim, 'All children should be treated alike. There should be no discrimination.' It must be conceded that to overlook individual differences and cultural differences and to treat everyone as though they were the same, does, indeed, involve a lack of discrimination. Think about it. It certainly is not in the child's interest. (Duquette 1992, p. 14)

We have ample evidence that the school performance of both mono- and bilingual children from economically disadvantaged areas is poor. The recent OFSTED report *Access and Achievement in Urban Education* (1993) stresses that teachers tend to generalise the effects of poverty and social disadvantage and to underestimate the potential ability of pupils. This is most marked in schools which have a high percentage of Asian pupils. Although there was much concern for underdeveloped language competence, no school provided a systematic programme of oracy. (p. 16)

The government-funded ALBSU (Adult Literacy and Basic Skills Unit) (see Resources Directory) programme also reflects the danger of equating 'equal treatment' with 'equality of opportunity'. Largely based upon evidence from the USA, ALBSU stresses the intergenerational effects of poor literacy, making no distinction between recently arrived immigrants and the indigenous population. Our pilot study, which compared the literacy histories of six Bangladeshi origin and six indigenous origin families, found a crucial difference between the two groups. Although both lacked confidence in their ability to assist their children's school reading, the English mothers interpreted this as due to 'being no good at reading in school', whereas those of Bangladeshi origin referred to a lack of opportunity. Significantly, there was no history reported of reading failure among these women, who reported leaving school 'because it was too far' or in order to 'get married' (Gregory *et al.*, 1993). It would seem vital that real equality of provision enables the next generation to escape this danger. Our work highlights the importance of other projects based on an understanding of community literacy practices and teachers' willingness to step outside recognized parameters of 'reading methods' to reflect carefully upon what will count as reading in their classrooms.

ACKNOWLEDGEMENTS

I should like to acknowledge the help of Nasima Rashid, Research Officer to the project, and to express thanks to Rani Shamas, headteacher, and to the staff of Canon Barnett School, London Borough of Tower Hamlets, where this work is taking place.

NOTE

This work has been supported by the Paul Hamlyn Foundation. A related research project on 'Family Literacy History and Children's Learning Strategies at Home and at School' is supported by the ESRC from 1994–95 (R000 22 1186).

REFERENCES

Anderson, A.B. and Stokes, S.J. (1984) Social and institutional influences on the development and practice of literacy. In H. Gelman, A. Oberg and F. Smith (eds) *Awakening to Literacy*. London: Heinemann Education.

Auerbach, E.R. (1989) Toward a social contextual approach to family literacy. *Harvard Educational Review*, 59(2), 165–81.

Bateson, G. (1979) *Mind and Nature*. London: Wildwood House.

Bhachu, P. (1985) Multicultural education – parental views. *New Community*, 12(1), 9–20.

Cochran-Smith, M. (1984) *The Making of a Reader*. Norwood, NJ: Ablex.

Duquette, G. (1992) The home culture of minority children in the assessment and development of their first language. *Language, Culture and Curriculum*, 5(1), 11–23.

Francis, H. (1993) Advancing phenomenography. *Nordisk Pedagogik*, 2, 68–75.

Freire, P. and Macedo, D. (1987) *Literacy: Reading the Word and the World*. London: Routledge & Kegan Paul.

Ghuman, P. (1980) Punjabi parents and English education. *Educational Research*, **27**(2), 121–30.

Gregory, E. (1988) Reading with Mother: a dockland story. In M. Meek and C. Mills (eds) *Language and Literacy in the Primary School*. London: Falmer Press.

Gregory, E. (1993a) Sweet and sour: learning to read in an English and Chinese School. *English in Education*, Autumn, 53–60.

Gregory, E. (1993b) Reading between the lines. *Times Educational Supplement*, 15 October, p. 4.

Gregory, E. (1993c) What counts as reading in the early years classroom? *British Journal of Educational Psychology*, **63**, 214–30.

Gregory, E. (1994) Cultural assumptions and early years' pedagogy: the effect of the home culture on minority children's interpretation of reading in school. *Language, Culture, and Curriculum*, **7**(2), 1–14.

Gregory, E. (1996). *Learning to Read in a Second Language: Making Sense of a New World*. London: Paul Chapman.

Gregory, E., Lathwell, J., Mace, J. and Rashid, N. (1993) *Literacy at Home and at School*. Literacy Research Group, Faculty of Education, London: Goldsmiths College.

Hancock, R. (1990) Positive parents. *Times Educational Supplement*, 9 November.

Hannon, P. and Weinberger, J. (1994) Sharing ideas about pre-school literacy with parents. Working with parents to involve children in reading and writing at home in Sheffield, UK. In H. Dombey and M. Meek Spencer (eds) *First Steps Together – Home–School Literacy in European Contexts*. Stoke on Trent: Trentham Books.

Heath, S.B. (1983) *Ways with Words: Language, Life and Work in Communities and Classrooms*. Cambridge: Cambridge University Press.

Macleod, F. (1985) *Parents in Partnership – Involving Muslim Parents in Their Children's Education*. Coventry: LEA.

Michaels, S. (1986) Narrative presentations: an oral preparation for literacy with 1st graders. In J. Cook-Gumperz (ed.) *The Social Construction of Literacy*. Cambridge: Cambridge University Press.

Murshid, T. (1990) Needs, perceptions and provisions – the problems of achievement among Bengali (Sylheti) pupils. *Multicultural Teaching*, **8**(3), 12–16.

National Curriculum Council (1988) *Introducing the National Curriculum Council*. London: National Curriculum Council.

OFSTED (1993) *Access and Achievement in Urban Education* London: HMSO.

Roc, M. (1992) *Discussions with Dra. M. Roc*. Barcelona: Autonomous University of Barcelona.

The Select Committee to the House of Commons (1986/87) *The Achievements of Bangladeshi Children in School*. London: HMSO.

Smith, D. and Tomlinson, S. (1989) *The School Effect – A Study of Multiracial Comprehensives*. London: Policy Studies Institute.

Tizard, J., Schofield, W. and Hewison, J. (1982) Collaboration between teachers and parents in assisting children's reading. *British Journal of Educational Psychology*, **52**, 1–15.

Tomlinson, S. and Hutchinson, S. (1991) *Bangladeshi Parents and Education in Tower Hamlets*. Research report, Advisory Centre for Education, University of Lancaster.

Topping, K. and Wolfendale, S. (eds) (1985) *Parental Involvement in Children's Reading*. Beckenham: Croom Helm.

Vygotsky, L. (1962) *Thought and Language*. Cambridge, MA: MIT Press.

Walton, C. (1993) Aboriginal education in Northern Australia: a case study of literacy policies and practices. In P. Freebody and A.R. Walch (eds) *Knowledge, Culture and Power*. London: Falmer Press.

Waterland, L. (1985) *Read with Me!* London: The Thimble Press.

Wells, A. (1993) *Family Literacy. Getting Started*. London: The Adult Literacy and Basic Skills Unit.

Chapter 9

Developments in Family Literacy in the United States

Lori J. Connors

INTRODUCTION

Family literacy or intergenerational programmes are based on the dual goals of increasing parents' literacy skills and improving the home learning environment for children. As such, they consider the 'family unit' as the client, rather than individual family members alone (Illinois Literacy Resource Center, 1992). Many disciplines – adult education, child development, family support – are often integrated in the goals and service delivery components of family literacy programmes.

The purpose of this chapter is to give the reader an introduction to the field of family literacy in the United States. First, one of the main theories guiding programme development and evaluation is offered. Next, the organization and implementation of one type of family literacy programme, a school-based programme serving young children and families, is presented. The chapter concludes with a brief discussion of some of the emerging issues in the field.

THE INTERGENERATIONAL TRANSFER HYPOTHESIS

The primary challenge for family literacy researchers and practitioners is to consider the dynamic nature of the transmission of educational beliefs and behaviours within the family. Equally important is to consider how the diversity of families – economically, educationally, and culturally – affect learning processes within the family (ILRC, 1992; Auerbach, 1989). How might parents participating in a family literacy programme affect their children's learning? Duffy (1992) suggests that parents indirectly influence their children's learning through the 'new attitudes and the new skills that the adult introduces into the house and into the pattern of family interaction' (p. 62). He further elaborates how parents' attitudes, skills, and interactions may influence their children:

(1) If parents' beliefs about the importance of education increase, then parents will communicate a more positive attitude toward education to their children.

(2) If parents learn more about parenting practices which support student success in school, then parents will more frequently use these skills at home with their children.

(3) If parents increasingly engage in literacy activities at home, then the children will have greater exposure to models of literacy and more frequent opportunities for parent–child teaching at home.

These three 'conditions' – a positive attitude towards education, improved parenting practices, and more exposure to literacy activities (Duffy, 1992) – are argued, according to this theory, to lead to better prepared and supported students in school. Other theories (e.g. social-contextual, critical, symbolic interactionism) are being tested in the field, but much more work remains to be done both in theory development and in data collection to demonstrate the effectiveness of family literacy programmes.

FAMILY LITERACY PROGRAMMES IN THE UNITED STATES

Many types of family literacy programmes currently operate throughout the United States, sponsored by community agencies, libraries, city or state governments, private foundations, and other federal funding streams (see Nickse, 1990 for further discussion of the types of programmes). One of the first family literacy programmes implemented in the US was Kentucky's Parent and Child Education (PACE) programme. PACE was piloted in 1986 and eventually implemented in 33 schools throughout Kentucky by 1990. This intensive model brought parents and preschool children to the school site (transportation was provided by the programme) four days per week to receive adult basic skill instruction, preschool education, and parenting education (including parent–child together activities). Heberle (1992) reports that results for the programme sample were positive. As compared to baseline data, parents' expectations for their children's future education improved, parents' literacy levels improved (70 per cent either received their Graduate Equivalency Diploma or raised their academic skills by two or more grade levels), and children's learning skills improved.

The Kenan Trust Family Literacy Project, operated by the National Center for Family Literacy, has replicated the PACE programme throughout the United States. Seaman (1992) and Darling and Hayes (1989) investigated the effects of the programme on parents and children who had participated in one of 14 programmes from 1986 to 1991. Parents completing the programme reported that they experienced changes in many areas of their lives. For example, many were proud of themselves for the first time and no longer afraid of challenges; many now read more, used the library, and had hopes for their own further education; and many were able to help their children with homework, read more to their children, and used more positive discipline techniques. Teacher ratings of children whose parents participated in the programme indicated that most were doing as well as or better than other students in their class and most were ranked in the upper half of the class.

The National Even Start programme is a US Department of Education grant programme to states to provide family literacy services to families with children from birth to age 7. From 76 funded programmes in 1989, it has grown to 503 programmes in 1994, serving approximately 35 000 families of preschool and early elementary children. An extensive, national evaluation of the Even Start programme is underway, including an in-depth study of 10 projects funded in 1989. (See St Pierre *et al.*, 1993a; St Pierre *et al.*, 1993b; St Pierre *et al.*, 1991 for further description of projects.) One study (St Pierre *et al.*, 1993a) found that children ($n = 1211$) participating in Even Start projects improved on tests of school readiness skills and language development at double the rate expected due to maturation (a control group was not used in this study). Adults in the programmes ($n = 550$) made small but positive gains on pre–post measures of adult literacy. Further analyses revealed that parents who had received more hours of parenting education had children who gained more on measures of language development.

The next section describes in greater detail one model of family literacy in order to ground our theoretical discussion and research review in local practice. While there is no one 'typical' model of family literacy, Project SELF HELP saw the family unit as the focus of service delivery, and specifically sought to increase parents' literacy and the home learning environment for children. We believe the project can be replicated in other locales with the commitment and dedication of the school principal and community organization staff.

PROJECT SELF HELP

> This is a story about me. I'm learning a lot about myself. I am learning to read and spell by helping my grandchildren with their homework, and reading lots of books. I encourage my grandchildren to read books every day. . . .

This story, written by a participant in Project SELF HELP, embodies the goals of many family literacy programmes – to give parents or other caretakers a second chance at education so they may provide their children with increased support for learning. However, it is a long and arduous road that leads an adult with low literacy skills to take the step to enrol in a programme and to reach their goals for themselves and their children. Family literacy programmes, particularly those based in schools, can eliminate some of the obstacles that parents face in improving literacy skills. They can also increase the co-ordination and collaboration with their children's teachers, other school staff, and the community.

The school-year programme

The SELF HELP programme was based at an elementary school in a high poverty area of Baltimore, Maryland. The principal of the elementary school contacted a local literacy provider in order to help some parents who were having difficulty assisting their children with homework because of their own low literacy skills. The literacy organization, school principal, and other members of a community task force wrote a grant proposal to fund the programme, which began in 1990.

Project SELF HELP delivered services to three target groups within the family: (1) parents or caretakers with reading levels below the fifth grade; (2) their academically at-risk elementary school children; and (3) their preschool children. The programme included adult education classes, homework and enrichment help for elementary students, and a developmental day care programme for preschoolers. Joint parent–child activities were held regularly. A summer reading programme exposed families to community based educational and recreational resources.

Project staff included:

- full-time adult education teacher/programme co-ordinator;
- part-time preschool teacher;
- part-time after-school tutor (also a first grade teacher at the school);
- part-time parent liaison.

The school-year programme operated three hours per day, two days per week, from October to June. Classes for adults, preschool children, and elementary children were held in separate rooms in the school building. Approximately two times per month, classes for parents and children met together.

The goals for parents/caretakers in the programme were to:

1. Increase literacy skills – learning to read, spell, write, and compute.
2. Increase parenting skills – how to praise, discipline, teach co-operative and responsible behaviour.
3. Increase life skills and personal growth – how to read, understand and use maps, common signs, and informational health literature.

The average length of a lesson was 30 minutes for all curriculum areas except parent–child time, which was held for one hour. Lessons focused on life skills, reading, personal growth, spelling, parenting, writing, and math.

Curriculum components were integrated where possible. For example, using a newspaper article on children's homework, five curriculum areas were addressed: (1) reading the article; (2) reviewing the spelling and meaning of words in the article; (3) using words from the article to introduce a grammar exercise; (4) using the homework advice given in the article to discuss parenting skills as they applied to their family situations; and (5) modelling life skills by using the newspaper to gain information for everyday life.

The goals of the elementary programme were to:

1. Assist children with homework and enrichment activities;
2. Increase exposure to positive experiences with parents and school staff.

In the elementary programme, children met with their instructor after school. When homework was completed, children worked with classroom materials of interest to them – such as maps and flags of the states, multiplication tables, and computer games. Sometimes parents worked individually with their own child on homework or games, or the elementary children read to the preschool children. In preparation for a parent–child time activity, elementary children often assisted in gathering necessary materials.

The goals of the preschool programme were to:

1. Increase reading readiness skills;
2. Increase exposure to positive experiences with parents and school staff.

In the preschool programme, three groups of children were served – 3- and 4-year-olds in no other programme, morning prekindergarten and kindergarten children, and afternoon prekindergarten and kindergarten children after school was out. The preschool teacher used a multi-sensory, thematic approach to introduce concepts of colour, numbers, and letters. The preschool children and their teacher 'played' together with developmentally appropriate materials such as puzzles, clay, paints, and books. They walked together, played games on the playground, and learned songs and rhymes.

The goals of parent–child time were to:

1. Increase parents' beliefs that parent–child activities could be fun and rewarding;
2. Increase parents' ability to respond positively to children's natural curiosity for learning;
3. Support and model the integration of parents' new literacy and parenting skills in natural learning opportunities.

Parent–child time was held approximately every other week. Parents who had children in both the preschool and elementary programmes alternated working with their children. Periodically, parent–child activities involved all family members.

The summer reading programme

The summer reading programme was available to families who attended the school-year programme. It operated three days per week for eight weeks. Families met at the local library for activities related to a weekly field trip to a community educational resource. Sites for field trips ranged from an art gallery and a museum in Baltimore, Maryland, to the FBI (Federal Bureau of Investigation) facility in Washington, DC. Various public transportation systems were used to get to the sites. Pre-trip activities included reading and discussing books related to the theme of the trip and related art activities. Post-trip activities included a discussion of the trip, telling stories related to the trip, related art activities, and problem solving.

The goals of the summer reading programme for parents were to increase awareness and independent use of community resources and modes of transportation, to increase positive interaction between family members, and to increase parents' ability to generalize learning opportunities from the community setting to home.

The goals for the children were to maintain reading and pre-reading skills over the summer, to increase the number of books read, and to improve social skills.

METHODOLOGY AND RESULTS

The families

On Monday I get out of bed at 7:00 AM and get my kids up. I make cereal for my kids every day. I tell my kids to get dressed. I go to school and help there. I make dinner every day. The kids take a bath every day. We go out every Friday to see my sister and mom. My kids like me to read a story to them. (Written by a SELF HELP participant)

The school-year programme began in October of 1991 with 12 parents, 11 elementary school age children and 13 preschool/kindergarten children. The highest grade completed by the adults in the SELF HELP programme ranged from the fourth grade to a special education tenth grade class, with the majority having completed eighth or ninth grade. No participants had graduated from high school or had completed a graduate equivalency exam (GED).

In the preschool sample, two of the children were enrolled in the school's prekindergarten programme for disadvantaged children and six of the children attended a half-day session of kindergarten, in addition to SELF HELP's day care programme. Five children were in no other day care or school programme. The elementary children were in grades one through four.

The summer programme began in July of 1992 with 12 parents and 22 children, all of whom had previously participated in the school-year programme (in 1990–91 or 1991–92).

Assessment instruments

Adult literacy was assessed with a test of basic skills, the Wide Range Achievement Test (WRAT; Jastok, 1984) in maths, reading, and spelling. The Maryland Adult Performance Program (MAPP; Maryland State Department of Education, 1987) and the California Adult Competency Assessment System (CASAS; California State Department of Education, 1985) were used as measures of functional literacy in reading/life skills and math. Within the first month of attendance the adults also completed assessments of their home educational environment (Dolan, 1983) and beliefs about their parenting role (Segal, 1985) in order to measure growth in parenting skills and attitudes related to children's success in school.

The preschool children who were in no other programme were assessed with an indicator of reading readiness, Concepts About Print (Clay, 1979); the comprehension subtest of the Merrill Language Screening Test (Mumm *et al.*, 1980); the receptive vocabulary subtest of the Test of Language Development (Newcomer *et al.*, 1988); and an inventory of letter recognition. Report card grades and attendance data were available for the prekindergarten, kindergarten, and elementary children.

Key issues for implementation

Recruitment and retention. The Chapter 1 liaison worker was instrumental in recruiting and retaining families and communicating the needs of the programme and families with teachers and other school staff. The liaison's effectiveness was enhanced by her long-standing relationship with the community and the school, having earned the trust of the principal, the school staff, and the parents. Sometimes the liaison worker helped parents approach school staff or negotiate unfamiliar or complicated school procedures. Parents saw her as a 'surrogate mother' figure. She often cajoled parents into attending and she praised and reinforced their progress at every opportunity.

The children's programmes were also an incentive for enrolment. The programme director reported that parents often said they attended Project SELF HELP so that their children could receive the homework help and enrichment activities of the elementary programme. The day care component allowed some parents to give their young children a preschool experience. Most of the children had never attended a preschool or other daycare programme. For parents with preschool children and elementary children, the developmental daycare provided a safe and fun activity for their children while they were attending classes.

Staff training. Parent–child time is often identified as one of the more difficult components to implement in family literacy programmes (ILRC, 1992). Staff training focused on three areas: (1) staff interactions with parents and children; (2) preparation and follow-up of parent–child time in the adult-alone and child-alone components; and (3) arrangement of the physical environment. Programme staff met periodically to plan parent–child activities and to choose the skills that teachers needed to reinforce in their classes. Parents and students became more actively involved in planning activities and preparing materials for parent–child time as the year progressed.

For example, the field notes from fall and spring observations of parent–child time reveal that staff made changes in the way they planned and structured parent–child time.

Fall 1991 observation
Preschool children and their teacher are seated on the floor reading a story. Parents are standing on the sidelines – some are talking, others just looking at the teacher, others are looking around the room. After the story, parents, children and the teacher go outside to the play ground. The teacher organizes a game of jump rope in one corner and relay races in another corner. Parents talk together on the sidelines or watch their children. Most of the interaction takes place between the children and the teacher. When they come back in, the teacher gives each parent a large sheet of paper and asks each parent to trace their child's body and label the body parts. One parent does not know how to spell 'forehead', another parent cannot get her active three-year-old to stay still long enough to trace her body, and the activity ends with this parent yelling at the child to stay still.

Spring 1992 observation
A shy three-year-old holding a hand-coloured drawing of 'Papa Bear' whispers, 'Someone's been eating my porridge!' His mother prompts him by reading the next line from her script, while his fourth-grade brother helps to keep the assemblage of props from tumbling off the stage. Meanwhile, another child holds her 'Mama Bear' figure by its popsicle stick handle and waits patiently for her mother's cue. Other adults and children form an excited audience and follow the action by reading from copies of the classic tale.

Other issues important to both the implementation of Project SELF HELP, and to replication by others, are discussed in the final section of this chapter and in Connors (1993, 1994). The project described here could be implemented in other locales for families and children with similar needs, with the commitment of the school principal and the community.

Does SELF HELP make a difference for families?

Approximately 62 sessions (186 instructional hours) were offered to participants in the school-year programme. Individual participants' attendance ranged from six sessions to 62 sessions. The average number of sessions attended was 32.

Project SELF HELP had an open entrance policy. Participants, therefore, could enter at any time in the school year. Between December and March, five families had moved away or had very limited attendance, and two new families were added. The school year ended with nine adults (eight mothers and one grandmother) in adult education classes, five children in the preschool programme, and 14 children in the elementary programme.

On average, parents and children that completed the project showed gains; however, the small sample size renders significance tests difficult to interpret. Preschool children made gains on all literacy assessments, and report card grades for school age children improved. Adults were functioning on average at the fourth grade level in reading, third grade level in spelling and fifth grade level in math on the WRAT on the pre-test. Mean math scores on the post-test improved by three grade level equivalents and mean reading and spelling scores rose slightly.

Scores on the CASAS and MAPP identify functional skill levels. On the CASAS, adults were functioning at the upper end of the entry level range (221) at the start of the programme and mean scores showed no significant change on the post-test. On the MAPP, they were functioning at the lower end of the entry level range (203) at the start of the programme and the mean scores realized an eight point gain on the post-test.

Two cases are presented below in order to give the reader a contextual understanding of the types of families served in Project SELF HELP and the types of outcomes to be expected.

Gloria's commitment to education increased in Project SELF HELP. She is 26 years old, married, and the mother of three school age boys. Her husband is employed and they are not receiving public assistance. Gloria completed the tenth grade, where she was in special education classes in math and reading. Both her parents and her four siblings dropped out of school. Her husband graduated from high school.

Gloria first began the SELF HELP programme in September of 1990, attended 20 sessions, and then dropped out in February 1991. She rejoined the programme in October 1991, and attended 38 sessions out of 62 sessions. Most of her absences were due to her own or her children's illnesses.

Gloria made important and impressive gains on all measures of basic literacy in 1991–92. Her WRAT scores improved two months in reading (3.1 to 3.3), seven months in spelling (2.4 to 3.1) and one grade level in math (4th to 5th). On the functional tests, her reading/life skills' scores improved 9 points (212 to 221) and her math scores improved 5 points (199 to 204). According to the authors of the test, a 3–4 point gain is the average per programme year. A score of 200–220 indicates entry level skills.

On the home educational environment assessment, positive changes in the way Gloria supported her children's learning at home were found. In October 1991, Gloria reported that she did not talk with her children about school at the dinner table, her children did not have a place to study privately, she seldom talked to her children about their future schooling, and she was not involved in any parent involvement activities at the school. In May 1992, Gloria reported that she talked to her children about school, they had a place to study, she sometimes talked to them about their future schooling, and she was actively involved in the Chapter 1 (a school-based programme for disadvantaged children) parent involvement activities.

Her involvement in Chapter 1 was confirmed by the parent liaison, who reported that Gloria volunteered on most of the school days that she was not attending SELF HELP. In addition, scores on the survey of parental beliefs about parenting changed from seeing her role as primarily a disciplinarian to one of 'parent as teacher'. The programme co-ordinator reported that 'Gloria is a very involved parent and gives her children lots of positive feedback.'

Gloria's second-grade boy is a student of average to above average ability. This child's grades improved from the first to the fourth quarter of the year in language and math, but not reading. The classroom teacher reported that he always completed his homework and that his parents often talked to her about how he was doing in school. In the after-school programme, this child often asked to learn new things. His parents supported his interests with activities at home.

Gloria's first-grade boy is a student of average ability. He showed no change in report card grades from the first to the fourth quarter on reading, language and math. The classroom teacher reported that he always completed his homework and her assessment of his ability as a student improved from fair to good over the programme year. The after-school teacher reported that he '. . . has come far this year. If you ask him to draw a picture he always includes words . . . he is confident about his work . . . enjoys school and likes challenges.'

The kindergarten child was having difficulty in school according to the classroom teacher's report. He improved on measures of literacy administered in the SELF HELP programme. The developmental day care teacher reported that he was an enthusiastic learner.

Gloria and her children attended 18 sessions of the summer programme and her husband joined the family for one field trip. Gloria and her children had the best attendance record of the summer programme. The family did not have a library card at the beginning of the summer but all members did by the end of the programme. The two oldest children read over 20 books each and their scores on the WRAT-reading subtest improved by six months for the second grader and five months for the first grader on the spring to the summer assessments.

Gloria has now 'graduated' from the SELF HELP programme to a more intensive, though still basic skill level, adult education programme in the community.

Lynn's significant gains were interrupted by family demands. She is 26 years old, divorced and the mother of two children. During her enrolment in the programme, Lynn was receiving public assistance. She reported that she completed the fifth grade and her parents and four siblings had all dropped out of school.

Lynn began Project SELF HELP in October 1990 and attended 55 sessions over the year. In 1991–92, Lynn attended 13 sessions before she suddenly dropped out of the programme. The parent liaison learned that she moved to another state to live with her mother because of her economic situation.

Lynn made significant gains in the first year of the project. The adult education teacher reported that she was very hardworking and often did extra homework activities or other writing assignments on her own. Her WRAT scores improved seven months in reading (3.7 to 4.4), one grade level in spelling (2.6 to 3.6), and one grade level in maths (fourth to fifth). On the reading/life skills functional test, Lynn improved six points (213 to 219). Post-testing for the 1991–92 year was not completed because of her sudden departure.

Lynn appeared to support her children's education at home. She reported on the home educational environment survey that her children did have a place to study, she sometimes talked to her child about future schooling, and she felt that her child's education was extremely important to his success in life. On the survey of parental beliefs about parenting, her score indicated that she viewed her role more as a 'disciplinarian' than a 'teacher'.

Her first-grade child had suspected learning disabilities and was evaluated by the school for placement in special education. This was a particularly difficult situation for Lynn because of the delays in getting her son tested and placed in a classroom where he could be successful. This child refused to attend the elementary programme and often caused Lynn to leave the adult education classes to attend to his needs.

Lynn's second-grade child was at risk of failing. The classroom teacher reported in November 1991 that she was 'probably failing', that she almost never completed assignments or stayed on task, and showed poor effort. This child attended the SELF HELP elementary programme.

In summary, both Gloria and Lynn achieved 'small wins' in Project SELF HELP. They both improved their own literacy skills and were supported in providing a positive home learning environment for their children. However, both also experienced 'stop outs' in participation in the programme. The term stop out, rather than drop out, recognizes the demands of family life, particularly for economically disadvantaged families. Seamless participation in intervention programmes may not be a realistic goal for many families. For Gloria, the relative stability of her family life during her participation in Project SELF HELP allowed her to move toward reaching her goals at a faster pace than Lynn. The competing needs of Lynn's family necessitated that she put on hold, perhaps just temporarily, her own goals.

FORGING NEW PATHS IN FAMILY LITERACY

Family literacy programmes are an emerging educational intervention. They need to be viewed realistically, however, as one piece of a comprehensive system to support families in their schools, neighbourhoods and communities. We need to recognize and applaud the sometimes small accomplishments made by children and families as they pursue long-term change. But family literacy programmes can be complex interventions to implement. There are many areas of the field which are still evolving and need continued thought and debate. We have selected three topics, based on our experiences with local programmes (see Dolan, 1992a; Connors, 1993, 1994 for further discussion of the issues) to further the discussion and conclude this chapter.

Developing successful collaborations

Funding sources for many family programmes increasingly require recipients to collaborate with existing community agencies in the delivery of services. Integrating multiple services to families at one location is intended to avoid duplication of services, reduce costs, share expertise, and provide a more holistic service delivery system for families (Dolan, 1992b; Sugarman, 1991). Schools and community literacy organizations are natural collaborators for delivering family literacy interventions; since schools rarely have the adult literacy expertise necessary for this type of project. Community organizations, also, may be seeking other sites to serve their clients.

Three steps appear to be necessary to set the stage for building successful relationships.

- First, planning together. School staff, community members, literacy providers and others need to be involved in identifying community needs, developing a pro-gramme that is responsive to these needs, and supporting the implementation of the programme.
- Second, sharing responsibilities. School staff and literacy staff must each take responsibility for specific tasks and goals of the project, relative to their expertise, knowledge of the system and the community, and ability to meet the needs of participants.
- Third, developing visibility. Throughout the year, or duration of the project, staff must work to build awareness of the programme with school staff, community members, families and others. Since school-based family literacy programmes are a relatively new phenomenon, many may be unaware of the purpose and goals of these types of services. Also, word-of-mouth and trust in programme staff are critical for participant recruitment and retention.

Melding two different cultures – a school culture and a community organization culture – with their different organizational structures, areas of expertise, and histories of purpose is never easy, and takes time to develop into a relationship of trust and respect. Two challenges will be faced by those implementing this type of programme.

Lack of time

School staff often have fairly structured schedules and limited flexible time for meetings or trainings. Community organization staff are often overburdened by multiple responsibilities, limiting the amount of time available to devote to the development of a particular programme.

The need to implement a programme almost immediately upon receipt of a grant severely limits the programme development phase of many projects. More critically for school–community collaborations, time for planning is most needed in the summer and early fall, precisely the time when school staff may be unavailable or busy with other preparations for their school responsibilities. Given the need to be responsive to local needs, slow and incremental implementation is preferable.

Use of school resources

The potential advantages for schools of housing a family literacy programme include extending the visibility of the school's programmes and goals to the community and greater efficiency in the use of a public space. However, schools are often faced with limited resources and see their primary purpose as one of meeting the needs of *children*. If schools see the family literacy programme as 'taking away' resources intended primarily for the 'children of the school', conflicts may arise. Sensitivity among collaborators and the 'host' school and a lengthy timeline to develop trust among those involved or affected by the collaboration may be needed to resolve these types of issues (Dolan, 1992b).

Meeting the learners' needs

Learner-centred instruction means that programme staff place great emphasis on determining the needs of the learner and responding to these needs throughout the curriculum. Duffy (1992) states: 'instruction will be most effective if it focuses on the particular tasks the individual will have to perform outside instruction, and if there is a bridge linking the new skills and knowledge to what the learner already knows' (p. 80). Programmes which embrace a learner-centred philosophy also see that improvement in participants' self-esteem and self-confidence are critical to the realization and maintenance of gains in literacy skills (Hypki, personal communication). This often results in fairly unstructured, but individualized educational experiences for learners. However, learner-centred instruction may not readily result in gains on standardized measures of adult literacy, which often measure isolated, out-of-context skills (Park, 1992).

Programme staff are often faced with the competing pressures of responding to participants' needs in order to keep them coming to the programme, and realizing significant gains on standardized measures in order to keep the programme funded. While it is possible to integrate activities that meet the personal and academic needs of learners, it takes great skill and training on the part of the instructor to achieve this balance successfully. Given that family literacy programmes are attempting to assist participants in meeting their adult education goals while developing greater personal and family competencies, the content of instruction and the types of measures used to evaluate gains need to reflect the broader focus of curriculum content.

Schools and family literacy programmes

When parents lack the literacy skills they need to be effective supporters of their children's education, or when parents have negative views of education because of their own previous failures, schools suffer in the form of less family involvement, less well prepared students, and less support for the school's educational goals for children. As schools continue to work to improve their efforts to involve all families, they will be called on by parents and community members to embark on this new educational intervention.

Can schools, which for some parents may recall unpleasant memories, or may appear large and impersonal, be effective collaborators in implementing family literacy programmes? Based on our experiences, we would say *yes* – if the design and expectations of the programme reflect the special needs, interests, and concerns of the families of the school. For schools, collaborating with a community agency to provide literacy services for parents and community members can result in:

- a responsive new practice to involve family and community members in the school, many of whom may be 'hard-to-reach';
- additional resources for the school in the form of the expertise of the community agency and the hiring of school staff or parents of children in the school as staff in the project;
- greater contact between parents of children attending the programme and the children's teachers, as well as the involvement of parents in new ways at the school;
- increased visibility and awareness of the school as a community resource; and
- more positive views of the school, and increased use of the school and school staff as a resource for parents' and children's needs.

School-based family literacy programmes may be one way of helping parents with low literacy skills to improve the success of their children in school and the quality of family life. This chapter has introduced the reader to family literacy as it is emerging and evolving in the United States. Family literacy programmes, run by a variety of entities, seek to increase adult literacy levels and the home environment for learning. Project SELF HELP, a school-based family literacy programme, was described as one model meeting these goals. The chapter concluded with a discussion of issues important for the further growth of the field.

ACKNOWLEDGEMENTS

Support for the completion of this paper was provided by the Center on Families, Communities, Schools and Children's Learning, funded by the Office of Educational Research and Improvement, US Department of Education (R117Q00031). The opinions expressed are the author's own and do not represent OERI positions or policies.

REFERENCES

Auerbach, E.R. (1989) Toward a social contextual approach to family literacy. *Harvard Educational Review*, **59**(2), 165–81.
California State Department of Education (1985) *California Adult Competency Assessment System*. San Diego, CA: Author.
Clay, M. (1979) *The Early Detection of Reading Difficulties: A Diagnostic Survey with Recovery Procedures*. Auckland, New Zealand: Heinemann Education Books.
Connors, L.J. (1993) *Project SELF HELP: A Family Focus on Literacy*. Baltimore, MD: Johns Hopkins University, Center on Families, Communities, Schools and Children's Learning.
Connors, L.J. (1994) *Small Wins: The Promises and Challenges of Family Literacy*. Baltimore, MD: Johns Hopkins University, Center on Families, Communities, Schools and Children's Learning.

Darling, S. and Hayes, A.E. (1989). *Breaking the Cycle of Illiteracy: The Kenan Family Literacy Model Program*. Kentucky: The National Center for Family Literacy.

Dolan, L. (1983) Prediction of reading achievement and self-esteem from an index of home educational environment. *Measurement and Evaluation in Guidance*, **16**, 86–94.

Dolan, L.J. (1992a) *Project SELF HELP: A First-Year Evaluation of a Family Literacy Program* (Report No. 8). Baltimore, MD: Johns Hopkins University, Center on Families, Communities, Schools and Children's Learning.

Dolan, L.J. (1992b) *Models for Integrating Human Services into the School* (Report No. 30). Baltimore, MD: Johns Hopkins University, Center for Research of Effective Schooling for Disadvantaged Students.

Duffy, T.M. (1992) What makes a difference in instruction? In T.G. Sticht, M.J. Beeler and B.A. McDonald (eds) *The Intergenerational Transfer of Cognitive Skills, Volume 1: Programs, Policy, and Research Issues*, pp. 61–83. Norwood, NJ: Ablex.

Heberle, J. (1992) Pace: Parent and child education in Kentucky. In T.G. Sticht, M.J. Beeler and B.A. McDonald (eds), *The Intergenerational Transfer of Cognitive Skills, Volume 1: Programs, Policy, and Research Issues*, pp. 136–48. Norwood, NJ: Ablex.

Hypki, C. (1994) Comments on first draft, Baltimore.

Illinois Literacy Resource Development Center (ILRC) (1992) *Fine Tuning the Mechanics of Success for Families: An Illinois Family Literacy Report*. Ranboul, IL: Illinois Literacy Resource Development Center.

Jastok Associates (1984) *Wide Range Achievement Test*. Wilmington, DE: Author.

Maryland State Department of Education (1987) *Maryland Adult Performance Program*. Baltimore, MD: Author.

Mumm, M., Secord, W. and Dykstra, K. (1980) *Merrill Language Screening Test*. San Antonio, TX: Psychological Corporation.

Newcomer, P. and Hammill, D. (1988) *Test of Language Development–2 Primary*. Austin, TX: Pro-Ed.

Nickse, R.S. (1990) *Family and Intergenerational Literacy Programs: An Update of 'The Noises of Literacy'*. Ohio: ERIC Clearinghouse on Adult, Career, and Vocational Education.

Park, R.J. (1992) Commentary on three programs for the intergenerational transfer of cognition. In T.G. Sticht, M.J. Beeler and B.A. McDonald (eds), *The Intergenerational Transfer of Cognitive Skills, Volume 1: Programs, Policy, and Research Issues*, pp. 159–68, Norwood, NJ: Ablex.

St Pierre, R., Swartz, J., Murray, S., Langhorst, B. and Nickel, P. (1993a) *National Evaluation of the Even Start Family Literacy Program: Second Interim Report*. Cambridge, MA: Abt Associates.

St Pierre, R., Swartz, J., Murray, S., Deck, D. and Nickel, P. (1993b) *National Evaluation of the Even Start Family Literacy Program: Report on Effectiveness*. Cambridge, MA: Abt Associates.

St Pierre, R., Swartz, J., Nickse, R., Gamse, B. and Hume, M. (1991) *National Evaluation of the Even Start Family Literacy Program: Status of Even Start Projects During the 1989–90 Program Year*. Cambridge, MA: Abt Associates.

Seaman, D.F. (1992) Follow-up study of the impact of the Kenan Trust model of family literacy. *Adult Basic Education*, **2**(2), 71–83.

Segal, M. (1985) A study of maternal beliefs and values within the context of an intervention program. In I. Sigel (ed.), *Parental Belief Systems: the Psychological Consequences for Children*. Hillsdale, NJ: Lawrence Erlbaum.

Sugarman, J. (1991) *Building Early Childhood Systems: A Resource Handbook*. Washington, DC: Child Welfare League of America.

Chapter 10

An Urban Parent Strategy for Accessing Achievement in Literacy: Experience in the London Borough of Newham

Ray Phillips

Mrs Finch was almost ready to start reading to her daughter at night; and with her go the many other mothers and fathers who would now welcome a partnership. It will not be long before they are demanding it, and at that point the old formal non-intervention agreement between teachers and manual workers will be dead. (Young and McGeeney, 1968, p. 118)

Newham Education Concern has always believed parents are the major neglected resource in education and we have felt that parents (as well as bringing pressure to bear when they see worrying situations) also have a positive role. Parents should be involved in education in a practical way. From the beginning we needed a centre to offer practical help to those parents who want involvement in school. (Newham Education Concern, 1976, p. 1)

INTRODUCTION

'Learning begins at home.' When Young and McGeeney 'coined' this sentence as a title for their research studies conducted for the Plowden Report (Plowden *et al.*, 1967), they were engaging in the early stages of a government inspired programme of social engineering in education. Since those heady days of the late 1960s, parental involvement in schooling has become an increasing, if shifting, focus of concern for policy-makers. Over the same period, the inspiration for parental assertiveness and empowerment has taken root at street level in the East End of London with the formation in 1973 of Newham Education Concern and, in 1975, of the Newham Parents' Centre.

The story of this parent action group, later to become a local educational charity, is available in more detail elsewhere (Phillips, 1989, 1992). For the moment, we might just usefully note the acknowledgement of the founders of the now twenty-year-old Parents' Centre to the post-Plowden 'social engineers':

We have been encouraged by the work of such people as Eric Midwinter, who has proved that it is lack of information, confidence and time that prevents working class parents from being involved in the education of their children and NOT apathy or want of interest. (Newham Education Concern, 1974, p. 1)

Slowly and deliberately over the past two decades, the Centre has evolved as the corporate subject of an innovatory urban parent strategy premised on the slogan: 'Parents helping parents help themselves!' In active defiance of comfortable text-book notions of inner-city parents being part of the educational problem Newham parents have used the Centre to seek out solutions to tackle the crowding crisis of urban illiteracy. Taken together, initiatives over the Centre's history reveal a vibrant definition of 'family literacy' in action.

PRACTICE

The parent-partnership model of family literacy being fostered at the Parents' Centre has, so far, assumed two distinctive forms: one avocational (PACER); the other, vocational (All About Us). Thus, whilst PACER (Parents and Children Enjoy Reading) is focused exclusively and unashamedly on enjoyment, All About Us is being developed as a means of achieving accreditation.

Notwithstanding the different orientations of the above two schemes, certain common features are discernible:

- encouragement of small groups and 1:1 tuition;
- use of school sites with crèche support;
- recruitment and training of volunteers;
- promotion of parent's/child's own writing;
- access to wide range of materials in Education Shop;
- holding of events as spur to creativity;
- availability of adult befriending/guidance/counselling/advocacy support.

PACER

The general aim of PACER is to initiate and develop literacy and numeracy support for parents who want to promote reading and writing as an enjoyable activity for their families. Since 1987, PACER Action Groups have been established in many local schools with some surviving far longer than others. Over this period, Groups have been established at 11 local school sites (four secondary and seven primary) as well as at two locations of the Parents' Centre. Although two Groups survived for only one year, the average life was two years, with two Groups underway for six years within the schools concerned. Up to 20 families have been attracted to each of these Action Groups with a sessional average of between six and ten families.

The sustainability of such Groups without the regular presence of a PACER worker has always been problematic. One tactic has been for PACER staff to offer introductory sessions on teaching methods for parents and carers to enable them to become more resourceful and self-sufficient. Although this was a standard element of support for the Action Groups; sometimes this was the only response PACER staff were able to offer a school. This has been especially the case in recent years with the reduction of resources available to the Project. Since 1989, PACER has undertaken Parent Training Schemes in 14 additional schools (all but one at primary level). These Schemes normally comprised four sessions with an average sessional attendance of ten families.

Parents and children at the weekly, two-hour PACER Action Group enjoyed a wide variety of activities involving the four core skills of listening, speaking, reading and writing. Reading was the key issue for most of the families. Parents would often be anxious because their child was not reading 'as well as the other kids in the class'. For those families where there was a history of poor reading, writing and spelling, the anxieties were manifestly greater.

PACER Groups have acquired a wide range of children's books, being fortunate to have the Parents' Centre's Education Bookshop staff to help select books found to be very popular with children. The books covered a wide range of topics and abilities, including some bilingual titles. Parents and children would take it in turns to read to each other. Sometimes a few adults and children would read together (many parents felt they had the patience to work with someone else's child rather than their own) or one child would read to another child, depending on the mood of the individuals in the group that particular week.

Given the concern for group interaction, reading plays became a popular choice. Certain selections involved writing for between two and ten parts, so there was usually a play that could be used with any given grouping. With forethought, roles could be identified for readers with variable skills. The PACER Groups were guided by the apprenticeship model:

> Reading is learned by reading. This is not as simple as it sounds, but is absolutely fundamental. Right from the start, learners have to behave as if they mean to become readers. Helpful adults must confirm them in the role by treating beginners as serious apprentices. (Meek, 1982, p. viii)

After reading, and especially the play-readings, the natural follow-up would be to do some writing. The adults were much more prepared to get involved in writing than their counterparts on the Centre's main literacy programme. There was a sense in which these parents felt they 'owed' it to the children to show them what to do and how – thus giving them extra courage. Play-writing was popular. One person would act as scribe (usually a PACER worker) to a group of adults and children. Each person would then assume a name and a few role characteristics and, whilst in character, would hold conversations with each other. This would all be copied down by the scribe who also had to help direct the 'play' into some order and towards a conclusion.

Once parents gained the confidence they needed to take more responsibility for the education of their children (and thereby themselves), they were more willing to take responsibility for preparing and organizing work at the Action Groups. One way they did this was to devise projects or themes. In carrying out such plans, children were often encouraged by the fact that they were more confident and more able artists than their parents.

In particular, book-writing and writing weekends in the country became a very productive activity. The first of these events was held in June 1988 at Debden House, Newham Council's Adult Education Centre in Epping Forest in Essex. To encourage

Table 10.1   *Writing weekend*

FRIDAY	Arrival, Reception and Welcome
	Dinner
	Introductions and Discussion
	Setting the scene
	The Parents' Centre
	Why do we write?
	Social Time
SATURDAY	Workshop 1 – Getting started: choosing a topic
	Coffee Break
	Workshop 2 – Getting down to writing
	Lunch – Free Time
	Workshop 3 – Carrying on
	Tea Break
	Workshop 4 – Editing: why it's done
	Barbecue, Disco – Social Time
SUNDAY	Workshop 5 – Editing our own work
	Workshop 6 – Where to next?
	– discussion and evaluation
	– forming an editing group
	Lunch and Depart

as many people as possible to attend, there was the additional provision of a crèche and youth group. Some parents wrote a book for their child, others helped their children write a book for themselves. There was an all-round boost in confidence as advantage was taken of all the resources made available by the Education Shop. (See Table 10.1.)

The strength of PACER, thus, lies in the informality and spontaneity of the Action Groups. With an emphasis on enjoyment, there is an implicit rejection of a 'curriculum' or 'syllabus' with which so many local parents identify their own often painful memories of schooling.

All About Us

This formal programme of family literacy was set up in 1994 by the Parents' Centre to raise standards of literacy among adults with literacy difficulties and their children. At the time of writing, two primary schools had been selected – one for the spring term and one for the summer term. The choice of title for this vocational programme was influenced by the concern, on the one hand, to recruit parents into a high profile school activity on a positive basis free from stigma and, on the other, to establish an inter-generational learning programme which started from where the parent and child were 'at'.

In this way, the Centre hoped to enable family members to develop self-esteem and to enhance mutual motivation and the family bond, through progressive individual and shared learning experiences. The emphasis was firmly on defining routes to accreditation whether, in the case of the child, to the National Curriculum or, in the case of the parent, to the City and Guilds 'Wordpower Certificate' (3793 Communication Skills). This accreditation scheme has been designed by the national Adult

Literacy and Basic Skills Unit (ALBSU) as a flexible framework, not a syllabus, to develop the competences of adults seeking to improve their basic skills.

In pursuit of the above general aim, several specific objectives were identified, including:

- to develop parents' skills in literacy through accreditation;
- to develop children's early literacy skills through a planned learning programme, in accord with the policy and approach of the schools;
- to promote enjoyment and sharing of reading and writing between parents and child through common learning activities;
- to make parents aware of how families can and do encourage the development of reading and writing skills in their children;
- to provide links with related agencies to promote literacy out of the school context;
- to increase family involvement in the school via such activities as monthly family literacy clubs open to all; ,
- to enable course members to adopt an inclusive approach to family literacy by encouraging others in learning.

All About Us specifically involved families whose children were taking the first steps on the road to literacy. These children were in the age range of 3 to 6 years and were attending nursery or infant school. The programme was deliberately school-based because it was felt that the positive familiarity of young families with early school would encourage enrolment and regular attendance. Later, the close partnership of home and school would stimulate a sense of joint ownership that would enable long-term involvement in family literacy to survive once the Centre staff had left the Scheme.

Feedback from parents revealed that the demand for course-based family literacy provision came from three distinct groups. Interest was shown by parents who wished to support their children in making a good start in literacy, but:

- were not sure of the best way to do so;
- felt unable to communicate comfortably in English and could not, therefore, encourage literacy in English;
- were not sufficiently confident of their own abilities in literacy to do so.

The first group prompted the organization of Family Literacy Learning Workshops which were the least intensive of the three course options. Here, the parent would be confident and competent in using the four core literacy skills of listening, speaking, reading and writing. The two-hour workshop sessions were once or twice a week for up to eight weeks. Parents were asked to focus on developing an understanding of the specific literacy skills needed by their children. Activities attempted to show how it feels to be a child approaching literacy and the importance for the child in gaining the confidence to 'have a go'.

The second group was involved in the ESOL (English for Speakers of Other Languages) Family Literacy Course. A typical candidate for the course would be a mother, largely responsible for the household duties and care of her family's children, with little experience of using English in her everyday life. Although her children might be bilingual, she would communicate with them largely in her mother tongue. The course, therefore, focused on giving her confidence in handling both spoken and

Table 10.2 *Family Literacy Course*

	Theme	Emphasis in combined and wordpower sessions
Intro. Week 1	Learning begins at home	Awareness of pre-school learning.
Week 2	Talking	Understanding of the purposes and development of talk. Eliciting information from children.
Week 3	Writing	Understanding of the purposes and development of writing skills and the difficulties faced by learners.
Week 4	Reading	Understanding of the purposes and development of reading skills and the difficulties faced by learners.
Week 5	Newspapers and magazines	Parent-planned activities, drawing on what has been learned about the four core literacy skills.
Week 6	Storytelling	Understanding of the 'performance' element in reading aloud.
Week 7	Play	The learning potential of different kinds of play.
Week 8	Family outings	Literacy in the environment. Mapping skills.
Week 9	School experiences	Comparison of parents' and children's experience of school. Understanding of the education system.
Week 10	Evaluation	

written English and in using English with her children. Tuition was based on six to eight hours per week for up to approximately ten weeks with the majority of time devoted to the development of basic skills in English. In parallel, the children received extra support in literacy activities at school. From time to time, parents and children engaged in common activities with an end 'product' (such as a book, conversation or game) which could be shared. Where appropriate, they might eventually move into the third group programme.

The final type of group was offered the accredited 'Wordpower' Family Literacy Course. Over ten weeks for up to eight hours per week, parents developed their literacy skills through a series of linked themes exploring the development of learning and literacy in their children, the difficulties children might meet as well as ways of supporting and encouraging young learners. Encouragement was given to the making of books and games to share at home.

The children involved in this third group received extra support in literacy activities from the Parents' Centre's early years' teacher and, where possible, were engaged in activities appropriate to each theme as presented to their parents. Regular sessions were timetabled for parents and children to undertake activities together.

As the parents become more confident in their awareness of their children's learning, they played a greater role in planning such activities both for the combined sessions at school and for use at home. Parents' work was also accredited towards the City and Guilds 'Wordpower' qualification and provision was made for them to continue and complete the relevant stage beyond the end of the course. As a vocational programme, the emphasis was very much on progression. The outline structure of the accredited course is shown in Table 10.2.

ORGANIZATION

My eldest daughter doesn't need help but she comes along [to PACER] each week just because she enjoys it so much. I've told my mates to come along – it's helped me and it'll help them too. (Newham Parents' Centre, 1989)

Having briefly described the avocational and vocational variants of the Centre's parent partnership model of family literacy, we might consider the linked issues of scheme promotion and member recruitment within PACER and All About Us. Here, word of mouth has no comparable substitute. Working at street level over 20 years, Newham Parents' Centre has adapted many forms of publicity – from the expensive publication or newspaper advertisement to the cheap 'tell your neighbour' approach. The latter may be slower but is usually more sure!

Even so, the formal launch of PACER or All About Us in any school does require as broad and assertive a declaration as resources will allow. One key difference in the substance of such promotion lies in the degree of engagement each scheme has with the mainstream curriculum of the school. Whereas the 'enjoyment' focus of PACER allowed the relative freedom of an 'extra-curricular' activity; the direct impact of All About Us on the day-to-day studies of the children involved did require the acceptance of a more rigorous, school-influenced discipline. Inevitably, this leads to distinctive approaches in terms of planning, promotion and organization.

Setting up a PACER Group

1. If you are a teacher and would like to set up a site within your school:
    - Consult with your head of department and head of school.
    - Call a meeting with parents and teachers keen to work together in partnership.
    - Approach your school governors and PTA.
    - Generate discussion on how PACER might work in your school.
    - If some parents are interested in working with their children at school, decide where, when and how it should happen:
      — during or after school;
      — who should attend (parents and/or teachers);
      — what books/materials;
      — how to raise funds;
      — how to share responsibilities.
    - Encourage a core group to supply and display materials. If money is available, get parents to purchase books/art materials they feel will be of interest to their children.
    - Support parents in designing/making posters, leaflets and letters to advertise the scheme.
    - Try to provide tea/coffee facilities and a lockable cupboard – something PACER can call its own.
    - Decide as a group what records needs to be kept – registers, library index, names, addresses, application forms, accounts, etc. Help parents to prepare this themselves.
    - Hold a social to launch PACER. At this meeting, set a regular time and day for the scheme.
    - Get going! Remember . . . if you have just one or two interested parents then go ahead . . . groups do build up and having a small core group to start will enable those parents to gain confidence at their own pace.

- Finally – don't let your teacher training get in the way! No one knows what is best for the children. Certainly, no one knows a child better than the parent. Give support and encouragement to parents at all times, even though they may use techniques you don't favour.

2. If you are a parent and would like to set up PACER in your school:
   - Talk to other parents, friends, PTA, school governors or local adult education/literacy groups.
   - Collect as much information on parental involvement as you can.
   - You are probably already aware of who, in your school, favours parental involvement. Ask for a meeting to talk about how you could set up PACER in your school. Take a friend with you to gain support.
   - If you are getting a positive response, then follow the teacher's points, above.
   - If you meet with resistance, then try to find out why. There may be ways you can negotiate with the school through the PTA or school (parent) governors. Don't give up, even if you are forced to work from home.
   - Remember, you are the person who taught your child to walk, talk, feed herself, dress herself, etc. and you are well qualified to help your child to read and write. In the process you will improve your own skills. You have influential support:

  > Parents know best the needs of their children – certainly better than educational theorists or administrators, better than our mostly excellent teachers. (Department for Education, 1992, p. 2)

Setting up All About Us

Once a school has registered interest in the programme, a series of information exchange meetings will need to take place. These should involve project staff, the headteacher, governors and other members of school staff. The purpose of the meetings will be:

- to provide information about family literacy – background, aims, development and potential;
- to gain relevant information about the school, including current policies and practices regarding teaching and parental involvement;
- to make staff aware of the needs of each of the three target groups and means of identifying members of those groups (see below);
- to establish the likely areas of demand within the school population;
- to establish appropriate means of meeting those demands.

The next stage will be to publicize the programme in the school, in order to raise parental awareness about family literacy. This will involve a consideration of the form or forms the scheme might take and will enable take-up levels to be gauged. The nature of any publicity will be dependent on the identified target group(s) and will involve close liaison with the staff room. There, letters home and in-school posters may be effective in attracting parents and children to the Learning Workshops but will, undoubtedly, be less effective in the case of the ESOL or Wordpower Courses. The successful identification of parents will require a careful selection process.

Parents for the Learning Workshop will possess basic skills in communication. They will probably have qualifications in English or in subjects requiring competence in written English and are likely to approach the school with confidence. Such parents are willing and able to ask questions about their children's progress and about ways of supporting learning.

Those parents likely to benefit from the ESOL Course will probably communicate with their children and others largely in their mother tongue, perhaps being unable or rarely choosing to speak English. Where they do speak some English, these parents may experience difficulty in understanding conversations and will require translation or simple rephrasings. They will all be anxious for their children to be well educated, even though their children will not necessarily experience similar difficulties in spoken English.

Parents for the Wordpower Course will have reasonably good conversational skills, whether English is their native or second language or they are bilingual. They will be able to follow and contribute to conversation of discussion, speaking competently enough to be understood, even if grammatical errors are made. They will probably lack confidence in reading and writing, and may avoid, or have difficulty in, completing forms, writing notes or letters. They will be concerned about their children's progress in reading and writing, and be keen that their children should not experience similar difficulties.

In all cases, one-to-one contact is likely to be effective, especially when the initiative has come from school staff. Parents will need the opportunity to discuss the course, ask questions and possibly sample activities. Pre-course measures might, therefore, include 'taster' sessions.

Given the commitment of many schools to community education and parental involvement, space may be available in community/parent rooms. Some schools will also be able to allocate space for a crèche, so that parents are encouraged to study free from concern over the care of their youngest children.

EFFECTIVENESS

> Literacy learners must be treated with respect. Children bring their language competence and their ability to learn language to development of literacy. We must rid ourselves of the pathological preoccupation with weakness in learners and take the positive view of building on strength. (Goodman, 1982, p. 346)

Whether avocational or vocational in form, the Parents' Centre's commitment to family literacy is based on certain broad criteria for measuring success. For both parents and children, evidence is gathered by students and tutor together in an agreed Personal Learning Plan and Record as to gains in the following areas:

- confidence in literacy skills to pursue interests and ambitions;
- development of a sense of independence, self-responsibility and self-esteem as well as a regard for the achievement of others;
- enhancement of parent–child relationships in the home based on mutual esteem;
- improvement in reading and writing;
- interest in and enthusiasm for literacy;

- time spent in reading and writing;
- using resources to develop literacy;
- confidence in approaching and using school.

PACER

Throughout the programme, PACER has challenged the role-model and structures that are often 'naturally' assumed. A parent, for example, will almost always assume a passive and compliant role when dealing with staff at school simply because of an inherent assumption that 'teacher knows best'. This is often reinforced by the child: 'My teacher says . . .'.

PACER has enabled families to change their perceptions of themselves and their families with regard to education. This has, in turn, enabled them to take on more responsibility for what happens in the class as well as at home. During the course of a year, a literacy student may make limited progress in terms of reading and writing skills, yet confidence and social skills will have progressed almost beyond recognition. The same may be said for a PACER parent.

There were five distinct groups of people who attended PACER Action Groups and who, therefore, had a role to play – the parent/carer, the child, the PACER worker, the teacher and the friend/relative. How these people related in a group was important and there were difficulties in ensuring smooth running. People needed to think about the roles they had to play as well as those they naturally assumed. Unless there were some definition, individuals could easily take on too much or too little or responsibilities that were inappropriate.

Some examples of role confusion were:

- when a parent assumed that the PACER worker or the teacher would teach the child rather than themselves;
- when a child or parent related to the PACER worker(s) or other parents in the group as though they were teachers – perhaps calling them 'Miss';
- when the teacher attending the site thought she had the right to interfere with the work that a parent and child were doing – perhaps because 'This is not the correct way!';
- when a parent brought along her child's friend and yet refused to discipline her when she ran riot around the room, disrupting the others.

In such situations, the PACER worker(s) usually had to take action. The most democratic approach was to raise the issue in group discussion. However, parents and children often felt 'chastened' and perhaps humiliated by this. The confidence-building work of many months was at risk of being destroyed.

Notwithstanding these trials, we might leave the last world with the PACER parents, themselves:

> D. has received his best report ever. This has happened since we've been coming to PACER and have got more support. D. also got his options this year simply because he's improved so much. I knew he could handle it.

L. has gone up three colour bands of reading at school. The teacher told me that she's grown in confidence and they think it's because I work with her at PACER.

E. has no confidence at all. She's nervous and shy and when she worries it brings out her speech impediment. Now her school says she is improving – she reads more quickly with confidence. You can see how her confidence has grown. (Newham Parents' Centre, 1989, p. 15)

All About Us

Each family member participating in the programme carried a personal profile. The specific content of these profiles varied from course to course, but each aimed to show progress in a pupil's understanding, approach, achievement and literacy behaviour. Comments were systematically gathered from more than one perspective.

Students, both parents and children, were involved in making initial self-assessments and setting themselves targets. They were also involved with family literacy staff, in monitoring their own progress and re-evaluating their targets. Additionally, each child's progress was monitored by his or her class-teacher. Parents were also involved in this process as part of their own developing understanding of their children's learning.

Developing a peripatetic, school-based model of family literacy brought challenges not faced by schemes with a permanent site. However, there were undoubted advantages. Schools could be made more accessible to families. They were used on a daily basis and so, siting courses within them brought learning opportunities directly to each family. The parent at the gate, lacking the confidence in literacy to seek out a course elsewhere, might find the courage to accept a place in the school. This was especially true of those parents (usually mothers) who experienced some degree of social isolation through lacking the confidence to speak English.

In operating from a school, recruitment and enrolment could be supported by drawing on the knowledge of teaching staff. They also could benefit from the scheme in terms of a growing awareness of literacy and of adults as learners. Parent–teacher relationships and concepts of parental involvement in education were also positively affected. Schools linked well into their local communities, were able to stimulate neighbourhood interest in family literacy and wider adult basic education.

With regard to the outcome of the programme against objectives in the first school, half of the parents on Course 1 and three-quarters of those on Course 2 were specifying new ways in which they supported their children's learning at home. Several parents commented that the course had given them time with their children and there was a general feeling that this was of great value. Two-thirds of parents also admitted that they often found themselves clashing with their children when their ideas differed. This was a useful discussion point!

Both parents and teachers were reporting better home–school relations in a third of the cases. Parents attributed this to their own increased confidence or ability to express themselves. By the end of the course, at least half of parents were reporting friendly contact with their child's teacher and two-thirds regular contact.

However, such a pre-structured context as a school did require firm liaison between project workers, headteacher and staff room in the formal preparation of a course. At least half a term was required to set the foundations. Yet, there was a danger in beginning the actual recruitment process too early. This needed to take place close to the beginning of each course to maintain the motivation and interest of each family. Moreover, the selection process was required to take especial care in not setting up parent/child groups that would cause too much disruption in the distribution of child withdrawals from their regular class. Family learning should not be at the expense of the child.

The children required either a sufficiently favourable adult–child ratio to allow each to be taught in his or her own class, or a separate classroom. This needed to be resourced to be stimulating and appropriate for children of different ages. Where numbers, space and activities permit, there was a definite advantage for parents and children to share teaching space. This also applied when they were engaged in separate activities, as sharing enabled them to see and respect each other as learners and facilitated the development of a cohesive and flexible programme.

This flexibility was especially important to recognize in a neighbourhood which was multicultural. A narrow approach could easily lead to the erroneous perception that family literacy schemes were exclusively targeted at bilingual families using little English. Programmes needed effective publicity at all levels to ensure that they were seen as relevant by all families in need.

CONCLUSION

> . . . most schools in these disadvantaged areas do not have within themselves the capacity for sustainable renewal. The rising tide of national educational change is not lifting these boats. Beyond the school gate are underlying social issues such as poverty, unemployment, poor housing, inadequate health care and the frequent break-up of families. Education by itself can only do so much to enable individuals to reach beyond the limiting contours of their personal and social circumstances and succeed. (OFSTED, 1993, p. 45)

Illiteracy is an enduring feature of poverty. Family literacy programmes in London's East End are essentially efforts to combat poverty. Since the early 1970s, the European Commission has struggled with a definition of poverty as 'social exclusion'. Fundamentally, measures to tackle poverty are about social access. Notwithstanding reservations about the European 'social contract', the United Kingdom government has responded to opportunities for social funding from the European Commission and to domestic demands for urban renewal by the setting up of the Single Regeneration Agency in the spring of 1994. The work of the Office for Standards in Education (OFSTED) has directly addressed the scope for educational innovation at all levels in meeting the challenge of urban regeneration with the 1993 Report on *Access and Achievement in Urban Education*. The key role, here, of family literacy strategies was recognized by the Department for Education in linking the launch of the above Report to the transfer to the Single Regeneration Agency of in-service support and training funds for Raising Standards in Inner-City Schools through measures such as the enhancement of parental involvement.

Working locally within a poverty priority area now recognized by both central government and the European Commission, Newham Parents' Centre has for 20 years sought to develop models of parent partnership built on effective home–school relations and collaboration between the voluntary and statutory sectors. In pursuit of this partnership, the Centre has combined elements of the postwar 'social engineering' tradition of parental involvement (Plowden, 1967; Warnock, 1978) with those of the 'adult education' approach to community learning (Russell, 1973). Indeed, the Russell Report not only recognized the status of parents as adult learners but also identified the real problem of adult illiteracy in contemporary Britain. This, in turn, ignited the Right to Read Campaign of the mid-1970s which led to the formation and development over 20 years of the national Adult Literacy and Basic Skills Unit.

Several of the street-level initiatives generated by Newham Parents' Centre have been funded by ALBSU which prioritized family literacy during the recent International Literacy Year. The Unit has, in particular, influenced both PACER and All About Us. The Centre has been able, in turn, to contribute to the production of national materials on literacy for parents and children, not only through the editing skills of professional workers but also through the responses of parents as students:

> My children are most important to me. Everything is geared around the family. I wasn't able to read and because I wanted to be able to help my girls I went to reading classes and now we read together. My daughter Karin is a good reader and she helps me. Family is so important to me because it's how I learnt. My mother brought up 8 children on her own and we never, ever went without. Love doesn't cost money! Because of my family I'll never be poor. (Jennings, 1987)

If education is to play a full part in the urban regeneration of areas like the East End of London, then we must continue to work hard to ensure that the path from Plowden to OFSTED has not been paved just with good intentions!

ACKNOWLEDGEMENT

Special thanks are due to Madeline Chapman, Lil Russell and Linda Sturman for their help and inspiration in writing this chapter.

REFERENCES

Department for Education (1992) *Choice and Diversity: A New Framework for Schools.* London: HMSO.

Goodman, K.S. (1982) The know-more and the know-nothing movements in reading. In F.V. Gollasch (ed.) *Language and Literacy: The Selected Writings of Kenneth S. Goodman Vol. II: Reading, Language and the Classroom Teacher.* London: Routledge & Kegan Paul.

Jennings, R. (1987) Talking about unemployment. In M. Walsh (ed.) *Parents and Children.* London: Adult Literacy and Basic Skills Unit.

Meek, M. (1982) *Learning to Read.* London: The Bodley Head.

Newham Education Concern (1974) *Application for Funding.* London: NEC.

Newham Education Concern (1976) *Three Years On.* London: NEC.

Newham Parents' Centre (1989) *PACER Report to ALBSU.* London: Newham Education Concern Services Association.

OFSTED (1993) *Access and Achievement in Urban Education.* London: HMSO.

Phillips, R.H. (1989) The Newham Parents' Centre. In S. Wolfendale (ed.) *Parental Involvement: Developing Networks Between School, Home and Community.* London: Cassell.

Phillips, R.H. (1992) Newham Parents' Centre: Parents as Partners in Education. In S. Wolfendale (ed.) *Empowering Parents and Teachers: Working for Children*. London: Cassell.

Plowden, J.P. *et al.* (1967) *Children and Their Primary Schools*. London: HMSO.

Russell, L. *et al.* (1973) *Adult Education: A Plan for Development*. London: HMSO.

Warnock, H.M. *et al.* (1978) *Report of the Committee of Enquiry into the Education of Handicapped Children and Young People*. London: HMSO.

Young, M. and McGeeney, P. (1968) *Learning Begins at Home*. London: Routledge & Kegan Paul.

Chapter 11

Developing Partnerships with Families in Literacy Learning

Trevor H. Cairney

INTRODUCTION

Although there has been long-term interest in family involvement in literacy and schooling, the last five to ten years has seen an increased recognition of the vital role that the family plays in children's success at school. Also, there has been a shift in emphasis from reading to literacy, and from what schools can do for parents, to how schools and families can form effective partnerships designed to benefit both children and schools. The purpose of this chapter is to describe an innovative programme that has been developed in response to this increasing understanding of the role that families play in literacy learning and schooling. The programme, Talk to a Literacy Learner (TTALL), was developed for families with children aged from 1 to 12 years. However, before describing TTALL and its evaluation it is important to trace the research work and theoretical development that influenced this programme.

Parent involvement in children's education is obviously an important element in effective schooling (Epstein, 1983; Delgado-Gaitan, 1991). There appears to be a high positive correlation between parent knowledge, beliefs, and interactive styles with children's school achievement (see Schaefer, 1991 for a detailed review). Differences in family backgrounds appear to account for a large share of variance in student achievement (Rutter *et al.*, 1970; Thompson, 1985). Unfortunately, many of the attempts to explain this relationship have reflected deficit models, and have been based on the assumption that some children receive 'good' or 'appropriate' preparation for schooling, while others receive 'poor' or 'inappropriate' preparation. This view has been criticized because of its failure to recognize that schooling is a cultural practice (Auerbach, 1989). In reality, much of the variability in student achievement in school reflects discrepancies that exist between school resources and instructional methods, and the cultural practices of the home (Au and Kawakami, 1984; Cazden, 1988; Heath, 1983; Moll, 1988).

Schools engage in specific discourses and hence inconsistently tap the social and cultural resources of society; privileging specific groups by emphasizing particular linguistic styles, curricula and authority patterns (Bourdieu, 1977). To be a teacher in any school demands specific ways of using language, behaving, interacting, and adherence to sets of values and attitudes (Gee, 1990). There is obvious potential for mismatches between these discourses and those which have been characteristic of some children's homes and communities. Children who enter school already having been partially apprenticed into the social practices of schooling (of which literacy is a part) invariably perform better at the practices of schooling than those who have not. It would appear that the literacy of schooling arbitrarily advantages some whilst disadvantaging others (Lankshear and Lawler, 1987; Street, 1984).

But how does one respond to the cultural mismatches of home and school? Should one focus on developing initiatives that provide parents with the cultural practices that enable them to cope with the limited practices of the school (Lareau, 1991), or find ways to help schools recognize the cultural practices of the home and community and build effective communication between these parties (Delgado-Gaitan, 1992)?

A combination of these two strategies appears to be the most effective way to counteract the effect of cultural mismatches. Involving parents more closely in school education has the potential to develop new understanding by each party of the other's specific cultural practices. This, in turn, may well enable both teachers and parents to understand the way each defines, values and uses literacy. In this way schooling can be adjusted to meet the needs of families. Teachers clearly have a significant responsibility to accept change. Parents in turn can also be given the opportunity to observe and understand the definitions of literacy that schools support, and which ultimately empower individuals to take their place in society (Cairney, 1995).

Some of the most significant early initiatives in this area occurred in the United Kingdom. The Plowden Report (Department of Education and Science, 1967) was one of several factors which probably influenced the significant number of projects that arose in the 1970s and 1980s. These early attempts to recognize the important role that parents play in children's literacy learning were typically based on a beginning premise that student achievement in school can be raised if parents are taught specific strategies which enable them to support their children in the literacy practices of schooling. One of the most commonly used strategies was Paired Reading. This simple technique was first designed by Morgan (1976) and was later refined (Topping and Wolfendale, 1985). However, while some of the programmes that focused on teaching parents specific strategies showed encouraging outcomes, there was a degree of inconsistency. For example, even the successful Haringey Reading Project (using a 'Parent Listening' approach) found that some of the children whose parents were involved in their programme made significant gains in reading achievement (irrespective of level of initial reading ability), while others made little advance (Tizard *et al.*, 1982).

There have been many attempts to describe the diversity of family literacy initiatives (see Epstein and Dauber, 1991; Fitzgerald and Goncu, in press; Petit, 1980; Rasinski and Fredericks, 1989; and Soliman, 1992). Nickse (1993) for example, has developed a classification system which is defined in terms of the target group (adults or children) and the relationship between the adults and children (adults and children working together, or only indirect contact). Power (1994) has suggested that these classification systems fall into two main groups. One group consists of typologies which are essentially hierarchical rankings of parent involvement. At the lowest level there is little contact between schools and families, while at the highest level there is a lot. The major assumption implicit within these typologies is that the higher the level of involvement the better. A second group of typologies assumes that varying levels of interaction can occur between schools and families, and that each can be acceptable; that is, there is no optimum level of involvement.

However, Cairney and Munsie (1992a) have suggested that all such typologies invariably mask diversity. While Nickse (1993) acknowledges this, her attempt to describe family literacy initiatives fails to address the issue. Cairney (1991) suggests that a more useful way to describe programmes that have been attempted may be to assess each project on a number of key variables, with the assumption being that on each of these there will be a continuum ranging from one extreme to another. He suggests four variables which might be used:

Content – What information is shared? What is the focus of group discussion, demonstrations, hometasks and so on? What is the stated purpose of the content?

Process – How is information shared? Who acts as the facilitator or leader for any programme and how does this person structure opportunities for discussion, observation, etc.?

Source – Who has initiated the involvement? Was it a parent, school, community, or government initiative?

Control – Who is in control of the programme? Where is the programme located (home, school, community building)? How do parents become involved in programmes (chosen, selected, parent initiative)?

In keeping with linear typologies Cairney and Munsie (1992a) adopt the assumption that many forms of family involvement can be worthwhile depending on the expectations of schools and families and the specific needs of each. When assessing the worth of any Family Literacy programme, consideration of a variety of criteria like the above is important. While many programmes claim to 'involve' parents, or attempt to develop 'partnerships', one needs to test the veracity of such claims. Can a programme lead to partnership if the initiator of the programme is a school which does not involve parents in its planning and conduct? While there may be a rich array of initiatives, some educators have begun to question the programmes that have been implemented. Auerbach (1989) has argued that some programmes are based on a model designed simply to transmit school practices to the home. Considerable criticism has been levelled at those programmes that are designed to exert a central influence on parents' caregiving roles. Many of these intergenerational literacy programmes aim to 'improve' the education of caregivers in order to bring about changes in children's learning. Frequently, these programmes focus on parenting as well as literacy (Neuman and Daly, in press).

It would appear that some schools and government agencies adopt very narrow definitions of parent involvement, which seek primarily to determine what parents can do for teachers, or how schools can make parents 'better' at their role in the home, rather than how schools and parents can develop close relationships of mutual support and trust.

Recently, there has been much attention in the literature to the need to view parents as equal partners. For example, Cairney and Munsie (1992a, 1995a) argue that we need to go beyond token involvement and recognize the vital role that parents play in education. Kruger and Mahon (1990, p. 4) also stress that 'parental involve-ment in literacy learning has much greater value than as an add-on to what teachers do'. Harry (1992) argues that such parent initiatives must forge collaborative rela-tionships that create mutual understanding between parents and teachers – a 'posture of reciprocity' – and which are associated with a shift from the school to parents and the community.

These educators argue that the aim should not be the transmission of knowledge from schools to parents and their children, but rather a process of reaching mutual consensus between the partners. This process of reaching shared understanding is what Vygotsky (1978) called 'intersubjectivity', and it requires a shared focus of attention and mutual understanding of any joint activity. Fitzgerald and Goncu (in press) suggest that participants need to reach agreement on the selection of activities, their goals, and plans for reaching the goals. Programmes that are imposed by teachers on communities 'for their own good' obviously fail to meet the conditions necessary for intersubjectivity to occur, and have little long-term benefit for parents and their children.

Involving parents more closely in school education has the potential to develop new understanding by each party of the other's specific cultural practices, and lead to the type of 'reciprocity' which Harry (1992) argues is needed. To achieve this teachers and parents need to understand the way each defines, values and uses literacy as part of cultural practices. Such mutual understanding offers the potential for schooling to be adjusted to meet the needs of families. It also offers parents the opportunity to observe and understand the literacy of schooling, a literacy which ultimately empowers individuals to take their place in society (Cairney, 1995).

It was with these assumptions in mind that the Talk to a Literacy Learner Programme (TTALL) was developed with funding from the New South Wales Ministry of Education and Youth Affairs. In the rest of this chapter I will describe the programme and its evaluation.

DESCRIPTION OF THE TALK TO A LITERACY LEARNER PROGRAMME

TTALL was developed as a vehicle for the development of effective relationships between parents, their children and schools or preschools. It is a parent education programme that was designed to provide parents and their children with access to the literacy of schooling. The programme was also designed as a vehicle to develop more effective relationships between schools and their communities. It was hoped that the basis of this relationship would be increased understanding by parents and teachers of each other's needs and expectations. The programme attempted to:

- provide parents with strategies and knowledge to enable them to more effectively support their children in school learning;
- lead to improvements in children's attitudes to literacy and a range of literacy practices;
- improve the relationship between parents and their children;
- improve the relationship between parents and schools or preschools;
- increase mutual understanding between all participants in schooling;

Table 11.1 *Overview of the content of Stage 1 of the TTALL programme*

Topic	Session	Focus of the session
1. LEARNING	1	Stresses that parents are their child's first teachers, and that children learn at different rates and in different ways. Shows how parents can support learning.
	2	Shows how parents can contribute to children's learning. Stresses that children's learning covers a wide range of experiences.
2. THE READING PROCESS	1	Explores the nature of the reading process.
	2	Encourages participants to examine their reading and that of their children.
3. SUPPORTING THE READER	1	Stresses that children need a stimulating home environment where reading is encouraged.
	2	Simple strategies introduced which assist the child's development as a reader (e.g. Paired Reading, Personal Spelling, Dictionaries, Directed Reading and Thinking).
4. USING THE LIBRARY	1	Aims to increase participant's knowledge of the function of the library, including its components and use.
5. THE WRITING PROCESS	1	Introduces parents to the understanding that children learn to write by writing and learn to spell by writing.
	2	Stresses that writing has one major purpose, to compose meaning for oneself, or others to read.
6. SUPPORTING THE WRITER	1	Introduces activities which support and encourage writing in the home.
	2	Gives participants an understanding of the features of quality writing.
	3	Introduces strategies which will assist in finding the standard spelling of words. Examines the importance of handwriting in assisting the writer to communicate their thoughts on paper.
7. RESEARCH	1	Provides participants with experiences which can assist children to research a topic.
	2	Shows participants how to categorize and organize information, locating and using suitable information.
	3	Introduces participants to notetaking and preparation of draft report.

- facilitate growth in the confidence, knowledge and self-esteem of parents, students and teachers.

The content of the programme (see Table 11.1) covered basic child development, the nature of the reading and writing processes, strategies for assisting children with reading and writing (e.g. directed reading and thinking, conducting writing conferences etc.), the use of the library for research, and the development of self-esteem (see Cairney and Munsie, 1992b for complete programme details).

The programme materials consist of a 250-page set of facilitator's notes covering every session, a 125-page photocopiable parent handbook, related overhead transparency masters, photographic resources, a video and two resource books.

ORGANIZATION OF THE PROGRAMME

The programme is presented using a mixture of short lectures, workshops, demonstrations, and apprentice teaching sessions (see overview of one session in Figure 11.1). An important part of the programme is the demonstration of all strategies. Each session is characterized by an interactive learning process involving a recursive cycle of activities (see Figure 11.2). These sessions do not always contain the same order of process elements (i.e. discussion, leader input, practical experiences, etc.), nor do these elements occupy the same proportion of each session. Since the sessions are very much learner centred they are very responsive to the needs and questions of the participants. Group members are given (and take) frequent opportunities to talk with each other, to share personal insights, to ask questions of each other, to provide opinions and to reflect on their own learning.

The role of the facilitator is to engage participants in discussion and to encourage them to reflect on their experiences of learning as well as those of their children. For example, within the first session of the final topic in this programme on research (see Figure 11.1), the facilitator begins by asking participants to share personal understandings of school research projects: What makes a good project? What do children learn from them? Are they too difficult at times (and if so, why)? Participants are also asked to discuss their role in the research project work completed at home: Which family members help at home? How do they help? This is followed by the sharing of an overhead transparency that indicates a number of characteristics of projects that teachers rate as important (also included in the Parent Handbook), and another which suggests the things that make completing projects more difficult. These overheads are discussed in groups. The facilitator then outlines one approach to research that is reproduced in their Parent Handbooks.

This involves selecting a topic, beginning a discovery draft, gathering some information, making notes, thinking about the form that the report will take, and finally completing the project. The facilitator then explains to parents that they will be given the chance to complete a project in this form with their children at home over the next two weeks. As a session break the facilitator then shares several pieces of literature (a normal part of each session). The first two steps of the research process are then demonstrated, allowing for discussion and questions as he/she proceeds. Participants then complete the first two stages of the process, working with a partner and utilizing a large collection of books assembled by the facilitator for this workshop. The session ends as usual with a hometask. This task involves the parents completing these same first two steps with one of their children before the next session.

The programme is introduced to parents in a variety of ways. Usually, this process begins with a series of written notices sent to all parents associated with the school or preschool. In communities where parents speak languages other than English the letters are translated and an undertaking given that the programme will be translated into and delivered in a number of specified community languages. This is also accompanied by whatever media publicity can be obtained in local newspapers, or even community radio if available. After several weeks of advertising, a public meeting is organized at the school, preschool or site for the programme. At this meeting the purpose of the programme is explained and a simple information sheet distributed requesting an indication of interest. This form requests details concerning

SESSION OVERVIEW

1. INTRODUCTION
   Aim of the session is to:
   – introduce activities which will enable
     participants to encourage writing at home.
   – stress the importance of talking to and
     encouraging children as they write.
   Review hometask activities.
   10 minutes

2. STORY READING
   Share a tale from *Hairy Tales and
   Nursery Rhymes* by Michael Rosen.
   Appendix 4, Literature Overview.
   5 minutes

3. WRITTEN CONVERSATIONS
   Group activity.
   Writing in pairs, no talking permitted.
   Blank OHT.
   30 minutes

4. REVIEW OF THE WRITING PROCESS
   Group discussion.
   Refer to OHT W:3 *Early Stages of
   Children's Writing Development.*
   5 minutes

5. CHILDREN AS WRITERS
   Leader input.
   Refer to OHT SW:1 *The Proficient Writer.*
   10 minutes

6. THE PROCESS OF WRITING
   Key statement: *Writing is a process in
   which meaning is constructed for an
   intended reader. It involves the writer
   in rehearsing, drafting, revising,
   editing and sharing.*
   Observation and discussion of first
   draft writing samples Years 2 to 6.
   Key statement: *A writing conference
   is a meeting that takes place between
   a teacher or other adult and students
   or among students themselves. The
   purpose of the conference is to talk
   with and help students with their
   writing. It should be a collaborative
   process.*
   Review video: *The Conference.*
   15 minutes

7. ENCOURAGING CHILDREN TO SPELL
   Key statement: *Learning to write involves
   learning to spell. Reading provides demonstration of standard spelling but reading
   alone is not enough. It is important that we
   become writers so that when we read we do
   so with a writer's sensitivity and are aware
   of correct demonstrations of spelling.*
   Review video: *Supporting the Writer.*
   Refer to OHT SW:2 *Stages of Spelling
   Development* and SW:3 *Observing Spelling.*
   25 minutes

8. 'PROCESS WRITING' IN ACTION
   Key statement: *Children involved in writing have a clear understanding of the
   purpose for writing. They are not writing
   to get a mark out of ten or to please the
   teacher. Children know their writing will
   be shared and discussed with others.*
   Parent/Child interaction.
   Parents talk and observe their child working on a piece of writing.
   30 minutes

9. HOMETASKS
   • Introduce 'Written Conversations'
     to the family.
   • Talk to your child about their writing.
     Remember to be interested and
     positive.
   • Select a favourite children's book to
     share with the group next session.
   5 minutes

Figure 11.1 *Sample session overview for Session 1 of Topic 7 (Research Writing) in the Stage 1 TTALL
Programme*

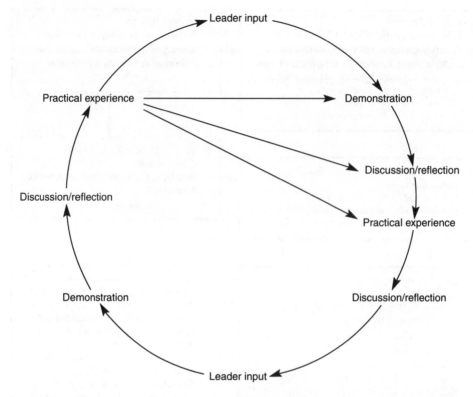

Figure 11.2 *Diagrammatic representation of the teaching/learning cycle used in the TTALL Programme*

their address, phone numbers, number and age of children, the class their child is in and the name of the teacher, and finally, their preferred meeting time and day.

From this initial information sheet groups are formed and an appropriate time selected for the programme to be conducted. Childcare is then arranged (if required); an appropriate venue secured, and arrangements made to commence the programme. A meeting is then held with the school or preschool staff to discuss the purpose of the programme and to consider their role in allowing parents to visit their rooms to observe literacy learners as well as to try a variety of literacy support strategies.

EVALUATION OF THE TTALL PROGRAMME

A comprehensive evaluation of TTALL was conducted to determine its impact on parents, students and the school and preschool. The TTALL programme was evaluated using the initial group to complete it. A total of 25 parents and their 34 children (aged from 1 to 12 years) served as the major participants in this evaluation. A further 75 students were selected randomly from all classes within the school to serve as a control group for comparison purposes.

The evaluation of the project was based on a variety of qualitative and quantitative measures. Pre- and post-test information (eight months apart) was obtained for all experimental and control students. This consisted of the ACER (Australian Council for Educational Research) primary survey comprehension and vocabulary tests, and the ACER spelling test. A test of reading attitudes was also devised and administered.

A variety of interviews (small group structured, large group unstructured interviews, and individual interviews) were also conducted with all parents before and after the programme. A written survey was also given to all parents at the conclusion of the programme.

Observations of class, group and home interactions were recorded in a variety of ways for later analysis. This included videotaping, detailed field notes, and the keeping of a reflective journal by the programme co-ordinator and assistant principal.

The quantitative test data were analysed using Analyses of Covariance (ANCOVA), while the qualitative data were analysed using a variety of procedures based on the principles of 'grounded theory'. This involved careful and repeated reading of the various sources of data to derive the major themes that were evident. Once these themes were identified, the data were analysed further using the constant comparative method (see Guba and Lincoln, 1981).

As a result of this process of inductive analysis nine major themes were identified.

The programme had an impact upon the way parents interact with their children

Analyses of parent interviews, and the post-programme survey, suggested that the programme led to changes in the way parents talk to and with their children. For example, when asked if the course had changed the way they talked to their children about school work, 19 parents (79 per cent) felt strongly that it had. The remaining five parents (21 per cent) felt less strongly about this, but agreed that it had affected them.

Analysis of video footage and direct observation of parent/child interactions also suggested that by the end of the programme parents were:

- offering more positive feedback;
- providing a different focus when listening to children reading (e.g. less emphasis on phonics);
- asking qualitatively different questions;
- providing qualitatively better responses to their children's writing and reading.

The programme offered parents strategies they did not have before

The data also suggested that the programme provided parents with new strategies for talking to their children about reading and writing. The post-programme survey showed that parents had begun to use a variety of new strategies. The strategies which were used most after the programme were personal spelling dictionaries (71 per cent), predictable books (67 per cent), Dialogue journals (59 per cent), Paired reading (54 per cent), and help with the editing of their child's work (50 per cent). Additionally, a majority of parents (92 per cent) indicated that they now listened regularly to their children reading.

The following journal entry shows how a research writing strategy was applied by one mother (Tracey). She shared how she had used a research strategy at home:

> We went through the steps just like you said, you know discovery draft, then we group the information and everything. I showed him how to use the table of contents and the index. He thought it was great, really easy. We grouped the information under the headings. It worked well, I didn't have to do all the work. I thought this session [i.e. the research session in TTALL] was the best.

The programme helped parents to choose resource material, help children with book selection, and use libraries more effectively

Parents in the TTALL programme were more aware of the diversity of resources available in the school and community. They were also more capable of finding appropriate resources within the community library, and could use a range of research skills that previously were not available to them.

Parents also demonstrated increased skill at selecting and making available a variety of literature for their children. Analysis of the earliest videos of parents reading to and with their children showed that over 55 per cent chose highly structured and uninteresting school readers. In contrast, in the final video session, not one school reading book was chosen. Instead children (and presumably parents) chose a variety of high quality fiction and non-fiction trade books. Parents also began regularly to seek advice on book selection, made frequent use of the library, and brought books along to sessions to share.

Parents gained new knowledge

When the post-programme evaluation was completed by parents it became clear that they firmly believed they had gained new knowledge about learning (100 per cent), writing (96 per cent), reading (100 per cent), and spelling (100 per cent). As well, all believed they were now more capable of dealing with their children's problems.

Observations of parents working with their own children also confirmed that this growth had occurred. As part of the evaluation many parents shared how the programme had helped them to gain confidence. Lynne was typical:

> I was saying to Sue today that I've noticed with Stephen he is best left by himself, he will get on and write, I mean he wrote all of this [Lynne produced some draft writing] by himself, umm while I was getting tea. Now the only word I had to help him with was 'hatched', he asked for that, but the rest he just sat down and wrote. But while we've been here this morning, I had to write the first sentence (he asked me) so he could think of the story, and he just fiddled and looked around the room, watched the other kids. I, I do find that he likes to be left on his own to just get on and do it.

The parents' families were affected

An interesting outcome of the TTALL programme was that it appeared to have an effect on the wider family. This was most evident in the way they spent their time. In parent self-reports 79 per cent suggested they now organized their homes in different ways in order to make time to help their children with their learning. During an interview one mother (Narelle) described how the programme had helped her to work with her eldest daughter, which in turn had influenced their relationship.

> I have found this activity [research skills] really great. It's brought my daughter and I closer together. The other smart one [meaning her son] just thought he was so clever, but my daughter and I have been working really hard. She really enjoys doing the project this way.

Another interesting outcome of the programme was that it led to changes in the reading and writing habits of specific children within families. For example, the following field note entry shows how the use of one of the programme strategies at home (research skills) had an impact upon the whole family.

> Deborah brought in her project today [which was done as part of the programme], beautifully illustrated . . . Deborah had done the writing, Dad had drawn the picture, and the boys had done the colouring, the paper crumpling, and had also collected some of the information. She commented: 'We all got down on the floor and worked on the project, it was great fun!'

The parents began to share their insights outside the family

One quite unexpected outcome of the project was that it had an impact on extended family members (e.g. sisters, brothers and their children, etc.), neighbours, and friends from other schools. Alice's comments illustrate this clearly:

> My sister's friend's kids can't read. My sister was telling them about the course I was doing. Anyway, they've asked me to help them out. I'm going to show this friend what to do. I'm really excited about it. I feel as if I can really do it now. I showed this friend all the books. She wants to do the course too, but I explained it was just for parents at this school. Anyway, we are making a bit of time for me to go over.

Parents gained a greater understanding of schools

An unexpected benefit of the programme was the finding that parents had an increased understanding of the ways schools operate. When asked in the post-programme evaluation if the TTALL programme had helped them to understand how schools worked, a majority (88 per cent) responded positively. This was confirmed through observations of the parents working in classrooms, and from the observations of the programme co-ordinator, classroom teachers and the school principal.

Parents grew in confidence and self-esteem

Participants in the TTALL programme also grew in confidence and self-esteem. The earlier reported observation that parents shared knowledge of the programme with people outside the school was evidence of this growing confidence. In the post-programme evaluation most parents indicated that they felt more confident working with their children (96 per cent), and when working as a parent in the school (92 per cent), and the majority (92 per cent) indicated that they wished to pursue further education. Parents expressed a desire to complete High School (two subsequently started), others wanted to enter the University of Western Sydney's community access programme (Unistart), one enrolled in the Bachelor of Education (Primary), two enrolled in adult literacy classes, and another became the co-ordinator of an adult literacy programme in the community.

Impact upon children's literacy performance levels, attitudes and interest

Although the TTALL programme was not designed to work with children directly, it was expected that the children of those parents involved would benefit. To gain some sense of the impact on children a variety of qualitative data were collected and confirmed that the children of TTALL parents were:

- more positive about themselves as learners;
- more confident readers and writers;
- reading more regularly;
- reading more difficult work;
- selecting a wider range of reading material;
- finding school work less difficult.

Analyses of a variety of standardized test measures also confirmed positive perform-ance gains for students of TTALL parents, relative to those students whose parents did not complete the programme.

Analyses of co-variance indicated statistically significant differences between the two groups in attitudes to literacy and vocabulary. This reflected the more positive attitude of the TTALL students on the post-test administration of this instrument, and their significant vocabulary gains relative to non-TTALL students. Significant gains in comprehension also occurred for TTALL subjects in grades 4 and 5. There were no statistically significant differences between the groups in spelling, although this was not surprising given the short length of the programme and the indirect nature of the intervention.

Impact of the programme on the school and preschool

Interviews with the staff indicated a number of specific ways in which the school and preschool were affected by the TTALL programme. The impact of TTALL took a number of forms. First, parents became more involved in school activities, classroom work, and school decision-making. As the elementary school principal commented:

> . . . there have always been interested parents, but to get them actually involved is another matter. You get some to turn up for special activities, but to actually get them involved in the classroom is difficult here . . . but they've become involved in classrooms and this makes them feel part of the school community rather than outsiders . . . as well, instead of 22 teachers, you've also got 25/30 trained people . . . not pencil sharpeners or

glue makers, but people who are actually involved in the learning process and who know what they are doing. . . .

A second major impact on the school was the development of more positive attitudes of teachers towards parents. This had many facets. Before TTALL many teachers had negative attitudes towards parents. One male teacher suggested: 'You'll never get these parents interested – no one will turn up.'

However, as the programme developed negativeness turned to guarded interest, and then finally changed attitudes. The principal provided an insight into this process of change:

> What we're trying to do is to create a culture where teachers are prepared to try things . . . if it's their project they'll make it succeed. This project fitted in perfectly. It opened a lot of teachers' eyes to what can be done with parent involvement.

Several teachers commented that they developed a better appreciation of the role that parents play in their children's education. A grade 3 teacher commented:

> I used to be fairly negative towards parents, they were a real threat to me – I saw them as the enemy almost. Now that I've had some of the TTALL parents in my classroom I've come to understand them more and see what they can do with their children. I've also seen that at times they know things about their children that I don't know.

Each of these comments indicated the shift in attitudes and perceptions that occurred for teachers. At the conclusion of the project teachers had gained new knowledge of parents, they had a better understanding of the role that parents play in their children's education, they learned to listen to parents and accepted the views expressed, and they began to engage more regularly with parents in conversations about educational issues and concerns. The 'reciprocity' that Harry (1992) speaks of had begun to develop.

A third major way in which TTALL affected the school and preschool was that it appeared to contribute to community development which had positive benefits for the teachers. The Deputy Principal explained this impact in the following way:

> The parents who've gone through TTALL have become quite a group, this is unusual in this community. They are the first ones to turn up for things, to sign up as committee members. They are the ones who are beginning to show an interest in forming a school council.

CONCLUSION

The TTALL programme has obviously been highly successful. It has obtained the participation of a number of parents who found it to be of great use to them. The evaluation of TTALL suggests that it leads to changes in the literacy practices of children and their families, and that teachers gain new knowledge and understanding of children and their families. The effect of these changes is to create a greater sense of partnership in the education of children involved.

While TTALL is a structured programme that has been designed and written by two literacy educators, its format and philosophy permits adaptations to be made to suit the needs of families and their children. For example, schools have adapted the content and delivery of TTALL to suit the needs of parents from diverse cultures. In some cases this has led to the presentation of the programme bilingually, while in others it has meant adaptations to programme content to match parent needs.

What TTALL offers is one starting point for the development of more effective partnerships with parents. Programmes like TTALL have the potential to facilitate the development of shared understanding, that is, 'intersubjectivity' (Vygotsky, 1978). The programme provides a vehicle to encourage a shared focus of attention through the literacy development of groups of children.

At the time this chapter was written over 200 schools were implementing the TTALL programme in Australia. This level of participation will permit further long-term evaluation to occur and new programmes to develop. An extension programme has already been developed for parents who have completed TTALL. This programme (the Parent Partnership Programme) is essentially a home-based programme that allows parents to share the insights gained as part of TTALL with other parents (Cairney and Munsie, 1995b). As well, additional funding has been obtained to develop a new programme for parents of secondary school children (Cairney and Munsie, 1993). This programme is particularly exciting because it has been initiated by parents in Western Sydney.

It is clear that TTALL has had an impact on the lives of the parents and children associated with the programme, as well as on the school and preschool in which it has been based. These findings support the claims of other researchers (e.g. Epstein, 1983; Topping and Wolfendale, 1985; Turner, 1987) that parent participation programmes have the potential to lead to significant gains in student ability to use literacy for a range of purposes.

The work in parent and family literacy in the past decade suggests that there is potential to develop more effective partnerships between schools and their communities. All schools have a responsibility to seek ways to facilitate partnership. As Cairney and Munsie (1992a) argue, all schools need to take positive steps to develop more effective partnerships with their communities. What is necessary is a preparedness to meet with and talk with parents about their hopes and aspirations for their children's education. Once this first step has been taken, schools need to look for starting points for the development of mutual responsibility for children's education. While parents and teachers can each have separate roles, there is much to be gained from partnerships.

The Talk to a Literacy Learner programme is one attempt to provide a vehicle for the development of such partnerships. The challenge for all of us is to seek to provide students with equal access to the literacy practices that they need to take their place in society. The development of close relationships between schools and their communities is an important starting point for the achievement of this outcome.

REFERENCES

Au, K. and Kawakami, A. (1984) Vygotskian perspectives on discussion processes in small-group reading lessons. In P. Peterson and L.C. Wilkinson (eds) *The Social Context of Instruction*, 209–25. Portsmouth, NH: Heinemann.

Auerbach, E. (1989) Toward a social-contextual approach to family literacy. *Harvard Educational Review*, **59**, 165–81.

Bourdieu, P. (1977) Cultural reproduction and social reproduction. In J. Karabel and A.H. Halsey (eds) *Power and Ideology in Education*. New York: Oxford University Press.

Cairney, T.H. (1991) Talking to Literacy Learners: the impact of an education programme upon parent/child interactions. Paper presented to the International Convention on Language and Learning, Norwich, 6–10 April.

Cairney, T.H. (1995) Family literacy: moving toward new partnerships in education. *Australian Journal of Language and Literacy*, **17**(4), 262–75.

Cairney, T.H. and Munsie, L. (1992a) *Beyond Tokenism: Parents as Partners in Literacy*. Melbourne: ARA.

Cairney, T.H. and Munsie, L. (1992b) *Talk to a Literacy Learner*. Sydney: UWS Press.

Cairney, T.H. and Munsie, L. (1993) *Effective Partners in Secondary Literacy Learning: Final Report to the Disadvantaged Schools Programme*. Sydney: UWS Press.

Cairney, T.H. and Munsie, L. (1995a) Parent participation in literacy learning. *The Reading Teacher*, **48**(5), 392–403.

Cairney, T.H. and Munsie, L. (1995b) *Parent Partnership Program*. Sydney: UWS Press.

Cazden, C. (1988) *Classroom Discourse*. Portsmouth, NH: Heinemann.

Delgado-Gaitan, C. (1991) Involving parents in schools: a process of empowerment. *American Journal of Education*, **100**, 20–45.

Delgado-Gaitan, C. (1992) School matters in the Mexican-American home: socializing children to education. *American Educational Research Journal*, **29**, 495–516.

Department of Education and Science (1967) *Children and Their Primary Schools: A Report of the Central Advisory Council for Education (England), Volume 1: Report, Volume 2: Research and Surveys* (Plowden Report). London: HMSO.

Epstein, J. (1983) *Effects on Parents of Teacher Practices of Parent Involvement*. Baltimore: Johns Hopkins University, Report No. 346, 277–94.

Epstein, J. and Dauber, S.L. (1991). School programmes and teacher practices of parent involvement in inner-city elementary and middle schools. *The Elementary School Journal*, **91**, 289–305.

Fitzgerald, L.M. and Goncu, A. (in press) Parent involvement in urban early childhood education: a Vygotskian approach. In S. Reifel (ed.) *Advances in Early Childhood Education and Day Care: A Research Annual*. Greenwich, CT: JAI Press.

Gee, J. (1990) *Social Linguistics and Literacies: Ideology in Discourses*. London: Falmer Press.

Guba, E. and Lincoln, Y. (1981) *Effective Evaluation*. San Francisco: Jossey-Bass.

Harry, B. (1992) An ethnographic study of cross-cultural communication with Puerto Rican-American families in the special education system. *American Educational Research Journal*, **29**, 471–94.

Heath, S.B. (1983) *Ways with Words: Language, Life and Work in Community and Classrooms*. Cambridge, UK: Cambridge University Press.

Kruger, T. and Mahon, L. (1990) Reading together: magical or mystifying. Paper presented to Australian Reading Association Conference, Canberra, 7–10 July.

Lankshear, C. and Lawler, M. (1987) *Literacy, Schooling and Revolution*. London: Falmer Press.

Lareau, A. (1991) *Home Advantage*. New York: Falmer Press.

Moll, L. (1988) Some key issues in teaching Latino students. *Language Arts*, **65**, 465–72.

Morgan, R.T.T. (1976) 'Paired Reading' tuition: a preliminary report on a technique for cases of reading deficit. *Child Care, Health and Development*, **2**, 13–28.

Neuman, S.B. and Daly, P. (in press) *Guiding Young Children: A Family Literacy Approach*. Unpublished report.

Nickse, R. (1993) A typology of family and intergenerational literacy programmes; implications for evaluation. *Viewpoints*, **15**, 34–40.

Petit, D. (1980) *Opening up Schools*. Harmondsworth: Penguin.

Power, J. (1994) Educating parents: improving literacy instruction in the home. Unpublished paper.

Rasinski, T.V. and Fredericks, A.D. (1989) Dimensions of parent involvement. *The Reading Teacher*, **43**(2), 180–2.

Rutter, M., Tizard, J. and Whitmore, K. (1970) *Education, Health and Behaviour*. London: Longmans.

Schaefer, E. (1991) Goals for parent and future parent education: research on parental beliefs and behaviour. *Elementary School Journal*, **91**, 239–47.

Soliman, I. (1992) Family and community participation in education. *Family and Community Participation in Education*, **2**, 1–8.

Street, B. (1984) *Literacy in Theory and Practice*. Cambridge, UK: Cambridge University Press.

Thompson, W.W. (1985) Environmental effects on educational performance. *The Alberta Journal of Educational Psychology*, **31**, 11–25.

Tizard, J., Schofield, W. and Hewison, J. (1982) Collaboration between teachers and parents in assisting children's reading. *British Journal of Educational Psychology*, **52**, 1–15.

Topping, K. and Wolfendale, S. (eds) (1985) *Parental Involvement in Children's Reading*. Beckenham, UK: Croom Helm.

Turner, R. (1987) *SHARE Project – Doveton Cluster: A Case Study*. Melbourne: Ministry of Education.

Vygotsky, L. (1978) *Mind and Society: The Development of Higher Mental Processes*. Cambridge, MA: Harvard University Press.

Part 3

Overview and Future Directions

Chapter 12

The Effectiveness of Family Literacy

Keith Topping

Defining 'family literacy' is difficult, and reviewing the effectiveness of family literacy programmes therefore even more difficult.

In this book, we have taken any small constellation of adult(s) and child(ren) committed to living closely together for an extended period to constitute a 'family'. We have taken 'literacy' to mean activities and competencies in oral language, reading, writing and spelling.

However, 'family literacy' cannot be defined merely by amalgamating these two sentences. Some of the additional identifying parameters of family literacy programmes are:

1. Family literacy targets gains in literacy competence, motivation and self-image for all participants – child and adult.
2. Family literacy seeks to enable family members to help each other to achieve such gains – both intergenerationally and intragenerationally – now and in the future.
3. Family literacy values the existing home culture and competencies of family members and builds on these.
4. Family literacy targets gains in literary competence in relation to the needs, uses, objectives and values of all participants, not just those of the school system. Family literacy seeks to link the needs and competencies of the home/community and school environments so far as possible.
5. Family literacy seeks to offer equal opportunities and access to all members of all families of all kinds.

It is clear that family literacy is about education, not schooling. It is not about the 'transmission of school practices' (Nash, 1987; Auerbach, 1989) from teacher to parent to child. Equally, family literacy is about empowerment, not remediation. It is not something that is done to families, to raise them to a fixed criterion of adequacy and increase their contribution to the engines of industry. It is done with families to give them greater adaptive control over their own future, as literacy demands are constantly increasing. Today's functionally literate adult might not be considered such in another decade.

Teachers and other professionals can be left wondering what they should do to serve their community best. Castigated in the early days of parental involvement for all too often speaking to parents in white middle-class vague generalities which many parents could not operationalize, those who moved to giving parents very specific structured training were sometimes accused of thereby disempowering those they sought to help – creating dependency and failing to value existing parental competencies. Establishing individually where each family was starting from and negotiating unique compromises seemed likely to prove highly consumptive of resources – with the result that only a few families could be helped and equal opportunity principles would be hopelessly compromised.

All of this is a quagmire for evaluators. Do we know what objectives have been, or should be, set for family literacy programmes? Is it possible to measure whether these have been achieved? How can we tell if some kinds of programme work better (or only) with some kinds of schools and families? And how can relative cost-effectiveness be estimated? These questions will be addressed, though not resolved, in this chapter.

The chapter commences by proposing a simple common framework for the review of family literacy initiatives. This is then applied to the effectiveness data provided by each contributed chapter to this book. Other evidence on the effectiveness of parental involvement in reading and on family literacy programmes is then considered. Studies discussed in detail in contributed chapters are not revisited at length. The chapter concludes with a brief summary and an indication of directions for future research.

Discriminating 'parental involvement in reading' and 'family literacy' programmes is problematic. Some of the early parental involvement in reading programmes always had strong family literacy overtones, while others have developed these over the years. Conversely, some more recent programmes may call themselves 'family literacy' programmes (this being currently fashionable), when on closer inspection they are found to feature few of the identifying parameters. As with any other educational development, faulty labelling and dilution through imperfect dissemination and incorrect replication can cause confusion.

AN EVALUATIVE FRAMEWORK

'Family literacy' includes a wide range of very varied practice, operating in very various contexts. Some specific interventions may only be effective in specific contexts. In other words, research must seek to identify interaction between treatment effect and aptitude to benefit from that treatment.

Evaluation is far from being an exact science, especially when applied to educational and community innovation in 'real life' settings. Family literacy initiatives are highly complex in the ways they produce their effects, even where the superficial organization is relatively simple. Furthermore, the hoped for effects are also subtle and complex, and extremely difficult to measure with adequate validity and reliability, even given an inexhaustible research budget.

In such a situation, apparently similar evaluative measures can yield very disparate results in a highly unpredictable manner. For instance, Topping (1995) noted that in his research on Paired Reading, norm-referenced reading tests of very similar type

Table 12.1   *Planning family literacy initiatives*

Stage I	Stage II
Starting points + first considerations	*Planning*
Objectives Current policy on parent– school relations School factors Current curriculum policies Other current initiatives Personnel Costing Clarification of aims	Objectives Target children Compatibility with existing provisions Reading method Materials Personnel Assessing, measuring, evaluating Record-keeping Training Time-scale Maintaining and monitoring
Stage III	**Stage IV**
Action	*Maintaining and monitoring*
Objectives Approaching parents Consideration in approaching parents Preparing children Preparing resources Training Terms of the agreement	Objectives Checking on the practicalities Monitoring progress: record keeping Feedback Meetings Home visiting Assessment
Stage V	
Measurement and evaluation	
Objectives Scope Design and methodology Measurement techniques Evaluation and types of evaluation Treatment of results Aftermath	

and construction produced very different results and test gains showed no relationship with the likelihood of practice effects, the availability or otherwise of parallel forms, or the ability range relevance of the instrument. Group reading tests did show greater variability than individual reading tests, but the latter were much more expensive in time to administer. From these data it was possible to list the reading tests most and least likely to give 'good' results when evaluating family literacy programmes.

It follows that if, unhappily, you do not demonstrate effectiveness in your family literacy programme, it may be because:

- the programme did not work;
- the programme did not work in your context, i.e. you chose a programme which could be effective elsewhere, but which is the wrong programme for you and your situation;

- the programme did work, but your measurements are too crude to capture the effects, i.e. you chose the wrong evaluative tool or methodology for the job;
- the programme was not made to work, i.e. the intended structure of the programme was fine for your context, but your organization of it was poor.

This last point is crucial. In reviewing evaluation research, it is not easy to be sure that like is being compared with like. Two programmes with the same name and structure operated at two sites offering identical contexts and populations may still yield very different outcome results on the same measures. Why? On one site the co-ordinator was always present, energetic, motivated and well-organized, while on the other . . . (A guide to the organizational elements of family literacy programmes is given in Table 12.1.)

This example highlights the dangers of making sweeping assertions or assumptions about particular programmes on the basis of evaluation data. Evaluations must themselves be carefully evaluated, although full information may not be available to the enquirer.

Additional problems arise when attempting to review studies which are overtly or covertly diverse, in an area of innovation. Many programmes in a rapidly expanding field are more concerned with the exigencies of survival than with the niceties of summative evaluation. If they have time for evaluation at all, it will be spent on formative evaluation, constantly fine-tuning the programme in response to ongoing informal (and often unsystematic) observation and feedback.

Thus, in a rapidly expanding innovative area, formal meta-analytic procedures are rarely usefully applicable, since they accept only data meeting traditional standards of scientific rectitude. Such data are often most available from student research theses, where much attention has been paid to 'proper' research design and often rather less to making sure that the programme actually worked to benefit its clients. Formal meta-analysis thus biases its outcomes by its selection processes, much as the published research literature is biased by submission and acceptance selectivities.

Given these caveats, formulating an overview of effectiveness in family literacy is obviously difficult. However, it is essential to make the attempt. A simple framework for appraising family literacy projects is offered in Table 12.2.

Where the meanings of the headings are not self-evident, they will be explored in the ensuing discussion of the contributed chapters. For those interested in evaluation, Auerbach (1990, pp. 204–5) offers a useful checklist for designing an evaluation of your own family literacy initiative – asking fundamental What? When? Who? How? questions.

REVIEW OF CONTRIBUTED CHAPTERS

The first four chapters concerned projects nominally listed under 'parental involvement in reading'. However, features of the family literacy approach are nonetheless evident.

Roger Hancock and Sarah Gale reported on the PACT scheme, involving parents reading with their early primary (elementary) school children at home and completing a home–school reading diary card. The project had operated for ten years, take-up had been high and work had flowed into numeracy, with all its implications for

Table 12.2 *An evaluative framework for family literacy programmes*

A. TARGETS AND METHODS

1.	Elements of literacy	(reading, writing, language)
2.	Lifespan	(of project, to date)
3.	Objectives	(cognitive, affective, social?)
4.	Method	(location, training, materials)
5.	Child age	(of primary target child)
6.	Child/parent ability	(? low literacy, special needs)
7.	Take-up	(total/proportional/dropout)

B. IDENTIFYING PARAMETERS

1. Builds on home culture
2. Enables client purposes
3. Links home and school
4. Equal opportunities/access

C. OUTCOMES

1.	Research design/type	
2.	Process data	(what happened during the project)
3.	Attainment gain	(for parent/child/teacher)
4.	Motivation/self-image	(parent/child/teacher)
5.	Subjective feedback	(on/by parent/child/teacher)
6.	Observations/behaviour	(of/by parent/child/teacher)
7.	Maintenance	(of gains at long-term follow-up)
8.	Generalization	(to other people, places, tasks)
9.	Spinoff	(unexpected/additional gains)
11.	Goal attainment	(see A.3)
10.	Cost-effectiveness	(known or estimated)

language development. The authors emphasized that wide dissemination brings great variety, not all of it necessarily productive, and commented that dissemination is itself another phase of testing. Nevertheless, the project was accessible to very many families on an equal opportunity basis.

Improved reading attainments were not considered the only indicator of success and formative evaluation via qualitative impressionistic data was preferred. Children spent more time with more books, were more interested in books, and library loans and family purchase of books increased substantially. There had been spinoff into other home–school activities, and changes to classroom and whole-school practice. Other benefits might be diffuse or long term and difficult or impossible to measure. The need to renew interest to cyclically revitalize the project was underscored.

The authors emphasized that the project was successful in enabling parents to share skills, ideas and knowledge with each other. They warned against omitting close parental consultation and attention to organizational detail at the planning stage, in the rush to implement. Family literacy was embedded in the social processes and cultural traditions of everyday life – family literacy was not schooled literacy. But the security of knowing there was no conflict between expectations at home and those at school could provide powerful support for children.

Peter Branston described the ten-year CAPER programme, involving parents in a variety of reading activities at home with their primary and secondary children via attendance at reading workshops and 'clinics', supplemented with a reading advisory centre. In the first three years of the project, 113 schools were involved and take-up had undoubtedly been high.

More formal evaluation focused only on nursery (kindergarten) children, not the main target group. One study comparing with a control group showed significant CAPER effectiveness on three norm-referenced tests and a criterion-referenced test, but in a second and larger study the differences were not significant. However, the second study found that CAPER children requested, borrowed and spent more time with books and their parents than did controls. Parents reported that their children were more interested in books, that they themselves felt more confident and that they expected their children to benefit in the future. CAPER was successful in drawing in fathers, extended families and members of the wider community. Spinoff included parental involvement in other areas and the teachers learning a good deal about parents, children and the reading process.

PACT and CAPER mainly focused on reading benefits for children, rather than wider literacy benefits for the whole family including those with restricted literacy. The chapters on Pause Prompt Praise (Glynn) and Paired methods (Topping) showed how workers began to broaden the scope.

Ted Glynn reviewed 18 years' work with Pause Prompt Praise, a specific technique for more able readers to tutor weak readers of primary or lower secondary age at home or in other settings, specifically to raise their reading competence. The PPP work was characterized by excellent process data, indicating that the training given did alter tutor behaviour. Approaching a score of studies had found norm-referenced reading test gains of between 1.5 and 11 times 'normal' rates of gain. Substantial gains for tutors had been demonstrated, but so far only with peer tutors. Both longitudinal single case study and group comparison data were available – the former difficult to summarize. A longer term follow-up study was reported to be in progress.

Glynn emphasized that learning in one environment did not automatically generalize to another, and indeed children might learn behaviours in one which were incompatible with learning in another – methods should therefore be designed to avoid 'instructional dependence'. His work with Khmer and Maori families testified to this, and the work on empirically evaluating training procedures which start 'where the parent is at' merits wider replication in other programmes. There is clearly great potential here for sibling tutoring, possibly in dual languages. Considering that this programme targets weak and disabled readers (who may be tutors or tutees) on the basis of structured but brief training, cost-effectiveness is likely to be comparatively high.

Some similarities with the Paired methods outlined in Keith Topping's chapter were evident, except that Paired Reading had developed into other literacy areas with Paired Writing and Cued Spelling. PR had been around since 1976, while Topping's own work with it spanned 14 years. All of these were structured methods in which participants were briefly trained, and which could be applied to any materials or task to hand and of interest, in any setting. They were effective with all children and should be offered on open access to all, irrespective of ability, although children with reading difficulties could be more persistently targeted, especially those of secondary age. When used at home, home–school diary cards sustained communication, and in a small minority of cases home visits might be added. The objective was to raise attainment, motivation and confidence.

Take-up of Paired Reading had been extensive, the published studies alone including almost 4000 subjects. However, dilution through dissemination had been a problem. PR had generated relatively little process data, what there was showing considerable variation in 'purity' of technique. Reading test gains had been large, certainly many times 'normal' rates, in controlled and baselined studies. Gains appeared to be sustained at short- and long-term follow-up. Cued Spelling had fared similarly well in eight small-scale studies, many of peer tutoring, while Paired Writing awaited further quantitative evaluation. Gains for tutors had been demonstrated for both PR and CS, but again only with peer tutors. For both, parents, teachers and children had given very positive structured subjective feedback, reporting improved motivation, interest and confidence in children.

Training in these methods was standardized, specific, structured and brief – the aim was to give all tutors a similar guaranteed experience of success, on which they could build their own individualized variations. Because the methods were materials-free, they were ideal for non-institutional operation for the client's own purposes, e.g. with adult literacy volunteers in the community. They could also be used in any written language – families for whom English was a second language participated using dual text books and tapes. Spinoff included developing confidence in both families and schools to proceed to Paired Maths and Paired Science. Longer-term generalization effects included many tutees becoming tutors.

Moving on to the chapters within the family literacy section proper, Hannon reported a recent pilot whole-literacy project emphasizing environmental print, narrative and story with preschool children aged 2 to 3 years, entailing six meetings at home and five at school. The project was open to all families within a geographical area, but the time costs of involvement were significant.

Interviews, work samples and field notes indicated that parents recognized their child's literacy activity, interacted with them and modelled more developed literacy related behaviour. Children experienced much greater contact with books than pre-project. Directions for further research were indicated. Hannon emphasized the need to build on and extend home literacy through tasks that were real and important to the child, rather than imposing school literacy.

A whole literacy approach was also taken by Kemp's Parents as Tutors Pro-gramme (PTP), developed over 20 years, which involved detailed training in 10 two-hour meetings for the parents of primary and secondary children with literacy difficulties. Catering for 120 families per year, it could be followed by the Individual Assistance Programme (IAP).

In two sample groups who completed both PTP and IAP, there was strong evidence of changed parental tutoring styles. Children improved from baseline on criterion-referenced measures of reading error rate and style, but it was unclear whether practice effects were controlled for by the distal comparison group, the more able of which showed less instructional dependence than the PTP group. In a mailed questionnaire survey with a 36 per cent response rate, the vast majority of parents felt their child was reading better. Process data were also kept on video by parents.

The programme commenced with individual parent consultative interviews, and this was followed through by an emphasis on parents helping each other. Spinoff included PTP parents becoming a resource for the whole class of school, as volunteers, trainers or monitors. Teachers in postgraduate study were involved in the programme delivery, a valuable learning experience for them. Although labour intensive, it should be remembered that the PTP targeted children with reading difficulty.

Gregory reported on a two-year programme targeted on bilingual families, using 'family literacy packs' on a structured home visiting basis, with the aim of raising reading attainment and *teacher* expectations of the 5- to 7-year-old children. Her chapter was an object lesson in building on the home culture, avoiding myths and false assumptions. She noted that parents and schools had very different objectives and expectations, and stressed the importance of fulfilling parents' own needs for their children.

The intensive programme operated with a small number of families, developing a deep individualized negotiated relationship with each. Gregory asserted strongly that equal treatment does not generate equal opportunity. Spinoff included a striking demonstration of how the education system could disempower children and *create* deficits. The cost-effectiveness of this intensive programme must be questioned, but compared to what? In comparison to Reading Recovery (Deford *et al.*, 1991), for instance, it may seem inexpensive.

Project SELF-HELP, reported by Connors, made a statement by its very name. This school-based programme targeted low-literacy parents and included adult education classes for parents (three hours two days per week), homework tasks, stimulatory day care for preschool children and a summer reading immersion aspect. Literacy, life and parenting skills were covered. Possible attendance was 62 sessions (total 186 hours), average attendance was 32 sessions. Twelve families were served per year.

On norm-referenced tests, *parents* made very large gains in maths and lesser gains in reading and spelling. Control groups were not available, but such gains could not plausibly be attributed wholly to practice effects. The children showed improved concepts about print, language comprehension and letter recognition. Observational data were kept in the form of field notes and case study data were also given.

Connors noted the very large parental time commitment, but access to the programme could be at any point. She commented that where educational objectives for each family were individualized, gains would not readily be apparent on crude norm-referenced tests of out-of-context skills – nevertheless her programme demonstrated such gains. Clearly, this programme was expensive and small in scale. Its cost-effectiveness must be considered in the light of the fact that it was one of the relatively few programmes to demonstrate substantial gains in parent literacy. Spinoff included more positive opinions of the school in the community and consolidation of contact with 'hard-to-reach' families.

Similarly, Phillips reported a programme working with parents alone and parent and child together, targeting gains for both and concerned with a very wide range of literacy-related activities. Parent 'Action Groups' met in local schools, continuing for periods as long as two years. Accreditation for parental learning gains was inbuilt. The Parents' Centre had developed its work over a 20-year period. The All About Us programme focused on children aged 3 to 6 years, but other work with primary and secondary aged children was undertaken.

A major emphasis was improving the confidence of disadvantaged parents – 'parents helping parents help themselves' – who kept personal records of achievement which were matched with the observations of professional staff. Parents' gains were individualized and not readily summarized, but a majority of parents reported helping their children in new ways at home. While the Centre was open to all families in the area, the parental time commitment was heavy. However, schools were seen as increasingly accessible by families.

The 'Talk To A Literacy Learner' programme described by Cairney dealt with reading and writing through a participative workshop approach, with the main objective of improving parent and child *attitudes* to literacy. Improvement in the confidence of parents, children *and* teachers was seen as vital. The programme was embodied in a 125-page parent handbook, co-ordinator's manual, video and other materials. Over a 12-year period, more than 100 schools had participated.

Good quality process data were available, showing changes in parental behaviour. Outcome data included pre–post test results for children on comprehension, vocabulary, spelling and reading attitudes, in comparison to a randomly selected control group. Participants did better on all measures except spelling, although comprehension improvement was more evident in older children. Parents felt more confident at home with their children and in school, and their own aspirations for themselves rose. In group and individual interviews and on a questionnaire, parents gave positive feedback and reported changing their helping style with their children at home in favour of new strategies. Observational data included field notes, video records and reflective diaries.

Cairney noted 'schooling is a cultural practice' and asked for 'genuine reciprocity' between schools and parents, involving true Vygotskian 'inter-subjectivity'. Spinoff included greater parental understanding of and involvement in the operation of schools and a more positive view of parents by teachers. Families came to organize their time in a different way to enable more contact between parents and children.

THE EFFECTIVENESS OF PARENTAL INVOLVEMENT IN READING

This area was covered in detail in the precursor to the current volume (Topping and Wolfendale, 1985), and material in that book will not be revisited here. Substantial new data have become available.

Perhaps most notable are the long-term follow-up data from the Haringey project (see Hewison in Topping and Wolfendale, 1985). The Haringey Reading Project was a two-year intervention with children aged 6 to 8 years in a disadvantaged area. Parents were encouraged to 'hear their children read' at home. Supportive home visits were made. At the end of the project, participant children performed significantly better on a range of norm-referenced reading tests than the control group of non-participants and a comparison group who received extra small-group reading tuition in school. Hewison (1988) conducted a follow-up three years after the end of the project, by which time some of the children were in different schools. The test result differences between the three groups was still evident.

The Belfield project in northern England also involved parents 'hearing' their children read, in a disadvantaged area, but for three years and without home visits (see Hannon *et al.* in Topping and Wolfendale, 1985). Participant children's reading test scores were compared with those of similar children who had passed through the school before the project, and no significant differences found (Hannon, 1987). While it is possible that the absence of home visiting accounts for some of the difference in test results between Haringey and Belfield, Topping (1995) found in Paired Reading projects that although home visiting improved test outcomes, disadvantaged families still registered significant test gains without it. It is possible that the Belfield test results were a case of research methods proving insufficiently sensitive, since by numerous other 'softer' process and outcome measures, the project was undoubtedly highly successful.

Significant reading achievement gains were recorded by Shuck *et al.* (1983) in their inner-city 'Parents Encourage Pupils' project. Webb *et al.* (1985) evaluated a project with 8-year-old children in an Armed Forces family school in Germany, a difficult transient population. Most families had just one home visit during the project. On reading tests, participant children gained twice as much as the control group. A comparison of parental involvement using reading books, reading games or a combination of these was reported by Loveday and Simmons (1988). The three matched experimental groups made similar gains on reading tests, but attitudes to reading improved most in the children who played reading games. There was also a suggestion that fathers might more readily involve themselves in games than books.

A more mixed picture emerged in a study of parental involvement in reading with 7- to 8-year-olds in a disadvantaged area reported by Ashton *et al.* (1986). No home visits were made. Subjective feedback was very positive and participant children read far more books than before. Three reading tests were used on a pre–post basis with a comparison group. Two of these showed no significant difference between participant and comparison children, but the third showed bigger gains for the project children, especially the weaker readers.

For younger children, there has been interest in the effects of encouraging parents to read to their offspring. Wade (1986) involved parents of 3- to 8-year-olds in telling and listening to stories, studying the children's ability to tell and retell stories on a pre–post basis over six months and at 18-month follow-up. At post-test participants significantly outperformed controls on both measures. At follow-up differences in subsequent gains were not significant, i.e. the experimental gains had not washed out.

France and Hager (1992) reported on a six-session read-aloud workshop for disadvantaged and minority parents and kindergarten children. Participants outperformed controls on two measures of listening comprehension over a 12-week period. Arnold and Whitehurst (1994) report similar work with disadvantaged 2- to 3-year-olds, gains being sustained at six-month follow-up.

Swinson (1985) demonstrated improvement in the language skills of nursery children as a result of parents' reading to them. He then replicated this (Swinson and Ellis, 1988) with children aged 3½ to 10 years with severe developmental delay, finding that participants made more than twice the progress in measured language skills than a comparison group.

Other projects have targeted children with special needs. Portsmouth *et al.* (1985) evaluated a parent 'hearing read' approach with moderately developmentally delayed children aged 8 to 15 who attended a special school. Substantial gains in reading accuracy for participants were claimed, compared to negligible gains for controls, although participants did not do better on reading comprehension or listening vocabulary tests and there are inconsistencies in the data presented. Special education students enrolled in an Intensive Learning Centre (learning disabled, emotionally disturbed and educable mentally retarded) were involved in a brief programme by Vinograd-Bausell *et al.* (1986). Students took home sight word flashcards with a sheet of instructions for parents, i.e. there was no direct professional/parent contact. After two weeks the participants significantly outperformed controls on a word recognition test. It is not stated what teaching the parents actually did, or whether the test gains endured or were generalized to meaningful reading.

A larger-scale approach to the question was taken by Rowe (1991), who gathered data on 5092 children aged 5 to 14 years in 100 Australian schools. Reading attitudes and activity levels were measured by pupil self-report and reading achievement by a reading comprehension test and teacher ratings. Family socio-economic status was found to account for a very small proportion of the variance in attitudes and achievement, while maternal educational level accounted for a good deal more. The amount of reading activity at home showed a substantial positive relationship to reading achievement (which increased with age), attitudes to reading and general attentiveness in school, regardless of gender.

The majority of the parental involvement in reading literature reporting 'objective' outcomes thus provides evidence of generally positive results. Subjective feedback from participants, gathered in various ways, is ubiquitously positive. Long-term follow-up data are very limited in quantity, but are positive. However, remembering the positive bias in published literature, the expectations of project leaders should remain realistic.

THE EFFECTIVENESS OF FAMILY LITERACY

Programmes with applications and objectives wider than parental involvement in children's reading are correspondingly more complex to evaluate.

A fascinating multiple case study account of untrained reading tutoring of children by their elder siblings was reported by Norris and Stainthorp (1991).

Very substantial contributions to progress in knowledge have been made by Toomey (1989, 1993) and Toomey and Sloane (1991, 1994), based on the West Heidelberg Early Literacy Project in Australia. Noting that more traditional forms of opportunity for parental contact and involvement might only serve to further advantage the already advantaged (Toomey, 1989), they operated their preschool programme for disadvantaged families through home visits until the prohibitive cost led to service delivery from local preschool day care facilities. Although the main focus was parents' reading and discussing books with children, there was also some emphasis on accessing environmental print, drawing and writing.

Results on the Sulzby test of emergent literacy (Sulzby, 1985) and other tests of literacy competence showed that although the comparison group was initially more competent than the experimental group, at post-test the programme participant children were significantly superior. However, these gains did not significantly carry over into measures of school literacy. Of course, it is not uncommon for interventions effective in raising attainment pre-school to fail to show significant measurable transfer effects to the school environment (Topping, 1986) – generalization is not automatic.

A three-month British parent involvement project targeted on 5-year-olds newly in school, involving all aspects of literacy and other curriculum and home activity areas, is reported by Dye (1989). Parents made weekly visits to the children's class and engaged in suggested activities with their child at home. Participants and controls were pre- and post-tested in 44 areas of competency, including mathematics and general knowledge. Participants showed significant gains in 22 of these, controls showed gains in only three. On norm-referenced tests of language and basic concepts, participants significantly out-performed controls.

Much of the other research on the effectiveness of family literacy comes from the USA, particularly the Kenan, Even Start and PACE models already referred to by Connors (see Chapter 9). Many other reports can be found on programmes claiming to be successful, but as Fisk (1990) noted in his review of intergenerational literacy programmes, a great deal of this 'evidence' is anecdotal. Franklin (1989) produced a useful survey of 16 intergenerational literacy projects, but some of these focused on adult literacy with only peripheral child involvement, and the evaluation details given are limited.

The PACE family literacy programme has demonstrated increased parental and child literacy, raised parental acquisition of formal qualifications, and raised parental expectations for their children (Heberle, 1992).

The Kenan programme has demonstrated over 14 sites increases in observed and self-reported literacy related behaviours and self-expectations, the child participants subsequently doing well in school. Participant children entered Chapter 1 or special education at lower rates than otherwise expected (Darling and Hayes, 1989; Darling, 1992, 1993; Seaman, 1992).

The Even Start programme has involved children aged 0 to 7 years, encompassing 503 sites and 35 000 families (by 1994). Gains on norm-referenced tests of school readiness and language development ($n = 1211$) at above 'normal' rates have been reported for participant children, but without control group data. A positive relationship between degree of child gain and degree of parental programme involvement was found. Participant adults have shown small pre–post gains on measures of literacy competence (St Pierre *et al.*, 1991, 1993).

None of these have provided long-term follow-up data, and Connors characterized the current scene as one of 'small wins'.

CONCLUSION

It seems that although the evaluation research on parental involvement in reading is generally positive, the picture for family literacy is still incomplete. Evaluative evidence to date is very various in quality and quantity. This is unsurprising for an innovatory type of intervention, especially one aiming at more numerous and more difficult targets. Nevertheless, there is much which is encouraging.

For the future, issues of generalization and maintenance of gains, and of cost-effectiveness, will be especially important. Do child gains evident out of school generalize into 'schooled literacy'? If not, why not, and what should and can be done about it? Does increased parental competence as prime community educator of one child automatically generalize to application with other family members – and if not, how can this be ensured? Whatever the immediate gains are, how can we be sure they do not wash out in the longer run?

Some family literacy programmes are very costly to operate. Funds will never be available to replicate them on a scale large enough to serve all who are in need. How can we produce similar positive effects more cheaply, maximizing cost-effectiveness and thereby widening access and equal opportunities? The costs of involvement to the families themselves must be scrutinized. Some of the intensive workshop programmes consume a great deal of parental time, inevitably excluding some otherwise well-motivated parents. Centre-based meetings can mean cash expenditure for parents on travel and care for smaller children. Cost-effectiveness must not be seen purely in terms of costs to professionals.

These large questions will only be finally answered some way down the road. For the present, as emphasized by Sheila Wolfendale in the following chapter, it is important that those working in the field speak the same language and share the same definitions so far as possible. What is 'family literacy'? The evaluation of Even Start is the evaluation of myriad disparate programmes, not a homogeneous entity – this becomes a problem if we and others are not aware of it and jump to faulty conclusions. Nickse (1990, 1993) has most helpfully offered the beginnings of a typology of programmes, objectives and methods of evaluation for family literacy.

We all need to be cultivating the host environment in government, schools and community – successful programmes do not spring up overnight. Better later and well than sooner and badly. We need to develop better methods of tutoring to propose to parents, which are widely acceptable and unlikely to clash with most home cultures. In concert, we need to develop inexpensive and more effective methods of recruiting, training and supporting parents and children.

To guide us on the way, we need more sensitive, more reliable and valid, less intrusive and threatening evaluation measures, particularly of adult literacy competence and child literacy competence out of school. We need better research designs, with meaningful but objective evaluation integrated into major programmes from the outset, especially to tease out aptitude × treatment interactions.

When linking home and school, we need to value and build upon the home culture and enable the clients' own purposes – beware pedagogical imperialism! Most of all, we need to offer wider access and more equal opportunities to all parents and children: irrespective of the age of the child(ren), socio-economic status, membership of ethnic, language or religious minorities, in rural and urban settings, whether with or without special educational needs.

As was noted by the Bernard van Leer Foundation (1986) from a truly international perspective:

> Much depends on the political, social and economic circumstances in which programmes operate. However, in the current economic circumstances, governments are not necessarily predisposed to increase spending on social programmes. The classical routes to institutionalisation and dissemination are via evaluation, publication and influencing of policy with a view to gaining access to national resources. These strategies do not always work. In situations of gross deprivation it is essential to look to other avenues which might ensure long-term continuity. The greatest single resource which the community can contribute is its own time, effort and dedication. (p. 12)

REFERENCES

Arnold, D.S. and Whitehurst, G.J. (1994) Accelerating language development through picture book reading: a summary of dialogic reading and its effects. In D.K. Dickinson, *Bridges to Literacy: Children, Families and Schools*. Oxford: Blackwell.

Ashton, C.J., Stoney, A.H. and Hannon, P.W. (1986) A reading at home project in a first school. *Support For Learning,* **1**(1), 43–9.

Auerbach, E.R. (1989) Toward a social-contextual approach to family literacy. *Harvard Educational Review,* **59**(2), 165–81.

Auerbach, E.R. (1990) *Making Meaning, Making Change: A Guide to Participatory Curriculum Development for Adult ESL and Family Literacy.* Boston, MA: University of Massachusetts.

Bernard van Leer Foundation (1986) *The Parent As Prime Educator: Changing Patterns of Parenthood* (Summary report and conclusions of the Fourth Western Hemisphere Seminar in Lima, Peru). The Hague, Netherlands: Bernard van Leer Foundation.

Darling, S. (1992) *Family Literacy: The Need and the Promise.* Louisville, KY: National Center for Family Literacy.

Darling, S. (1993) Family literacy: an intergenerational approach to education. In Adult Literacy and Basic Skills Unit (ed.) *Family Literacy* (Viewpoints No. 15). London: ALBSU.

Darling, S. and Hayes, A.E. (1989) *Breaking the Cycle of Illiteracy: The Kenan Family Literacy Model Program.* Louisville, KY: National Center for Family Literacy.

Deford, D.E., Lyons, C.A. and Pinnell, G.S. (1991) *Bridges to Literacy: Learning from Reading Recovery.* Portsmouth, NH: Heinemann.

Dye, J.S. (1989) Parental involvement in curriculum matters: parents, teachers and children working together. *Educational Research,* **31**(1), 20–35.

Fisk, W.R. (1990) *Intergenerational Literacy: A Review of Programs.* Clemson, SC: Clemson University.

France, M.G. and Hager, J.M. (1992) Effects of an intergenerational reading workshop on the listening comprehension of at-risk kindergarten students. Paper presented at the Annual Convention of the International Reading Association, Orlando, Florida.

Franklin, M. (1989) *Intergenerational Literacy Projects: What Works.* Little Rock, AK: Arkansas Department of Education.

Hannon, P. (1987) A study of the effects of parental involvement in the teaching of reading on children's reading test performance. *British Journal of Educational Psychology,* **57**, 56–72.

Heberle, J. (1992) PACE: Parent and Child Education in Kentucky. In T.G. Sticht, M.J. Beeler and B.A. McDonald (eds) *The Intergenerational Transfer of Cognitive Skills, Vol. 1: Programs, Policy and Research Issues.* Norwood, NJ: Ablex.

Hewison, J. (1988) The long term effectiveness of parental involvement in reading: a follow-up to the Haringey Reading Project. *British Journal of Educational Psychology,* **58**, 184–90.

Loveday, E. and Simmons, K. (1988) Reading at home: does it matter what parents do? *Reading,* **22**(2), 84–8.

Nash, A. (1987) *English Family Literacy: An Annotated Bibliography.* Boston: University of Massachusetts at Boston.

Nickse, R. (1990) Family literacy and community education: prospects for the '90s. *Journal of Community Education,* **3**(2), 12–18.

Nickse, R. (1993) A typology of family and intergenerational literacy programmes: implications for evaluation. In Adult Literacy and Basic Skills Unit (ed.) *Family Literacy* (Viewpoints No. 15). London: ALBSU.

Norris, E. and Stainthorp, R. (1991) Reading tuition by elder siblings. *Reading,* **25**(1), 13–18.

Portsmouth, R., Wilkins, J. and Airey, J. (1985) Home based reading for special school pupils. *Educational Psychology in Practice,* **1**(2), 52–8.

Rowe, K.J. (1991) The influence of reading activity at home on students' attitudes towards reading, classroom attentiveness and reading achievement: an application of structural equation modelling. *British Journal of Educational Psychology,* **61**, 19–35.

St Pierre, R., Swartz, J., Nickse, R., Gamse, B. and Hume, M. (1991) *National Evaluation of the Even Start Family Literacy Program: Status of Even Start Projects During the 1989–90 Program Year.* Cambridge, MA: Abt Associates.

St Pierre, R., Swartz, J., Murray, S., Deck, D. and Nickel, P. (1993) *National Evaluation of the Even Start Family Literacy Program: Report on Effectiveness.* Cambridge, MA: Abt Associates.

Seaman, D.F. (1992) Follow-up study of the impact of the Kenan Trust model of family literacy. *Adult Basic Education,* **2**(2), 71–83.

Shuck, A. *et al.* (1983) Parents Encourage Pupils (PEP): an innercity parent involvement reading project. *The Reading Teacher*, **36**(6), 524–28.

Sulzby, R. (1985) Children's emergent reading of favourite story books: a developmental study. *Reading Research Quarterly*, **20**, 458–81.

Swinson, J. (1985) A parental involvement project in a nursery school. *Educational Psychology in Practice*, **1**, 19–22.

Swinson, J. and Ellis, C. (1988) Telling stories to encourage language. *British Journal of Special Education*, **15**(4), 169–71.

Toomey, D. (1989) How home–school relations policies can increase educational inequality: a three-year follow-up. *Australian Journal of Education*, **33**(3), 284–98.

Toomey, D. (1993) Parents hearing their children read: rethinking the lessons of the Haringey Project. *Educational Research*, **35**(3), 223–36.

Toomey, D. and Sloane, J. (1991) Developing 'emergent literacy' for children of low-socio-economic status: a pre-school based programme. *Australian Journal of Reading*, **14**(1), 40–9.

Toomey, D. and Sloane, J. (1994) Fostering children's early literacy development through parent involvement: a five-year programme. In D.K. Dickinson, *Bridges to Literacy: Children, Families and Schools*. Oxford: Blackwell.

Topping, K.J. (1986) *Parents as Educators: Training Parents to Teach Their Children*. Beckenham: Croom Helm/Cambridge, MA: Brookline.

Topping, K.J. (1995) *Paired Reading, Spelling and Writing: The Handbook for Parents and Teachers*. London: Cassell.

Topping, K. and Wolfendale, S. (1985) (eds) *Parental Involvement in Children's Reading*. Beckenham: Croom Helm/New York: Nichols.

Vinograd-Bausell, C.R., Bausell, R.B., Proctor, W. and Chandler, B. (1986) Impact of unsupervised parent tutors on word recognition skills. *The Journal of Special Education*, **20**(1), 83–90.

Wade, B. (1986) *Story at Home and School (Educational Review No. 10)*. Birmingham, UK: Faculty of Education, University of Birmingham.

Webb, M., Webb, T. and Eccles, G. (1985) Parental participation in the teaching of reading. *Remedial Education*, **20**(2), 86–91.

Chapter 13

Transitions and Continuities in Home–School Reading and Literacy

Sheila Wolfendale

INTRODUCTION

The aim of this chapter is to trace the evolution from parental involvement in reading to family literacy; describe a relationship between these two phenomena; examine some of the influences upon a number of related initiatives; and provide a commentary upon a number of features characteristic of parental and family involvement in literacy.

The preceding chapters in this book represent the many facets of literacy teaching and learning initiatives. They are predicated on the premise that by involving parents/ families in these processes, children's achievement in and out of school will be fostered and enhanced. By linking a number of the chapters with the earlier book (Topping and Wolfendale, 1985), we hope to demonstrate continuity (longer term outcomes, wider take-up, generalizability and applicability elsewhere). We also hope to demonstrate the transition from narrow school-focused pedagogical considerations (improving early reading skills by involving parents in school- and home-linked projects) towards broader educational and ecological impact (Thomas, 1992). We have witnessed, and a number of the chapter authors have participated in, an evolution. This chapter considers the impetus behind recent and current literacy teaching/learning initiatives that include the family (not just parental) domain as a key component in the delivery of literacy skills acquisition.

EMPHASIS UPON LITERACY: PREMIUM FOR A PRODUCTIVE SOCIETY

The social context of literacy cannot be defined without reference to broader economic and political frames. Tensions inherent in reconciling disparate aims on the part of educationalists and politicians are not a new phenomenon, but in an era where state responsibility may equal intervention may equal control, conflicts between pedagogical and political aspirations are peculiarly hard to resolve (Resnick and

Resnick, 1977). Even amongst educationalists there is not always a consensus about definitions of literacy, its purpose and functions.

In the United Kingdom, political control over the taught formal curriculum is evinced in the advent of the National Curriculum legally mandated in the 1988 Educational Reform Act. It is not surprising that any government that seeks to influence education to the extent of prescribing the school curriculum should also perceive that it has a right to dictate the form and content of literacy teaching, ostensibly for broader, national, and ultimately intra-national competitive purposes.

The historical backdrop to changing views about literacy in different societies is explored in Wolfendale (1990); Levine (1986); Houston (1988); Brooks *et al.* (1993). An historical-comparative perspective illuminates not only how relative and context-bound are definitions of literacy, but also how ever-changing are concerns about literacy standards. Brock (1990) examines five myths about literacy which, he avers, have shaped the social contexts within which literacy education has had to operate. He contends that throughout this century, it has been hard to dispel the myth that reading standards have declined. The debate continues to rage, with proponents of this view (Turner, 1990) ranged against other educationalists and researchers proposing, on the basis of *their* evidence, an alternative view (Gorman and Fernandez, 1992; Pumfrey, 1991; and, for a comparative view, a report to the Australian government by a House of Representatives Standing Committee, 1992).

A debate about reading and literacy standards in any country is an entirely legitimate and integral part of the perennial desire to maintain and raise standards of functional literacy amongst all groups within a given society. The 1990 International Literacy Year focused attention upon many countries, those in the main which are not yet able to provide universal, free education (UNESCO, 1993) and which thereby disadvantage whole sectors of the population, for example, women (Wagner and Puchner, 1992). At the 1994 UNESCO World Symposium on literacy, it was estimated that worldwide there are 386 million children and young adults from 6 to 17 years of age who are at risk of becoming the next generation of illiterate adults. Within the United Kingdom, one such identified 'sector' – young adults – has been the focus of concern in respect of literacy achievement; and a recent report highlighted the serious literacy problems of a small but significant minority of young adults (Elkinsmyth and Bynner, 1994).

Undoubtedly, aspirations for a literate society and workforce are and should be of collective concern and responsibility, and there are inherent issues of access and equal opportunities to be tackled at all societal levels; government, school, community and within families.

The idea of national literacy campaigns is not new, as Houston (1988) notes. Within the United Kingdom there are currently two national organizations that aim to promote and publicize the notion of life-long literacy and the many means by which such goals can be achieved.

The National Literacy Association (Griffiths, 1995) and address in the Resource Directory, p. 187 below), which came into existence during 1992, combines representation on its national executive committee of major organizations and key people involved in literacy with a grass-roots populist approach to proselytizing the importance of literacy skills acquisition. Its campaign thrust is to promote the idea of 99 per cent literacy achievement by the year 1999. The National Literacy Trust (address in

Resource Directory), which was formed during 1993, likewise aims to encourage more reading and writing for pleasure and to enhance literacy standards. Taking a positive view, the NLT states (in *Literacy Today*, 1994)

> perhaps the key issue we need to face nationally is what might be called the 'literacy gap' not necessarily produced by a fall in educational standards but by a rise in the literacy levels required by society and the work place. (p. 1)

So, in a context of various changes to the content of English and therefore to literacy teaching in the National Curriculum in the United Kingdom, there are concerted efforts to ensure that literacy (learning, teaching, through and post-school) remains on the collective societal agenda. In addition, it is crucial that access to the tools and skills of literacy are widened to encompass groups that might otherwise remain on the periphery of formal education and hence excluded from these opportunities – for example, working-class parents of young and older school-aged children (see Hancock, Hannon and Phillips, Chapters 2, 6 and 10) and Bangladeshi mothers (Gregory, Chapter 8).

REVIEWING PARENTAL INVOLVEMENT IN READING INITIATIVES

Many of the seminal projects reported in Topping and Wolfendale (1985) and elsewhere were predicated on a number of 'equal opportunities' premises. That is, they were not only targeted to increase the reading and literacy achievement of pupils, but were aimed also at empowering those parents and carers who participated in joint home–school programmes (Wolfendale, 1992). By giving them access to and training in reading teaching methods, the taught formal curriculum was opened up to them and they were introduced to the notion of the 'equivalent expertise' of teachers and parents operating in the interests of children.

Schools were not abdicating their own responsibilities, nor were they prepared to surrender control of the curriculum, but in keeping with the spirit of 'parents as educators' (Topping, 1986) they were increasingly prepared to share the educational process with home. Many of the chapters in this book attest to these developments. Over the past 10 to 15 years or so, parent–child reading activities have become routine in many schools, and there have been parallel developments within the special educational needs area. Indeed such initiatives are not discrete, but are overlapping and cross-influential. Partnership between teachers and parents/carers is now an explicit and fundamental principle within the *Code of Practice on the Identification and Assessment of Special Educational Needs* (Department for Education, 1994) which the United Kingdom government regards as the cornerstone of the most recent legislation on special educational needs. At each of the Code's stages of identification, assessment and intervention with special educational needs, schools are expected to involve parents fully. For a significant number of children, their individual education plans will include home–school reading programmes, utilizing one or more of the methods described in Topping and Wolfendale (1985) and in this volume.

The influence of 'parental involvement in reading' has pervaded other areas – for example in a number of the UK government-funded City Challenge projects. These are targeted to inner city and other areas deemed to be in need of urban regeneration.

Improving literacy is included as a key attainment target and home–school reading schemes are an integral means of achieving these goals (Bentley *et al.*, 1995).

Endorsement of these approaches has come from influential national reports on future directions of education within the United Kingdom (Institute for Public Policy Research, 1993; National Commission on Education, 1993). Both these reports call for Home School Policies, and suggest that a Home–School Contract or Agreement could strengthen parents' rights to become involved in their children's learning. A further influential marker was the recommendation contained in the report on the National Curriculum commissioned by the government (The Dearing Report, 1993) that schools should actively seek to involve parents:

> If ways could be found to involve more mothers and fathers in the initial teaching of reading, we would make a huge contribution to the raising of educational standards. (p. 24)

Chapters 7 and 11 in this volume testify to similar developments in Australia. In North America, the Goals 2000: Educate America Act calls upon schools to 'promote partnerships that will increase parental involvement', and the United States Department of Education has released a report entitled 'Strong Families, Strong Schools'. The United States also has the Federal Even Start Family Literacy Program for families with children from 0 to 8 years, and now has a 'National Family Literacy Centre'. The first National Family Literacy Day was held on 1 November 1994.

The key emphasis in the above quotation is on the word *ways* – that is, the translation of such rhetoric into realities for *all* schools, on behalf of *all* children. In a survey undertaken by the National Literacy Trust (NLT, 1993) of 1000 adults, there was a consensus view that education should be a shared home–school undertaking. Worryingly, what also came to light in this survey were the large numbers of adults who confessed to having literacy problems themselves, a finding which in itself endorses the philosophy that an alliance between home and school can promote literacy achievement.

This section has provided a short review of the impetus towards involving parents in their children's reading development. In the previous chapter the effectiveness of such initiatives was critically examined. A number of these initiatives have provided the seminal influence and foundation for the succeeding generation of family literacy work, to which we now turn.

THE TRANSITION TOWARDS FAMILY LITERACY

Earlier work involving parents in their children's reading development tended to concentrate efforts on enhancing children's reading *attainment*. As researchers and practitioners gained experience and hindsight wisdom, they began to consider broader family dimensions, such as: the effects upon other family members of a home–school reading programme; the literacy levels and language skills of other family members; and the extent to which such a programme was meeting needs other than fostering children's reading.

Elsewhere (Wolfendale, 1993) it has been asserted that even within these earlier projects, spanning the first years of the 1980s, the common agenda and mutual aspirations of teachers and parents were insufficiently explored. In school and home settings, there is a common desire for children to develop competence in: reading for pleasure and for information; to use the printed word to understand and make sense of the world; to become familiar with multi-media usage; to question, weigh arguments critically and to appraise evidence; to be functionally at ease with completing forms, comprehending signs and instructions in public places; to use language competently in all its richly varied ways – in other words, to acquire 'literacy for life'.

The contention is that with the earlier focus on reading development, wider literacy dimensions were overlooked – understandably, since practitioners and researchers were exploring and accumulating an invaluable store of appropriate methodologies and resources in home–school reading schemes.

The common agenda alluded to above can be appraised within conventional definitions of literacy. One received and oft-quoted definition is that which was formally adopted by UNESCO:

> A person is literate when he [*sic*] has acquired the essential knowledge and skills which enable him to engage in all those activities in which literacy is required for effective functioning in his group or community. (Oxenham, 1980, p. 87)

This definition is subject to a critique by Jackson (1993) who argues that it insufficiently reflects the role of literacy as an agent of change, and that it fails to take into account cultural contexts and imperatives. The definition of literacy provided by Botkin *et al.* (1979) identifies the potential of literacy as an empowering tool:

> Despite the difficulties inherent in articulating new measurable standards, efforts should be encouraged to conceive of literacy as a means of increasing people's consciousness and their ability to participate constructively and ethically. (Botkin *et al.*, 1979, p. 43)

Jackson (1993) distinguishes between 'schooled literacy' and home literacy – the latter she takes to encompass a myriad of learning opportunities for the child. This theme is further explored later in this chapter when discussing home–school connections.

Wolfendale (1993) provides a view, albeit in compressed form, of the evolution from the essentially hypothesis-testing nature of earlier parental involvement in reading projects towards those which embrace broader family/contextual dimensions and which might, therefore, be characterized as 'family literacy'. These offer the potential for the 'common agenda' to be realized.

DEFINITIONS, RATIONALE AND CHARACTERISTICS OF FAMILY LITERACY

Definitions

Much seminal work has emanated from the United States of America (see Connors, Chapter 9 of this book) as well as from Australia (see Kemp and Cairney, Chapters 7 and 11; Walker, 1993; Rivalland, 1994; Toomey and Sloane, 1994; Spreadbury, 1995). This and other work indicates that there cannot be one simplistic definition of family literacy and that it would be invidious to pigeon-hole the rich array of practice into one overarching defining statement.

That said, we can conceive of family literacy practice as epitomizing 'literacy-specific experiences' (Dickinson, 1994, p. 3) involving some or all family members (within the parameters of a given family as defined by the family itself). Features which define the activities include: sharing reading/language experiences; linking 'schooled literacy' with that of the home; equal value being placed by all participants upon influences of home and school upon children's learning.

Dombey and Meek Spencer (1994) express the twin influences upon children of home and school in these words:

> At home, in the company of their family, caregivers and neighbours, children learn to speak their mother tongue. In doing so they learn their culture . . . school is both the society of children and the place of official instruction and institutionalised learning. Children's entry into the world of written language spans this transition. (p. xi)

Essentially, then, family literacy is about enabling children and their families to participate in and benefit from and shape the future of their cultural heritage, by equipping them with the appropriate tools and techniques, derived from and applicable to formal schooling and the 'natural' resources of their home and community environment.

Rationale

Again, there is no uniform, standard rationale common to all family literacy endeavours, which can be predicated upon a number of underlying assumptions and sets of values. But what emerges from the burgeoning literature on family literacy are predominating rationales, one which emphasizes the 'deficit' or 'needs' model, and the other, a 'wealth' model which attempts to avoid such labelling by adopting an alternative value position.

The deficit model can be seen to have its roots in the seminal United States Head Start work of the 1960s (Meisels and Shonkoff, 1990), which was often experimental, testing hypotheses that targeted educational programmes could compensate for socio-economic deprivation. This model assumed that children and families disadvantaged by their deprived status could be positively assisted, via educational intervention to combat their situation, and become enabled, even empowered, to compete on equal terms with their less socio-economically deprived peers.

This rationale has been adopted to some extent by the United Kingdom government-funded ALBSU (Adult Learning and Basic Skills Unit) family literacy initiative. The aim of this is to provide learning opportunities for parents with literacy difficulties and their children, so as to enhance skills in both generations and empower parents by developing with them strategies they can use to support their children's literacy acquisition (Hemstedt, 1995). This four-year project is multi-faceted, centring upon school, home and local communities. Dissemination is integral to the project's aims and goals and ALBSU produces a periodic newsletter describing events and developments.

The ALBSU family literacy initiative shows that even the deficit model is not now applied simplistically. In fact, as Meisels and Shonkoff (1990) describe, the initial 'compensatory' approaches gave way to a broader view which perceived the child as part of a viable, vibrant, dynamic family unit that was socially valid (even if economically deprived) and which acknowledged the 'equivalent expertise' of parents as educators (as was alluded to earlier in this chapter).

Running in parallel with the 'deficit/needs' model inherent in a number of family literacy schemes is a 'wealth' model, which assumes a value position that children are the inheritors and inhabitants of a family domain with its own rich, cultural, linguistic and domestic traditions. Family literacy endeavours in this context aspire to effect a rapprochement between the different milieux in which children exist, notably, home, school, community. Bentley *et al.* (1995) in describing a UK government City Challenge family literacy project in the north-west of England, explored the ambiguities and tensions posed by dealing simultaneously with both deficit and wealth models and aimed to reconcile these by their integrated approach.

All family literacy work is driven and informed by an overriding rationale, be it political/economic/social/pedagogical, and/or combinations of these (Snow *et al.*, 1991; Sticht and Phillips, both in ALBSU *Viewpoints*, 1993). That a congruence between and among approaches is possible is demonstrated by Sticht in these words:

> All societies must prepare each generation of its human resources with the knowledge and skills needed to perpetuate and extend the culture of the society. (p. 9)

Characteristics

From the above discussion, the reader will doubtless begin to form an idea of some of the characteristics of family literacy programmes which are integral to their definition and scope. There are other characteristics or features which are common to a number of programmes, although not universal. For example:

Intergenerational family literacy

This goes beyond the traditional parent–child dyad in service delivery to a less linear approach which not only spans two or more generations within the same family, but branches outwards to siblings (Norris and Stainthorp, 1991) and other relatives (Nickse, 1993, and see Connors, Chapter 9 of this book). This is an amalgam of the ecological/systemic model referred to at the beginning of the chapter.

Early years focus

In the United Kingdom, leading researchers include Hannon and colleagues (see Chapter 6 of this book). The rationale for their Sheffield-based study (Weinberger, 1990) is that knowledge of literacy at school entry is a strong predictor of later attainment, so clearly home environment and parents have a key role to play. The authors refer to the preschool stage of emerging literacy as the 'roots' of literacy (also see Athey, 1990).

Typologies

These are often advanced in research and application work as a tool to facilitate conceptual clarity, and within the realm of family literacy several have been proposed. For example, Walker (1993) offers five areas: planning; practice (home–school); communication; training and evaluation. He then presents a matrix setting these against a continuum from nil parental involvement to parents as partners. The matrix can be used as an analytical tool. Nickse (1993) proposes a wider classification system or typology. Walker's was developed for use within a single project, whereas Nickse's is a schematic macro-matrix on which are plotted other American family literacy programmes, and which she suggests would be amenable to use in evaluating such programmes.

THE HOME AS A CONTEXT FOR LEARNING

School as a milieu for children's learning is well-trodden ground and Sylva (1994) provides a comprehensive review of school influences upon children's development. The milieu of home/family has recently received a fair amount of attention as educators realize the potential of maximizing children's learning in both their main environments. The purpose of this section of the chapter is to consolidate the earlier description of family literacy by reference to contemporary views on the place of the home in children's development and progress, as well as to draw attention to a perceived mismatch between home and school in respect of literacy experiences and expectations.

Dunn (1989) reviews research in this topic area and concludes that there are four major features of family interactions that may contribute to the learning that takes place:

- the emotional significance of family interactions;
- discourse about cause and consequence;
- children's pleasure in mastery over the social world;
- the focused, individual nature of interactions at home.

Parenting functions, which have such a crucial bearing upon the formation of children's attitudes and constructions of the world, and parenting styles, which likewise affect and influence later behavioural outcomes, are explored in Wolfendale (1992).

The family context for language development is well chronicled (Brice-Heath, 1983). A number of projects have sought to enhance language development by invoking what Fox refers to as the 'rich granary' of naturalistic language (Fox, 1993) by involving parents and carers – see for instance storytelling initiatives (Swinson and Ellis, 1988; Fox, 1993), the use of the Primary Language Record which involves parents in the assessment of language (James and Wyeth, 1994), running family reading groups (Beverton *et al.*, 1993).

The home as a springboard for literacy acquisition has been a recurring theme of this chapter and indeed is the *raison d'être* of this book; but now let us examine the proposition, expounded by a number of writers, that at the interface between home and school, there has been a mismatch between school and home expectations (see Gregory, Chapter 8 of this book), and that further, teachers have insufficiently absorbed and valued literacy-relevant home experiences.

This 'gap' has been explored by Weinberger (1993, 1995), whose studies found that most children's homes were 'rich, complex and powerful' environments for literacy learning. She commented on 'how many literacy experiences children were involved in at home, and what a central role parents played in early literacy development' (1993, p. 91). Another finding was that parents whom she interviewed expressed the view that they did not know much, if anything, about how their children's teachers taught reading and literacy skills, and so she advocated schools 'taking more of the initiative in communication with parents about literacy, and finding ways to allow the literacy learning that takes place at home to become more visible' (p. 91).

In reporting upon related research, Kohl (1995) asserts that if teachers do not build upon children's previous literacy experiences, they will undermine the effectiveness of their teaching practices. What is highlighted in these studies are the differential prior experiences that children have that are rarely incorporated into formal educational processes. Spreadbury's studies (1995) lead her to propose a continuum from home-based to school-based learning which would redress the power balance and restore some equity in the relations between parents/carers and teachers in literacy teaching.

FAMILY LITERACY AS PART OF THE EDUCATIONAL AGENDA: PROSPECTS AND PREDICTIONS

Some of the family literacy work reported in this book and elsewhere (e.g. Dickinson, 1994) has been inspirational. Are we witnessing a burgeoning of family literacy? Does the current work herald significant consolidation and expansion as we head towards the millennium?

Some signs and portents point in that direction, based on evidence to date and taking into account a number of other influences upon schools that are propelling them towards increasing the extent of co-operation with parents. We can make a reasonable prophecy about these continuing directions:

- That for the foreseeable future, government-funded projects in the area of urban regeneration involving local schools will continue to insist upon parental involvement linked to children's achievement as performance indicators. (See also Phillips, Chapter 10 of this book.)
- That schools will be anxious to demonstrate, for the purposes of the mandatory periodic school inspection, that they are involving parents actively in the life and routines of the school, since this is one of the performance indicators that inspectors and evaluators will be required to explore and on which to seek evidence.

For these imperatives, parental involvement in reading/literacy provides an effective vehicle.

We can anticipate, again with some confidence, that many initiatives have now taken root and become embedded in local and educational routine: a perusal of the UK Directory of Home–School Initiatives (Bastiani, 1993) shows that in many parts of the United Kingdom parental involvement/partnership schemes, including literacy-focused ones, are flourishing. Some of them have demonstrated close links with the taught curriculum (Dye, 1989).

Perhaps all these initiatives will encourage more schools, in keeping, too, with the requirement for them to forge active partnerships with parents in the realm of special educational needs (see above), to adopt a whole school policy on involving parents with the teaching/learning of reading and literacy (Topping, 1989).

Can we foresee that schools will readily incorporate parental dimensions as they become assured, from the research and literature on school effectiveness, as well as from political imperatives, that the degree and quality of home–school links denotes one of the key indicators of school effectiveness (Hargreaves and Hopkins, 1991; Reynolds and Cuttance, 1992)?

All these possible trends and prognostications are based on present practice, whether established or emerging. However, they are essentially school-based and educationally oriented. What of influences from other sources which could have a bearing upon directions of family literacy?

The advent of information technology (IT) and multi-media approaches pervade an increasing number of homes and affect the lives of families. In different ways – at school, in the work place, as well as at home – we are all actually or potentially subject to the demands made upon our expertise, or lack of it, by the 'new' technology. We respond differentially, according to our inclination, to external imperatives, and to the availability of funds to support the introduction into our lives of IT equipment. Yet it impinges upon our lives in all sorts of ways.

The demands upon children now are to become familiar with IT and to be able to marry traditional literacy skills with those required for electronic literacy, or, as it has been referred to, the 'new literacy'; that is, to be able to combine skills with print and the telephone with familiarity with computers, IT networks, fax machines, CD ROM access to information and electronic mail. Dombey and Meek Spencer (1994) aver 'nor can modern electronic systems replace the "handiness" of books as sources of information' (p. xiii), yet there are other realities for children reared in an electronic age, and for whom work and leisure activity may be synonymous with the use of such equipment, rather than library and print-based pursuits.

There is potential to harness and exploit these media to (a) develop the requisite skills that children need to function and compete and (b) bring together home and school in ways that will be mutually beneficial. Otherwise, as IT ware is expensive, poorer families may be increasingly disadvantaged.

Firstly we need to note that the incorporation of 'technology' into teaching is hardly new, as many years of schools' radio and television broadcasting attests. Formal education must be ever interactive with all developing forms of media and communication. Initial doubt, reserve, scepticism, and fear of the unknown give way to acceptance and constructive exploitation of new opportunities (Educational Television Company, 1994). Noted is a glossary of 'new information literacy' terms provided to members of the United Kingdom Reading Association (Language and Literacy News, 1994) to assist their introduction to the UKRA Internet connection.

As with radio and television, computers – including routine domestic access to the international interactive electronic mail network, e.g. INTERNET – will undoubtedly become standard in homes, as will the other 'new' IT mentioned above. Abbott (1994) predicts that before long each of us will have a miniaturized electronic notebook into which we will download digitized books, either directly from a modem or by going to the library where we will be able to 'pump' it in, as we pump in petrol to our cars. Tuman (1994) tells us that new forms of technology, e.g. hypertext, multimedia, digital text and virtual reality, will fundamentally affect our conceptions and usage of literacy. The 'Talking Computer' already exemplifies the match between the technology and the teaching of basic literacy skills (contact Jersey Advisory Service about one such trial – address in Resource Directory).

There is undoubted scope in all of these fast-moving developments to involve parents in the 'new literacy', wherein the rationale could be an amalgam of the so-called deficit model (in that so many adults have learning needs to become familiar and competent with IT – often children are better informed than their parents or their teachers!) and the 'wealth' model, that is, that there is a match between what parents can already offer with the educational opportunities. Such a triangular learning partnership (teachers, children, parents) could be one of the most positive developments we could aim for.

Indeed it is beginning to happen – at the time of writing, a project is getting under way in the London Docklands area (an area under regeneration) involving up to 20 primary schools in three local education authorities. This partnership between the London Docklands Development Corporation and the National Literacy Association aims to develop literacy amongst primary age pupils and try out Open Integrated Learning Systems (NCET, 1993) utilizing multi-media computer networks and Integrated Learning Systems literacy software, such as Global English, and Talking Screen.

One of the aims of the project is to 'foster parental and community involvement in support of literacy and related IT-based communication skills'. This aim will be pursued via equipping the pupils with portable 'laptop' personal computers with appropriate software designed to encourage child/parent partnership in learning activities in the home. With the support of a home–school liaison officer, work with parents in families and in community groups will seek to engender positive and supportive attitudes to the families' acquisition of literacy through computer technology. It is also planned to work with parents in reviewing the family use of television as an entertainment and information-giving medium (contact this author for further information at Psychology Department, University of East London, Stratford Campus, Romford Road, London E15 4LZ).

PARTNERSHIP IN LITERACY – FROM TRANSIENCE TO PERMANENCE?

The work described in this book and overviewed in this chapter is impressive and exciting; some of it has been subjected to evaluation of its effectiveness. Yet a number of these projects are temporary – time-limited because they are hypothesis-testing research, or because the pump-priming funds supporting their inception and implementation inevitably run out.

If family literacy partnerships are to take root, pedagogical aims on the part of schools need to be aligned with social/political/economic imperatives. We need to explore rationales that realistically combine the 'deficit/wealth' models, so that we can constructively target adults with expressed learning needs and their children who have developmental and educational learning needs. All citizens should have the right to become empowered via access to the media available at that time in that society. By taking that statement as a fundamental assertion of rights and entitlement, we can transcend individual needs to make an ambitious case for the inclusion into the taught school curriculum of family literacy, as it is an extension of schools' basic responsibility to teach literacy skills.

The goal is and should be one of collective responsibility. There are now sufficient methodologies, tools and techniques to convince teachers, governors, educational administrators and other educationalists that family literacy could be a powerful, enabling vehicle to enhance literacy and educational standards. The cost implications of a family literacy policy can range, reassuringly, from negligible to vast, depending on the level and scale of any initiative.

Can we move towards the point where family literacy activities are so embedded within and integral to school, home and community that the word 'initiative' becomes inappropriate? Whilst not the only panacea to perceived problems of inequality, disadvantage and the felt alienation of so many mothers and fathers towards school, it offers immediate and accessible ways to parents into the educational process. The 1994 International Year of the Family put the spotlight on the societal need to cherish and invest in the family unit – let the last word come from an article in a United Kingdom national daily broadsheet, *The Guardian*, in 1994 describing the creation of a Parents' Centre at St Anne's Primary School, Toxteth, Liverpool:

> Children who see their parents involved with the school take schoolwork seriously themselves.

REFERENCES

Abbott, C. (1994) *Reading IT*. Reading: Reading and Language Information Centre, University of Reading.

Athey, C. (1990) *Extending Thought in Young Children: A Parent–Teacher Relationship*. London: Paul Chapman.

Bastiani, J. (1993) *UK Directory of Home–School Initiatives*. 2nd edn. London: Royal Society of Arts.

Bentley, D., Cook, M. and Harrison, C. (1995) Family literacy: ownership, evaluation and accountability. In B. Raban-Bisby (ed.) *Developing Language and Literacy*. Stoke on Trent: Trentham Books.

Beverton, S., Hunter Carsh, M., Obrist, C. and Stuart, A. (1993) *Running Family Reading Groups*. Widnes: UKRA.

Botkin, K., Elmandjra, M. and Malitza, M. (1979) *No Limits to Learning: Bridging the Human Gap*. Oxford: Pergamon.

Brice-Heath, S. (1983) *Ways with Words*. Cambridge: Cambridge University Press.

Brock, P. (1990) A review of some of the literacy, political and mythological contexts of reform and regression in literacy education. In Proceedings of the 15th Australian Reading Association Conference, 7–10 July. Victoria, Australia: ARA.

Brooks, G., Pugh, A.K. and Hall, N. (1993) *Further Studies in the History of Reading*. Widnes: UKRA.

Code of Practice on the Identification and Assessment of Special Educational Needs (1994). London: HMSO.

Dearing, R. (1993) *The National Curriculum and Its Assessment: Final Report*. London: School Curriculum and Assessment Authority.

Dickinson, D. (ed.) (1994) *Bridges to Literacy: Children, Families and Schools*. Oxford: Blackwell.

Dombey, H. and Meek Spencer, M. (eds) (1994) *First Steps Together: Home–School Early Literacy in European Contexts*. Stoke on Trent: Trentham Books.

Dunn, J. (1989) The family as an educational environment in the preschool years. In C. Desforges (ed.) *Early Childhood Education*. Edinburgh: Academic Press and the British Psychological Society.

Dye, J. (1989) Parental involvement in curriculum matters; parents, teachers and children working together. *Educational Research*, **31**(1), 20–35.

Educational Television Company Research Paper for Channel 4 (1994) *The Use of Television in the Development of Early Literacy*.

Elkinsmyth, C. and Bynner, J. (1994) *The Basic Skills of Young Adults*. London: ALBSU.

Fox, C. (1993) *At the Very Edge of the Forest: The Influence of Literature on Storytelling by Children*. London: Cassell.

Gorman, T. and Fernandez, C. (1992) *Reading in Recession*. Slough: National Foundation for Educational Research.

Griffiths, C. (1995) The '99 × 99' Campaign – the pledge for literacy. In B. Raban-Bisby (ed.) *Developing Language and Literacy*. Stoke on Trent: Trentham Books.

Guardian (1994) Back to school for success, 21 December.

Hargreaves, D. and Hopkins, D. (1991) *The Empowered School*. London: Cassell.

Hemstedt, A. (1995) The ALBSU family literacy initiative. In B. Raban-Bisby (ed.) *Developing Language and Literacy*. Stoke on Trent: Trentham Books.

House of Representatives Report (1992) *The Literacy Challenge: Strategies for Early Intervention for Literacy and Learning for Australian Children*. Canberra: Australian Government Publishing Service.

Houston, R.A. (1988) *Literacy in Early Modern Europe: Culture and Education 1500–1800*. London: Longman.

Institute for Public Policy Research (1993) *Education: A Different Vision*. London: IPPR.

Jackson, M. (1993) *Literacy*. London: David Fulton.

James, H. and Wyeth, M. (1994) The primary language record: parents and teachers learning together. In H. Dombey and M. Meek Spencer (eds) *First Steps Together, Home–School Early Literacy in European Contexts*, ch. 6. Stoke on Trent: Trentham Books.

Kohl, K. (1995) Connections and negotiations: early literacy learning at home and school. In B. Raban-Bisby (ed.) *Developing Language and Literacy*. Stoke on Trent: Trentham Books.

Language and Literacy News (Newsletter of the United Kingdom Reading Association) (1994), No. 15, Autumn, 9–11.

Levine, K. (1986) *The Social Context of Literacy*. London: Routledge & Kegan Paul.

Literacy Today (1994), **1**, 1. London: National Literacy Trust.

Meisels, S. and Shonkoff, J. (eds) (1990) *Handbook of Early Childhood Intervention*. Cambridge: Cambridge University Press.

National Commission on Education (1993) *Learning to Succeed: A Radical Look at Education Today and a Strategy for the Future*. London: Heinemann.

NCET (National Council for Educational Technology) (1993) *See IT in the USA: Report of a Study Visit*. Coventry: NCET.

Nickse, R. (1993) A typology of family and intergenerational literacy programmes: implications for evaluation. *Viewpoints*, **15**. London: ALBSU.

Norris, E. and Stainthorp, R. (1991) Reading tuition by elder siblings. *Reading*, **25**(1), April, 13–18.

Oxenham, J. (1980) *Literacy: Writing, Reading and Social Organization*. London: Routledge & Kegan Paul.

Phillips, R. (1993) Parent involvement in family literacy: an anti-poverty perspective. In *Family Literacy* (Viewpoints No. 15), 16–21. London: ALBSU.

Pumfrey, P. (ed.) (1991) Reading standards: issues and evidence. Papers presented at the

London Conference of the British Psychological Society, December, Division of Educational and Child Psychology of the BPS, 1–59.

Resnick, D. and Resnick, L. (1977) The nature of literacy, an historical exploration. *Harvard Educational Review*, **47**(3), August, 370–85.

Reynolds, D. and Cuttance, P. (1992) *School Effectiveness: Research, Policy and Practice*. London: Cassell.

Rivalland, J. (1994) Women's work: the shaping of literacy practices. *Australian Journal of Language and Literacy*, **17**(4), November (special issue on literacy and family).

Snow, C., Barnes, W., Chandler, J., Goodman, I. and Hemphill, L. (1991) *Unfulfilled Expectations: Home and School Influences on Literacy*. London: Harvard University Press.

Spreadbury, J. (1995) Families matter: adults reading aloud to children at home and at school and its implications for language education. In B. Raban-Bisby (ed.) *Developing Language and Literacy*. Stoke on Trent: Trentham Books.

Sticht, T. (1993) Workforce education, family literacy, and economic development. In *Family Literacy* (Viewpoints No. 15), 9–16. London: ALBSU.

Swinson, J. and Ellis, C. (1988) Telling stories to encourage language, *British Journal of Special Education*, **15**(4), December, 169–71.

Sylva, K. (1994) School influences on children's development. *Journal of Child Psychology and Psychiatry*, **35**(1), January, 135–70.

Thomas, G. (1992) Ecological interventions. In S. Wolfendale, T. Bryans, M. Fox, A. Labram and A. Sigston (eds) *The Profession and Practice of Educational Psychology: Future Directions*, ch. 4. London: Cassell.

Toomey, D. and Sloane, J. (1994) Fostering children's early literacy development through parent involvement: a five year program. In D. Dickinson (ed.) *Bridges to Literacy, Children, Families, Schools*, ch. 6. Oxford: Blackwell.

Topping, K. (1986) *Parents as Educators*. Beckenham: Croom Helm.

Topping, K. (1989) A whole school policy on parental involvement in reading. *Reading*, **23**(2), 85–97.

Topping, K. and Wolfendale, S. (eds) (1985) *Parental Involvement in Children's Reading*. Beckenham: Croom Helm.

Tuman, M. (1994) *Word Perfect (Literacy in the Computer Age)*. Basingstoke: Falmer Press.

Turner, M. (1990) *Sponsored Reading Failure*. Warlingham: Education Unit.

UNESCO (1993) *Education for All: Status and Trends*. Paris: UNESCO.

Wagner, D. and Puchner, L. (1992) World literacy in the year 2000. *Annals of the American Academy of Political and Social Science*, March. London: Sage Publications.

Walker, I. (1993) Parental involvement in literacy – a fourth generation. In A. Littlefair (ed.) *Literacy for Life*. Widnes: UKRA.

Weinberger, J. (1993) Children's early literacy experiences at home, the role of parents and children's subsequent literacy development. In A. Littlefair (ed.) *Literacy for Life*. Widnes: UKRA.

Weinberger, J. (1995) Parents' contribution to children's literacy learning. In B. Raban-Bisby (ed.) *Developing Language and Literacy*. Stoke on Trent: Trentham Books.

Weinberger, J., Hannon, P. and Nutbrown, C. (1990) *Ways of Working with Parents to Promote Early Literacy Development*. Sheffield: University of Sheffield Publication Sales.

Wolfendale, S. (1990) The social context of literacy: towards a partnership in the promotion of literacy. In Proceedings of the 15th Australian Reading Association National Conference, Canberra. 7–10 July. Victoria, Australia: ARA.

Wolfendale, S. (1992) *Empowering Parents and Teachers: Working for Children*. London: Cassell.

Wolfendale, S. (1993) Acquisition of literacy for life: teachers and parents sharing responsibility. In A. Littlefair (ed.) *Literacy for Life*. Widnes: UKRA.

Resource Directory

Listed below are the resources for practitioners recommended by the contributors to this book, organized by relevant chapter. After this, there is a general section by the editors covering additional resources which are not necessarily recommended, but may well be found useful. Finally, a list of further useful addresses is appended. Resources which were listed in Topping and Wolfendale (1985) are generally not repeated here.

Chapter 2   Hackney PACT

PACT materials

PACT Home Reading Record Booklets (19 pages including parent guidance notes). In English, Turkish and Bengali.

PACT Bookmarks (giving guidance to parents about helping beginning readers). In English, Turkish, Chinese and Bengali.

PACT 1991 Hackney Survey Report.

PACT 1984 Handbook.

Helen Oxenbury PACT Poster.

Available from: PACT, Queensbridge Building, Albion Drive, London E8 4ET.

Traditional Storytelling: A Sourcebook and Directory (compiled by Tony Aylwin, Storyteller).

Available from: The School of Primary and Secondary Education, The University of Greenwich, Avery Hill Campus, Mansion Site, Bexley Road, Eltham, London SE9 2PQ.

The 'Good Time' Reading Guide (written by parents of the Eveline Lowe Primary School, Southwark).

Available from: The Parent and Family Education Unit, The City Lit, Stukeley Street, Drury Lane, London WC2B 5LJ.

Videos

Adults and Children Reading Together (5 mins)

Available from: Blue Gate Fields Infant School, London Borough of Tower Hamlets, King David Lane, London E1 0EH.

The Chinese Independent School of Tower Hamlets (17 mins)

Available from: Learning by Design, Tower Hamlets PDC, English Street, London E3 4TA.

Dual language story books

The Fox and The Crocodile Eddie McParland and Omar Mohammed (Somali/English) (ISBN 1-873928-00-9)

The Fox and The Crocodile Eddie McParland and Sharifa Chowdhury (Bengali/English) (ISBN 1-873928-02-5)

Hungry But Free Eddie McParland and Omar Mohammed (Somali/English) (ISBN-1873928-12-4)

The Old Woman and the Pumpkin Michael Rosen and Urmi Rahman (Bengali) (ISBN 1-873928-24-6)

The Old Woman and the Pumpkin Michael Rosen (English) (ISBN 1-873928-19-X)

The Old Woman and the Pumpkin Michael Rosen and Suleiman Abdi (Somali) (ISBN 1-873928-29-7)

The Selfish Sparrow/The White Cat and the Wicked Wolf Edward Korel (Kurdish/English) (ISBN 1-873928-05-X)

The Golden Finger Edward Korel (Chinese/English) (ISBN 1-873928-30-0)

The Bharunda Bird Edward Korel (Bengali/English)

The Kicking Bird Edward Korel (Somali/English) (in press)

The Rainstone Edward Korel (Kurdish/English) (ISBN 1-873928-10-6)

Other relevant publications

Telling Tales Jenny Quintana (ISBN 1-873928-64-5)
Language Works Robin Shell (ISBN 1-873928-79-3)
Language Activities Cecile Buxton (ISBN 1-873928-12-2)

Available from: Learning by Design, Tower Hamlets PDC, English Street, London E3 4TA.

Chapter 3 Children and Parents Enjoying Reading (CAPER)

Branston, P. and Provis, M. (1986) *Children and Parents Enjoy Reading (CAPER)*. London: Hodder & Stoughton.
Ready for Reading video and notes. From Promotions Sound and Vision, 2 Hill Grove, Caswell, Swansea SA3 4RQ, Wales.

Chapter 4 Pause Prompt Praise

Videotapes and training booklets

A 30-minute videotape and accompanying training booklet are available, depicting the background and the approach to understanding the reading process, and demonstrating the use of the Pause Prompt Praise procedures.

Title: *Pause Prompt Praise Reading Tutoring Procedures* (1992)
Authors: Dick, M., Glynn, T. and Flower, D.
Production: Audiovisual Section, University of Otago
Distribution: The Learning Shop, New Zealand Special Education Service, P.O. Box 12–188 Thorndon, Wellington, NZ.
                Fax: 64-4-499-2591

A 30-minute videotape and accompanying training booklet are also available in the Maori language, covering similar content but presenting the material in a Maori-preferred context and style.

Title: *Tautari Tautoko Tauawhi: Hei Awhina Tamariki ki te Pānui Pukapuka* (1992)
Authors: Atvars, K. and Glynn, T.
Production: Audiovisual Section, University of Otago
Distribution: New Zealand Special Education Service, Tauranga Field Office, 17 Wharf Street
                Tauranga, NZ.
                Fax: 64-7-571-0455

A bi-cultural Tautari Tautoko Tauawhi Resource Manual for Staff is also available from the Tauranga Field Office of the New Zealand Special Education Service (address above). This manual is designed for use in training workshops and hui (gatherings) in which parents and grandparents and other family members are trained in the delivery of the programme. The training is delivered and the resource materials are demonstrated in both Maori and English. The Resource Manual for Staff contains examples of teaching and learning materials presented in both languages, as well as details of the requirements for the award of two different Certificates, one for tutors, the other for trainers of tutors.

Chapter 5   Tutoring Systems for Family Literacy

Topping, K.J. (1986) *Parents as Educators*. Beckenham: Croom Helm/Cambridge, MA: Brookline.

Topping, K.J. (1988) *The Peer Tutoring Handbook: Promoting Co-operative Learning*. Beckenham: Croom Helm/Cambridge, MA: Brookline.

Topping, K.J. (1995) *Paired Reading, Spelling and Writing: The Handbook for Parents and Teachers*. London: Cassell.

Topping, K.J. and Croft, S. (1992) *Paired Science*: a resource pack for parents and children. (Further details of this pack to aid setting up a project to develop scientific knowledge and language in children aged 5 to 7 years and their families is available from the Centre for Paired Learning, Department of Psychology, University of Dundee, Dundee DD1 4HN, Scotland.

Setting Up a Paired Reading Programme: PAL VHS video and accompanying booklets from The Educational Resource Service, Woodlands Conference Centre, 315 Woodlands Road, Glasgow G3 6NG (Tel 0141 339 3108). The video covers school planning, home visiting, preparing the children, setting up a Paired Reading library and evaluation and is very useful for the in-service training of teachers.

Paired Reading: A Resource Pack is available from St Annes RC Infants and Nursery School, Overbury Street, Liverpool L7 3HJ. Of particular interest are the very high rates of take-up in this school and their arrangements for accreditation. (A Paired Reading module, validated through the Merseyside Open College Federation, enables the parent to gain 1 credit in a Credit Accumulation and Transfer scheme.)

A Teacher's Manual and NTSC training video *Paired Reading: Positive Reading Practice* are available from the North Alberta Reading Specialists' Council, Box 9538, Edmonton, Alberta T6E 5X2, Canada, or from the International Reading Association, 800 Barksdale Road, P.O. Box 8139, Newark, DE 19714-8139, USA.

Chapter 6   School Is Too Late

Hannon, P. (1995) *Literacy, Home and School: Research and Practice in Teaching Literacy with Parents*. London: Falmer Press.

(Discusses practical issues in programmes for school-age as well as preschool involvement. Argues the case for involvement and offers a theoretical framework for practice. Places involvement in a broader context of the historical exclusion of parents from the curriculum and the nature of literacy in society. Critiques some aspects of family literacy.)

Weinberger, J., Hannon, P. and Nutbrown, C. (1990) *Ways of Working with Parents to Promote Early Literacy Development*. USDE Papers in Education, No. 14. Sheffield: University of Sheffield Division of Education.
(Booklet for practitioners, describing methods devised in the Sheffield Early Literacy Development Project.)

Chapter 7   Parents, Teachers, Children

Brown, H. and Cambourne, B. (1988) *Read and Retell*. Melbourne: Thomas Nelson.

Cambourne, B. (1988) *The Whole Story: Natural Learning and the Acquisition of Literacy in the Classroom*. Auckland: Ashton Scholastic.

Christie, F., Gray, P., Gray, B., Macken, M., Martin, J., Macken, M. and Rothery, J. (1991) *Language: A Resource for Meaning and Report Writing*. Marrickville, NSW: Harcourt Brace Jovanovich.

Collerson, J. (ed.) (1988) *Writing for Life*. Rozelle, NSW: Primary English Teaching Association (PETA).

Derewianka, B. (1990) *Exploring How Texts Work*. Rozelle, NSW: Primary English Teaching Association (PETA).

Graves, D. (1983) *Writing: Teachers and Children at Work*. Exeter, NH: Heinemann.

Holdaway, D. (1979) *The Foundations of Literacy*. Gosford, NSW: Ashton Scholastic.

Kemp, M. (1985) *Transformations ACT*. Australia: University of Canberra.

Kemp, M. (1987) *Watching Children Read and Write: Observational Records for Children with Special Needs*. Melbourne: Thomas Nelson.

McGregor, R. (1989) *Working Together: The Co-operative English Classroom*. Melbourne: Nelson.

McGregor, R. and Meiers, M. (1991) *Telling the Whole Story*. Hawthorn, Victoria: Australian Council for Educational Research (ACER).

McKay, F. (1991) *Public and Private Lessons*. Melbourne: Australian Reading Association (ARA).

McNamara, J., McLoughlin, R. and Baker, G. (1987) *Putting Pen to Paper*. Melbourne: Victoria Non-Government Schools.

Rickwood, J. and Satrapa, J. (1989) *When It's Fun You Learn*. Adelaide: Australian Association for the Teaching of English (AATE).

Wallace, C. (1988) *Learning to Read in a Multicultural Society: The Social Context of Second Language Literacy*. New York: Prentice-Hall.

Chapter 8   Learning from the Community

Breakthrough to Literacy materials, especially: *The Children's Sentence Maker*, 2nd edn; *Word Maker*; *Sentence Stands*; *Teacher's Manual*. Harlow, Essex: Longman.

Ladybird *Read-it-Yourself* traditional tales. Loughborough: Ladybird Books.

Listen, Discuss and Do, Unit 4. London: LEA Learning Materials. Available for reference only at the Centre for Language in Primary Education, Webber Row, London SE1, and many teachers' centres.

The Talking Pendown computer program for use with the Acorn computer. Harlow, Essex: Longman.

Chapter 9   Developments in Family Literacy in the United States

ERIC Search on Family Literacy. US Department of Education, Division of Adult Education and Literacy, Washington, DC 20202-7240, USA.

Chapter 10　An Urban Parent Strategy for Accessing Achievement in Literacy

An extensive range of adult/family literacy materials is available from the Adult Literacy and Basic Skills Unit, Kingsbourne House, 229/231 High Holborn, London WC1V 7DA. Tel 0171-405 4017. Fax 0171-404 5038.

These include *Family Literacy News*, a regular newsletter. Other leaflets include *Family Literacy: Getting Started* and *Parents and Their Children: The Intergenerational Effect of Poor Basic Skills*. See also *Family Literacy* (Viewpoints No. 15) (1993).

Chapter 11　Developing Partnerships with Families in Literacy Learning

Cairney, T.H. (1990) *Teaching Reading Comprehension: Meaning Makers at Work*. Milton Keynes: Open University Press.

Cairney, T.H. (1990) *Other Worlds: The Endless Possibilities of Literature*. Melbourne: Nelson.

Cairney, T.H. (1990) *Balancing the Basics*. Gosford, NSW: Ashton Scholastic.

Cairney, T.H. (1995) *Pathways to Literacy*. London: Cassell.

Cairney, T.H. and Munsie, L. (1992). *Beyond Tokenism: Parents as Partners in Literacy*. Melbourne: Australian Reading Association.

Cambourne, B. (1988) *The Whole Story: Natural Learning and Acquisition of Literacy in the Classroom*. Gosford, NSW: Ashton Scholastic.

Derewianka, B. (1990) *Exploring How Texts Work*. Sydney: Primary English Teaching Association.

ADDITIONAL RESOURCES

Auerbach, E. (1990) *Making Meaning, Making Change*. A guide to participatory curriculum development for adult ESL and family literacy. (From the English Family Literacy Project, University of Massachusetts, Boston, MA 02124-3393.) Other titles available are: *English Family Literacy: An Annotated Bibliography*; *Non-traditional Materials for Adult ESL*; and *Participatory Approaches to Adult ESL: A Resource Book for Teachers*.

Bastiani, J. (1989) *Working With Parents*. London: Routledge.

Bastiani, J. and Doyle, N. (1994) *Home and School: Building a Better Partnership*. (Available from the National Consumer Council, 20 Grosvenor Gardens, London SW1S 0DH.)

Bennett, J. *Reading: How Parents Can Help*, National Association for the Teaching of English, 50 Broadfield Road, Broadfield Business Centre, Sheffield, S8 0XJ (Tel: 0742 555419). A5 size six-page booklet, answering questions such as When to start? What books to use? What to do? What if my child makes a mistake? Also contains a 'Basic books list' for parents and books about reading for parents.

Bloom, W. (1987) *Partnership with Parents in Reading*. Sevenoaks: Hodder & Stoughton.

Body, W. (ed.) (1990) *Help Your Child with Reading*. London: BBC Books.

Boehnlein, M.M. and Hager, B.H. (1985) *Children, Parents and Reading: An Annotated Bibliography*. Newark, DE: International Reading Association. (Includes substantial listings of books and pamphlets for parents, reading material for children, and resources for professionals.)

Brizius, J.A. and Foster, S.A. (1993) *Generation to Generation: Realizing the Promise of Family Literacy*. High Scope Press, 600 N. River Street, Ypsilanti, MI 48198-2898, USA.

Child's Play: Computing and Technology for Parents. This is a regular newsletter for parents about using computers with their children. From Face to Interface Ltd, Suite 403 Argyll House, 6–13 Chamber Street, London E1 8BW. The National Council for Educational Technology also offers some support to parents in this area – contact NCET, Milburn Hill Road, Science Park, Coventry CV4 7JJ. Another relevant contact is the Parent Information Network (PIN) Redhatch House, St John's Road, Ascot, Berks SL5 7NH.

Clark, L. (1994) *Help Your Child with Reading and Writing: A Parents' Handbook*; and Shaw, C. (1993) *Talking To Your Child: A Parents' Handbook*. In the Positive Parenting series, published by Hodder and Stoughton. Both these paperback books are very practical with plenty of ideas and strategies.

Colmar, S. and Wheldall, K. (1987) *Supertalkers: Helping Your Child Learn to Talk.* Birmingham, UK: Positive Products.

Culkin, M.L. (1993) *Family Literacy Evaluation Report* (includes useful interview guides and questionnaire formats). From the Adult Learning Source, 1111 Osage Street, Suite 310, Denver, CO 80204-3400, USA, which has also developed a comprehensive curriculum guide for family literacy.

Currie, L. (1992) *Learning to Read: Putting Parents in the Picture.* Windsor: NFER-Nelson. This comprises a teacher's handbook and 10 booklets in a plastic wallet.

Cutting, B. (1985) *Reading Matters: Helping Your Child with Reading*; and (1988) *Talk Your Way to Reading: Helping Your Child with Language.* Leeds: Arnold.

Davis, C. and Stubbs, R. (1988) *Shared Reading in Practice.* Milton Keynes: Open University Press.

Dialogue is a participative learning game about the involvement of home and school in the curriculum (in this case the 5–14 and National Curriculum in the UK, although the original was developed in Denmark). It is used with parents, teachers, school governors, administrators, etc. in groups of four to seven. There are primary (elementary) and secondary (high school) versions. Available from the Department of Education, 8 University Gardens, University of Glasgow, Glasgow G12 8QQ.

Dickinson, D. (1994) *Bridges to Literacy: Children, Families and Schools.* Oxford: Blackwell.

The Directory of Child-to-Child Activities Worldwide. Available from The Child-to-Child Trust, Institute of Education, 20 Bedford Way, London WC1H 0AL.

Dombey, H. and Meek Spencer, M. (eds) (1994) *First Steps Together: Home–School Early Literacy in European Contexts.* Stoke on Trent: Trentham Books.

Dundas, P. and Strong, T. (1988) *Readers, Writers and Parents Learning Together.* Melbourne: ASCCO.

Edwards, P. (1990) *Parents as Partners in Reading.* Chicago: Children's Press. (A six-week plan including three videos.)

Fisk, W.R. (1990) *Intergenerational Literacy: A Review of Programmes.* Clemson, SC: Clemson University.

Franklin, M.R. (1989) *Intergenerational Literacy Projects: What Works?* (for the International Reading Association 34th Annual Convention, Institute on Intergenerational Literacy). Little Rock: Arkansas Department of Education.

Fredericks, A. and Taylor, D. *Parent Programs in Reading: Guidelines for Success.* Newark, DE: International Reading Association.

Geere, B. *Seven Ways to Help Your Child with Reading.* Available from 15 Stamford Drive, Bromley, Kent BR2 0XF. The practical suggestions in this 41-page booklet cover: making reading fun; developing attention and discrimination; practice; pre-reading activities; booklist; phonics; addresses of suppliers; book clubs and book reviews.

Griffiths, A. and Hamilton, D. (1984) *Parent, Teacher, Child.* London: Methuen.

Griffiths, A. and Hamilton, D. (1987) *Learning at Home.* London: Methuen.

Hall, Rachel (1990) *Talking Together* (shared language activities for adults and young children: developed from original work in the Department of Speech, University of Newcastle upon Tyne). STASS Publications, 44 North Road, Ponteland, Northumberland NE20 9UR (Tel 01661 22316). Exercises in 10 sections in ring binder, with teaching 'tips' for adults/parents. The sections are: Making Music; Sounds Fun; Action Packed; Can You Remember?; Storytime; Copy Cats; Hide and Seek; Guess What?; Listen and Do; Good Ideas.

Heald, C. and Eustice, V. (1988) *Ready to Read: Your Child 2–6 Years.* Leamington Spa: Scholastic.

Herrmann, B.A. (ed.) (1994) *The Volunteer Tutor's Toolbox.* Newark, DE: International Reading Association.

Literacy Links (Teacher's Resource) (1990). Kingscourt Publishers Ltd, P.O. Box 1427, London W6 9BR.

Long, R. (1986) *Developing Parental Involvement in Primary Schools.* London: Macmillan.

MacBeath, J. and Turner, M. (1994) *Learning Out of School: Homework, Policy and Practice.*

Quality in Education Centre, Faculty of Education, University of Strathclyde, Glasgow. (Considers the role of parents in homework, particularly with older schoolchildren.)

McNamara, D., Morgan, A., Slingsby, K. and Sutcliffe, S. *Home School Liaison in Humberside: Teachers' Practices and Professional Expertise.* Available from the School Community Office, Hull Education Centre, Coronation Road North, Hull HU5 5RL (see also Organizations below).

Manley, D. (1986) *Look, No Words.* A guide to text-free materials which can be used to teach any language. York: Longman for the School Curriculum Development Committee.

Merttens, R. and Vass, J. (1990) *Sharing Maths Cultures.* Lewes: Falmer Press.

Merttens, R. and Vass, J. (eds) (1993) *Partnership in Maths: Parents and Schools.* Lewes: Falmer Press.

Morgan, R. (1986) *Helping Children Read.* London: Methuen.

Morrow, L.M. (1993) *Literacy Development in the Early Years: Helping Children Read and Write,* 2nd edn. Boston: Allyn & Bacon.

Morrow, L.M. (ed.) (1995) *Family Literacy Connections in Schools and Communities.* Newark, DE: International Reading Association.

Morrow, L.M., Burks, S.P. and Rand, M.K. (1992) *Resources in Early Literacy Development: An Annotated Bibliography.* Newark, DE: International Reading Association.

Morrow, L.M., Tracey, D. and Maxwell, C.M. (eds) (1995) *A Survey of Family Literacy.* Newark, DE: International Reading Association.

Munn, P. (ed.) (1993) *Parents and Schools: Customers, Managers or Partners?* London: Routledge.

No Limit: A Blueprint for Involving Volunteers in Schools. Available from Community Service Volunteers, 237 Pentonville Road, London N1 9NJ, as is a video entitled *Community Partnerships in the Making.* Many useful checklists, guides and reproducibles are included.

Nutbrown, C. (199) *Early Literacy Development and Work with Parents: Putting the Theory into Practice.* Available from OMEP, 753 Bury Road, Rochdale, Lancs OL11 4BB. This 28-page pamphlet includes many ideas and activities, based on earlier research and development.

Participatory Evaluations of Child-to-Child Projects in India. Available from the Aga Khan Foundation, P.O. Box 435, 1211 Geneva 6, Switzerland.

Pearce, L. (1990) *Parents as Partners in Literacy.* Published by LDA. The materials include a video and handbooks in a ring-binder. They are based on the author's extensive work with children, teachers and parents in primary schools.

Pugh, G., De'Ath, E. and Smith, C. (1994) *Confident Parents, Confident Children: Policy and Practice in Parent Education and Support.* London: National Children's Bureau. (Includes a wider listing of resources, mostly on education for parenthood.)

Rasinski, T. (1995) *Parents and Teachers: Helping Children Learn to Read and Write.* Fort Worth, TX: Harcourt Brace.

Reach and Teach: A Guide for Parents and Family Agencies: Learning Activities for Children from Birth to Five (1992) (ERIC ED367861). Produced by Pinellas County School Board, Clearwater, Florida. *Reach and Teach* is a Family Literacy project.

Reading Together: How Mums and Dads Can Help Their Children to Extend Their Reading Skills (video). Newspapers in Education Project, Lancashire Evening Post (Tel 01772 54841).

Root, B. (1988) *Helping Your Child Learn To Read.* London: Usborne.

Shockley, B., Michalove, B. and Allen, J. (1995) *Engaging Families: Connecting Home and School Literacy Communities.* New York: Heinemann.

Strickland, D.S. and Morrow, L.M. (1989) *Emerging Literacy: Helping Young Children Learn to Read and Write.* Newark, DE: International Reading Association.

Strong, G. and Dundas, V. (1991) *Readers, Writers and Parents: Learning Together.* Resource pack including Facilitator's Manual and Parent Handbook. It covers reading, writing and spelling. Available from R.C. Owen Publishers Inc., P.O. Box 585, Katonah, NY 10536.

Taylor, D. (1983) *Family Literacy: Young Children Learning to Read and Write.* Exeter, NH: Heinemann.

Taylor, D. and Dorsey-Gaines, C. (1988) *Growing Up Literate: Learning from Inner-city Families.* Portsmouth, NH: Heinemann.

Topping, K. and Wolfendale, S. (eds) (1985) *Parental Involvement in Children's Reading*. Beckenham: Croom Helm/New York: Nichols.

UKRA (United Kingdom Reading Association) (1993) *Running Family Reading Groups*. Warrington Road Primary School, Naylor Road, Widnes, Cheshire WA8 0BP. A 40-page manual, describing earlier work and the operation of family reading groups.

USDHHS (1991) *Promoting Family Literacy Through Head Start* (Publication No. AFC 91-31266). Washington, DC: United States Department of Health and Human Services.

Weinstein, G. (1990) *Family and Intergenerational Literacy in Multilingual Families*. Washington, DC: Office of Educational Research and Improvement.

Wolfendale, S. and Bryans, T. (2nd edn 1994) *WORD-PLAY: Language Activities for Young Children and Their Parents*. Available from NASEN (National Association for Special Educational Needs), NASEN House, 4/5 Amber Business Village, Amber Close, Amington, Staffs B77 4RP. A 47-page booklet written for collaborative work between nursery and infant staff and parents in a jointly planned programme of language activities and games. It comprises the introduction, which includes guidance notes, and activities listed in nine sections. There are references and suggestions for further reading.

Wragg, T. and Williams, M. (eds) (1993) *Parents' File*. Includes photocopiable workcards for a wide range of home activities linked with National Curriculum objectives. Available from Southgate Publishers, Glebe House, Church Street, Crediton, Devon EX17 2AF.

Young, P. and Tyre, C. (1985) *Teach Your Child to Read*. London: Fontana/Collins.

Young, P. and Tyre, C. (1983) *Dyslexia or Illiteracy: Realising the Right to Read*. Milton Keynes: Open University Press.

Organizations

The Adult Learning Source, 1111 Osage Street, Suite 310, Denver, CO 80204-3400, USA, has developed a comprehensive curriculum guide for Family Literacy.

The Community Education Development Centre, Lyng Hall, Blackberry Lane, Coventry CV2 3JS, produces a catalogue of resources for community education, which includes: *Parents as Co-educators: A Handbook for Teachers*; *Partnerships with Parents in the Primary School*; *Home–School Partnerships*; and *Reading: Involving Parents*, as well as a newsletter, *Partnerships*.

The ERIC Clearinghouse on Reading and Communication Skills, Indiana University, Smith Research Centre, 2805 East 10th Street, Suite 150, Bloomington, IN 47408-2698, USA, produces a digest, *Resources for Involving Parents in Literacy Development*. ERIC-RCS also produces a Learning Package on *Involving Parents in the Reading Process*, including selected abstracts and articles and various listings of resources. The Family Literacy Center at the same address produces two catalogues packed with useful resources: *Harness the Tremendous Potential of Parent Involvement: Resources for Parents and Educators* and *ERIC-REC/ EDINFO Press Resources: Effective Strategies to Enhance Education For All Learners*.

Humberside Education Authority, The School Community Office, Hull Education Centre, Coronation Road North, Hull HU5 5RL, produces *Eurodetective* (a European awareness pack for home–school use); *Finding Out Together: At Home and School: Tools, Machines, Containers* and *Food* (closely related to National Curriculum targets) and a number of other resources in various curricular areas. Alwyn Morgan, the School Community Officer, also masterminds a wide range of creative courses for parents and others.

The International Reading Association produces a video package for early childhood teachers, parents and caregivers, *Linking Literacy and Play*. This includes a video, facilitator's guide and ten books of readings. Details from the International Reading Association, 800 Barksdale Road, P.O. Box 8139, Newark, DE 19714-8139, USA.

The Jersey Advisory Service produces *The Jersey Computer-Assisted Reading Development Programme* (1993). Contact the service at P.O. Box 142, Highlands, St Saviour, Jersey DE4 8QJ, Channel Islands.

The National Association for the Teaching of English (50 Broadfield Road, Broadfield Business Centre, Sheffield S8 0XJ) publishes a booklet titled *Helping Your Child With Reading and Writing*, in English, Punjabi, Gujarati, Bengali and Urdu.

The National Center for Family Literacy in the USA produces a substantial manual on implementing programmes following the 'Toyota' model (see 'Useful Addresses' section, below).

The National Library for the Handicapped Child, 20 Bedford Way, London WC1H 0AL, offers assistance in the selection of reading materials (in paper, audio-visual and micro-electronic form) for children with special needs and has a great interest in parental involvement.

The Reading and Language Development Centre, Nene College, Boughton Green Road, Northampton NN2 7AL, UK, has leaflets for parents in many languages on helping children with reading.

The Reading and Language Information Centre, University of Reading, Bulmershe Court, Earley, Reading RG6 1HY, UK, publishes a series of parent–teacher guides on *Helping Children With Reading, Spelling, Reading Difficulties, Handwriting, Maths*. It also publishes Dee Reid (new edn 1990) *101 Good Read Alouds for 5–11 Year Olds* and *Working Together: Parents, Teachers and Children* (1987).

The Royal Society of Arts funds and hosts the Parents in a Learning Society Project and generates various materials including a regular *Project Newsletter* and a *Directory of Home–School Initiatives in the UK*. Further details from the RSA, 8 John Adam Street, London WC2N 6EZ.

Roy Yates Books, Smallfields Cottage, Cox Green, Rudgwick, Horsham, West Sussex RH12 3DE, is a supplier of children's books in a vast range of different languages, including dual-language books. Substantial catalogue available.

La Ventana Magica is a voluntary organization dedicated to the participatory enrichment of children and families through literary, musical and audio-visual media. Contact at Urbanización Santa Cecilia, Calle 3–12, Caracas 1071, Venezuela.

Rendimiento en el Estudio is a Family Literacy programme which uses radio programmes to reach families in remote rural areas. Details from REEE, Dpto. Educación a Distanci, Universidad Catolica del Uruguay, Damaso Antonio Larranaga, Avenida 8 de Octubre 2738, CP11600 Montevideo, Uruguay.

Programme kits

Many commercial publishers now produce 'Home Learning' kits for parents, increasingly closely tied to the demands of the National Curriculum (e.g. Pan/Macmillan, Longman, Reed International, Oxford University Press, Hodder & Stoughton). (To be used with care if at all.)

Reporting to Parents (a whole school in-service training package for teachers, focusing on more effective communication with parents). Developed by John Bastiani with Warwick University and LEA. Available from: EDS Publications, Manor Hall, Sandy Lane, Leamington Spa CV32 6RD.

Strathclyde Parent Prompts (materials for parents and children at home closely linked to the requirements of the National (5–14) Curriculum in Scotland, in many curricular areas). Available from Strathclyde Regional Council Education Department, Glasgow, Scotland.

USEFUL ADDRESSES

United Kingdom

Adult Dyslexia Organisation, 336 Brixton Road, London SW9 7AA.

Book Trust, 45 East Hill, London SW19 2QZ.

Book Trust Scotland, The Scottish Book Centre, 137 Dundee Street, Edinburgh EH11 1BG.

British Association for Literacy in Development (BALID), School of Social Sciences, University of Sussex, Falmer, Brighton BN1 9QN. Contact: Brian Street (Chair). BALID is a voluntary association of literacy professionals and practitioners who are committed to the sharing of experience of adult literacy between Britain and the developing world.

British Dyslexia Association, 98 London Road, Reading, Berks RG1 5AU.

Centre for Language in Primary Education (CLPE), Webber Row, London SE1 8QW.

The Dyslexia Institute, 133 Gresham Road, Staines TW18 2AJ.

European Research Network About Parents in Education. The chair of the English language section of this organization is Dr Alistair Macbeth, Department of Education, University of Glasgow, 8 University Gardens, Glasgow G12 8QQ.

Federation of Children's Book Groups, 6 Bryce Place, Currie, Midlothian EH14 5LR.

National Literacy Association, 5 Airspeed Road, Priory Industrial Park, Christchurch, Dorset BH23 4HD. (Aims to ensure that 99 per cent of all children leave school with adequate literacy for work and life by 1999.)

National Literacy Trust, 1A Grosvenor Gardens, London SW1W 0BD. (Aims to 'Empower parents and families to maximize their capacity to develop their literacy skills' and publishes a newsletter *Literacy Today*.)

The School Bookshop Association, 1 Effingham Road, Lee, London SE12 8NZ.

School Library Association, Liden Library, Barrington Close, Liden, Swindon SN3 6HS.

United Kingdom Reading Association (UKRA), c/o Warrington Road CP School, Naylor Road, Widnes, Cheshire WA8 0BP.

Volunteer Reading Help (VRH), Room 438, High Holborn House, 49/51 Bedford Row, London WC1V 6RL.

Australia

ACLD, 804 Forest Road, Peakhurst, NSW, Australia.

Children's Book Council of Australia, 35 Mitchell Street, North Sydney, NSW 2060, Australia.

Dyslexia Foundation of NSW, P.O. Box 63, Camperdown, NSW 2050, Australia.

SPELD, 16 Coronation Avenue, Mosman, NSW 2088, Australia.

Canada

The Children's Book Centre, 229 College Street, 5th Floor, Toronto, Ontario, M5T 1R4, Canada.

New Zealand

Children's Literature Association of New Zealand Inc., P.O. Box 36036, Auckland 9, New Zealand.

SPELD, P.O. Box 24042, Royal Oak, Auckland, New Zealand.

USA

American Library Association, 50 East Huron Street, Chicago, IL 60611.

Association of Community Based Educators, Case studies of exemplary educational practices of community based organizations (Project SELF HELP and others). Pat Jackson, 1805 Florida Avenue NW, Washington, DC 20009.

Association for Supervision and Curriculum Development, Intergenerational/Family Literacy Professional Network, 1136 West Knox, Tucson, AZ 85705.

The Barbara Bush Foundation for Family Literacy, 401 South 4th Avenue, Suite 610, Louisville, KY 40202-3449.

Center on Families, Communities, Schools and Children's Learning, Johns Hopkins University, 3505 North Charles Street, Baltimore, MD 21218.

The Children's Book Council Inc., 76 Irving, New York, NY 10001.

Family Resource Coalition, 200 South Michigan Avenue, Suite 1520, Chicago, IL 60604.

Illinois Literacy Resource Center, 200 South Frederick, Rantoul, IL 61866.

International Reading Association, 800 Barksdale Road, PO Box 8139, Newark, DE 19711.

National Center for Family Literacy, Waterfront Plaza, Suite 200, 325 West Main Street, Louisville, KY 40202-4251.

National Center on Adult Literacy, University of Pennsylvania, 3910 Chestnut Street, Philadelphia, PA 19104-3111.

Name Index

Subject Index